PILGRIMAGE OF PEACE

PILGRIMAGE OF PEACE

*The Collected Speeches of John Paul II
in Ireland and the United States*

FARRAR   STRAUS   GIROUX
New York

Photographs by Arturo Mari
© *L'Osservatore Romano* 1980

© in the English translation *L'Osservatore*
Romano and William Collins Sons and Co. Ltd., 1980

© Marietti Editori Torino, 1980

© Libreria Editrice Vaticana, Vatican City, 1980
The official texts in the original languages are
published in *Acta Apostolicae Sedis*

Phototypeset by MS Filmsetting Ltd.,
Frome, Somerset, England
Printed in the United States of America

Library of Congress catalog card number: 79–6704

Library of Congress Cataloging in Publication Data
John Paul II, Pope.
   Pilgrimage of peace.
I. Title.
BX1751.2.J627   230'.2   79–6704

IRELAND

29 September – 1 October

Saturday, 29 September

DEPARTURE FROM FIUMICINO AIRPORT

Pope John Paul II travelled by military helicopter to Fiumicino Airport, Rome. He was greeted there by Carlo Confalonieri, Dean of the Sacred College, Cardinal Ugo Poletti, Vicar of Rome, Cardinal Polobertoli, who as *camerlengo* is responsible for the administration of the Church in the absence of the Pope, and by many other prelates, diplomats and representatives of the Italian Republic. The Pope gave a short farewell address before leaving Rome at 8.12 am.

My heartfelt thanks go to all here present, especially the Cardinals, the members of the Diplomatic Corps, and the representatives of the Italian Government. My gratitude also goes to all those who are now following me with their affection and hope.

I am leaving Rome and the beloved soil of Italy to make a long journey of an eminently pastoral nature, in harmony with my supreme service to the Church.

I am first going to Ireland, the 'Island of Saints', on the occasion of the centenary of the Shrine of Our Lady at Knock, in response to the invitation of the Episcopate. I wish to express to the people of that country my dutiful appreciation of the firm fidelity they have shown, down the centuries, to Christ, the Church and the Apostolic See. I also wish to offer my lively thanks for the dynamic missionary zeal that has always animated them in spreading the Gospel message throughout the world. I truly hope that this visit will contribute to changing that atmosphere of tension that, especially in recent times, has provoked disunity and, unfortunately, destruction and death.

I am then going to the United Nations Organization, in response to an invitation from the Secretary General, Dr Kurt Waldheim. In this, I am following in the footsteps of my predecessor, Paul VI of venerable memory, who fourteen years ago, on 4 October 1965, in that prestigious forum gave an address that had a wide influence on international opinion. The words that I shall speak at that Assembly will be, as it were, a continuation of the great Pope's prophetic appeal for peace and harmony between peoples.

Finally, at the invitation of the Episcopal Conference of the United States and also of President Carter, I shall visit a number of cities of the great American nation. In particular I shall meet the sons and daughters of the Catholic Church, to confirm and strengthen them in the faith. I shall also meet other Christian brethren and the members of non-Christian communities, in order to intensify common efforts towards that perfect unity willed by Christ.

May the Lord guide my steps during these coming days and assist me with his grace, in order that the spiritual aims of this latest journey may be attained. For this purpose I ask everybody, especially the sick and the children, to remember me in their prayers.

With my Apostolic Blessing.

ARRIVAL AT DUBLIN AIRPORT

After a flight lasting less than three hours, the papal plane known as St Patrick, landed at 9.48 am, local time, on Saturday 29 September, at Dublin Airport. The Pope was welcomed by Dr Patrick J. Hillery, President of Ireland, and by Dr Tomas O Fiaich, Primate and Archbishop of Armagh. Then John Paul II addressed the following greeting to the faithful gathered at the airport:

Praised be Jesus Christ!

It is with immense joy and with profound gratitude to the Most Holy Trinity that I set foot today on Irish soil.

I come to you as a servant of Jesus Christ, a herald of his Gospel of justice and love, as Bishop of Rome, as Successor of the Apostle Peter. And in the words of Peter I offer you the greeting of my heart: 'Peace to all of you who are in Christ' (1 Pt 5:14).

I deeply appreciate the welcome of His Excellency the President of Ireland who, as the representative of all upright citizens, extends to me the warm hospitality of this land.

I am grateful moreover to my Brothers in the Episcopate, who are here to greet me in the name of the whole Church in Ireland, that I love so much. I am very happy to walk among you – in the footsteps of Saint Patrick and in the path of the Gospel that he left you as a great heritage – being convinced that Christ is here: 'Christ before me, Christ behind me . . . Christ in the heart of every man who thinks of me, Christ in the mouth of every man who speaks of me.'

At this moment of my arrival I feel the need to express my esteem for the Christian traditions of this land, as well as the gratitude of the Catholic Church for the glorious contribution made by Ireland over the centuries to the spreading of the Faith. From this capital city I send my greetings to all the Irish throughout the world.

And as I invoke God's blessings on Ireland, I commend all her people to the prayers of our Blessed Lady, to the intercession of Mary, Mother of Jesus and Queen of Peace, under whose patronage I place my pastoral visit.

Praised be Jesus Christ!

DUBLIN, HOMILY AT PHOENIX PARK

The first religious act of the Holy
Father on his pilgrimage to Ireland
began at noon on Saturday, 29
September, about two hours after his
arrival in the land of St Patrick. An
immense crowd had gathered around
the altar erected in Phoenix Park
with its vast expanse of green,
popularly known as the Fifteen Acres.
Once before, during the 1932
Eucharistic Congress, Phoenix Park
served as the centre of Eucharistic
devotion. After the Gospel of the
Mass, the Holy Father delivered the
following homily:

Your Excellency, the President of Ireland,
Your Eminence, the Cardinal Primate,
Your Grace, the Archbishop of Dublin,
My Brothers in the Episcopate:
    Bishops of Ireland,
    Visiting Bishops,
Your Excellency, the Taoiseach and Members of the Irish Government,
My Lord Mayor and the City Council of Dublin,
Dear brothers and sisters in Jesus Christ,

1   Like Saint Patrick, I too have heard 'the voice of the Irish' calling to me, and so
I have come to you, to all of you in Ireland.
    From the very beginning of its faith, Ireland has been linked with the
Apostolic See of Rome. The early records attest that your first Bishop, Palladius,
was sent to Ireland by Pope Celestine; and that Saint Patrick, who succeeded
Palladius, was 'confirmed in the faith' by Pope Leo the Great. Among the sayings
attributed to Patrick is the famous one addressed to the 'Church of the Irish, nay of
the Romans', showing them how they must pray in order to be 'Christians as the
Romans are'.
    This union of charity between Ireland and the Holy Roman Church has
remained inviolable and unbreakable down all the centuries. You Irish Catholics
have kept and loved the unity and peace of the Catholic Church, treasuring it above
all earthly treasures. Your people have spread this love for the Catholic Church
everywhere they went, in every century of your history. This has been done by the
earliest monks and the missionaries of Europe's Dark Ages, by the refugees from
persecution, by the exiles and by the missionaries – men and women – of the last
century and this one.
    I have come to you as Bishop of Rome and Pastor of the whole Church, in
order to celebrate this union with you in the Sacrifice of the Eucharist, here in
Ireland's capital city of Dublin, for the first time in Irish history. As I stand at this
moment, a pilgrim for Christ to the land from which so many pilgrims for Christ,

9

peregrini pro Christo, went out over Europe, the Americas, Australia, Africa, Asia, I am living a moment of intense emotion. As I stand here, in the company of so many hundreds of thousands of Irish men and women, I am thinking of how many times, across how many centuries, the Eucharist has been celebrated in this land. How many and how varied the places where Mass has been offered – in stately medieval and in splendid modern cathedrals; in early monastic and in modern churches; at Mass rocks in the glens and forests by 'hunted priests', and in poor thatch-covered chapels, for a people poor in worldly goods but rich in the things of the spirit, in 'wake-houses' or 'station houses', or at great open-air hostings of the faithful – on the top of Croagh Patrick and at Lough Derg. Small matter where the Mass was offered, for the Irish, it was always the Mass that mattered. How many have found in it the spiritual strength to live, even through the times of greatest hardship and poverty, through days of persecution and vexations. Dear brothers and sisters, dear sons and daughters of Ireland, permit me, together with you, to glance back over your history, in the light of the Eucharist celebrated here for so many centuries.

2   From the Upper Room in Jerusalem, from the Last Supper, in a certain sense, the Eucharist writes the history of human hearts and of human communities. Let us reflect on all those who, being nourished on the Body and Blood of the Lord, have lived and died on this island, bearing in themselves, because of the Eucharist, the pledge of eternal life. Let us think of so many generations of sons and daughters of this country, and, at the same time, sons and daughters of the Church. May this Eucharist of ours be celebrated in the atmosphere of the great communion of the saints. We form a spiritual union in this Mass with all the generations who have done God's will throughout the ages up to the present day. We are one in faith and spirit with the vast throng which filled this Phoenix Park on the occasion of the last great Eucharistic hosting held on this spot, at the Eucharistic Congress in 1932.

Faith in Christ has profoundly penetrated into the consciousness and life of your ancestors. The Eucharist transformed their souls for eternal life, in union with the living God. May this exceptional Eucharistic encounter of today be at the same time a prayer for the dead, for your ancestors and forebears. With their help, may it become more fruitfully a prayer for the living, for the present generation of sons and daughters of today's Ireland, preparing for the end of the twentieth century, so that they can meet the challenges that will be put before them.

3   Yes, Ireland, that has overcome so many difficult moments in her history, is being challenged in a new way today, for she is not immune from the influence of ideologies and trends which present-day civilization and progress carry with them. The very capability of mass media to bring the whole world into your homes produces a new kind of confrontation with values and trends that up until now have been alien to Irish society. Pervading materialism imposes its dominion on man today in many different forms and with an aggressiveness that spares no one. The most sacred principles, which were the sure guides for the behaviour of individuals and society, are being hollowed-out by false pretences concerning freedom, the sacredness of life, the indissolubility of marriage, the true sense of human sexuality, the right attitude towards the material goods that progress has to offer. Many people now are tempted to self-indulgence and consumerism, and human identity is often defined by what one owns. Prosperity and affluence, even when they are only beginning to be available to a larger strata of society, tend to make people assume that they have a right to all that prosperity can bring, and thus they can become more selfish in their demands. Everybody wants a full freedom in

all the areas of human behaviour and new models of morality are being proposed in the name of would-be freedom. When the moral fibre of a nation is weakened, when the sense of personal responsibility is diminished, then the door is open for the justification of injustices, for violence in all its forms, and for the manipulation of the many by the few. The challenge that is already with us is the temptation to accept as true freedom what in reality is only a new form of slavery.

4   And so, it becomes all the more urgent to steep ourselves in the truth that comes from Christ, 'who is the way, the truth and the life' (Jn 14:6), and in the strength that he himself offers us through his Spirit. It is especially in the Eucharist that the power and the love of the Lord are given to us.

The Sacrifice of the Body and Blood of Jesus Christ offered up for us is an act of supreme love on the part of the Saviour. It is his great victory over sin and death – a victory that he communicates to us. The Eucharist is a promise of eternal life, since Jesus himself tells us: 'He who eats my flesh and drinks my blood has eternal life, and I will raise him up at the last day' (Jn 6:54).

The Holy Sacrifice of the Mass is meant to be the festive celebration of our salvation. In the Mass we give thanks and praise to God our Father for having given us Redemption through the precious blood of Jesus Christ. The Eucharist is also the centre of the Church's unity, as well as her greatest treasure. In the words of the Second Vatican Council, the Eucharist contains 'the Church's entire spiritual wealth' (*Presbyterorum Ordinis*, 5).

Today I wish to express the gratitude of Jesus Christ and his Church for the devotion that Ireland has shown to the Holy Eucharist. As successor of Peter and Vicar of Christ, I assure you that the Mass is indeed the source and summit of your Christian life.

On Sunday mornings in Ireland, no one seeing the great crowds making their way to and from Mass could have any doubt about Ireland's devotion to the Mass. For them a whole Catholic people is seen to be faithful to the Lord's command: Do this in memory of me. May the Irish Sunday continue always to be the day when the whole people of God – *the pobal De* – makes its way to the House of God, which the Irish call the House of the People – *the teach an pobal*. I have learned with great joy that large numbers also come to Mass several times each week and even every day. This practice is a great source of grace and of growth in holiness.

5   Yes, it is from the Eucharist that all of us receive the grace and strength for daily living – to live real Christian lives, in the joy of knowing that God loves us, that Christ died for us, and that the Holy Spirit lives in us.

Our full participation in the Eucharist is the real source of the Christian spirit that we wish to see in our personal lives and in all aspects of society. Whether we serve in politics, in the economic, cultural, social or scientific field – no matter what our occupation is – the Eucharist is a challenge to our daily lives.

Dear brothers and sisters: there must always be consistency between what we believe and what we do. We cannot live on the glories of our past Christian history. Our union with Christ in the Eucharist must be expressed in the truth of our lives today – in our actions, in our behaviour, in our life-style, and in our relationships with others. For each one of us the Eucharist is a call to ever greater effort, so that we may live as true followers of Jesus: truthful in our speech, generous in our deeds, concerned, respectful of the dignity and rights of all persons, whatever their rank or income, self-sacrificing, fair and just, kind, considerate, compassionate and self-controlled – looking to the well-being of our families, our young people, our country, Europe and the world. The truth of our union with Jesus Christ in the

Eucharist is tested by whether or not we really love our fellow men and women; it is tested by how we treat others; especially our families: husbands and wives, children and parents, brothers and sisters. It is tested by whether or not we try to be reconciled with our enemies, on whether or not we forgive those who hurt us or offend us. It is tested by whether we practise in life what our faith teaches us. We must always remember what Jesus said: 'You are my friends if you do what I command you' (Jn 15:14).

6   The Eucharist is also a great call to conversion. We know that it is an invitation to the Banquet; that, by nourishing ourselves on the Eucharist, we receive in it the Body and Blood of Christ, under the appearances of bread and wine. Precisely because of this invitation, the Eucharist is and remains the call to conversion. If we receive it as such a call, such an invitation, it brings forth in us its proper fruits. It transforms our lives. It makes us a 'new man', a 'new creature' (cf. Gal 6:15; Eph 2:15; 2 Cor 5:17). It helps us not to be 'overcome by evil, but to overcome evil by good' (cf. Rom 12:21). The Eucharist helps love to triumph in us – love over hatred, zeal over indifference.

The call to conversion in the Eucharist links the Eucharist with that other great Sacrament of God's love, which is Penance. Every time that we receive the Sacrament of Penance or Reconciliation, we receive the forgiveness of Christ, and we know that this forgiveness comes to us through the merits of his death – the very death that we celebrate in the Eucharist. In the Sacrament of Reconciliation, we are all invited to meet Christ personally in this way, and to do so frequently. This encounter with Jesus is so very important that I wrote in my first Encyclical Letter these words: 'In faithfully observing the centuries-old practice of the Sacrament of Penance – the practice of individual confession with a personal act of sorrow and the intention to amend and make satisfaction – the Church is therefore defending the human soul's individual right: man's right to a more personal encounter with the crucified forgiving Christ, with Christ saying, through the minister of the sacrament of Reconciliation: "Your sins are forgiven"; "Go, and do not sin again".' Because of Christ's love and mercy, there is no sin that is too great to be forgiven; there is no sinner who will be rejected. Every person who repents will be received by Jesus Christ with forgiveness and immense love.

It was with great joy that I received the news that the Irish Bishops had asked all the faithful to go to Confession as part of a great spiritual preparation for my visit to Ireland. You could not have given me a greater joy or a greater gift. And if today there is someone who is still hesitating, for one reason or another, please remember this: the person who knows how to acknowledge the truth of guilt, and asks Christ for forgiveness, enhances his own human dignity and manifests spiritual greatness.

I take this occasion to ask all of you to continue to hold this Sacrament of Penance in special honour, for ever. Let all of us remember the words of Pius XII in regard to frequent Confession: 'Not without the inspiration of the Holy Spirit was this practice introduced into the Church' (*AAS* 35, 1943, p. 235).

Dear brothers and sisters: the call to conversion and repentance comes from Christ, and always leads us back to Christ in the Eucharist.

7   I wish also at this time to recall to you an important truth affirmed by the Second Vatican Council, namely: 'The spiritual life, nevertheless, is not confined to participation in the liturgy' (*Sacrosanctum Concilium*, 12). And so I also encourage you in the other exercises of devotion that you have lovingly preserved for centuries,

especially those in regard to the Blessed Sacrament. These acts of piety honour God and are useful for our Christian lives; they give joy to our hearts, and help us to appreciate more the liturgical worship of the Church.

The visit to the Blessed Sacrament – so much a part of Ireland, so much a part of your piety, so much a part of your pilgrimage to Knock – is a great treasure of the Catholic faith. It nourishes social love and gives us opportunities for adoration and thanksgiving, for reparation and supplication. Benediction of the Blessed Sacrament, Exposition and Adoration of the Blessed Sacrament, Holy Hours and Eucharistic processions are likewise precious elements of your heritage – in full accord with the teaching of the Second Vatican Council.

At this time, it is also my joy to reaffirm before Ireland and the whole world the wonderful teaching of the Catholic Church regarding Christ's consoling presence in the Blessed Sacrament: his real presence in the fullest sense: the substantial presence by which the whole and complete Christ, God and man, is present (cf. *Mysterium Fidei*, 39). The Eucharist, in the Mass and outside of the Mass, is the Body and Blood of Jesus Christ, and is therefore deserving of the worship that is given to the living God, and to him alone (cf. *Mysterium Fidei*, 55; Paul VI, Address of 15 June 1978).

And so, dear brothers and sisters, every act of reverence, every genuflection that you make before the Blessed Sacrament, is important because it is an act of faith in Christ, an act of love for Christ. And every sign of the Cross and gesture of respect made each time you pass a church is also an act of faith.

May God preserve you in this faith – this holy Catholic faith – this faith in the Blessed Sacrament.

I end, dear brothers and sisters, beloved sons and daughters of Ireland, by recalling how Divine Providence has used this Island on the edge of Europe for the conversion of the European continent, that continent which has been for two thousand years the continent of the first evangelization. I myself am a son of that nation which received the Gospel more than a thousand years ago, many centuries later than your homeland. When in 1966, we solemnly recalled the millennium of the Baptism of Poland, we recalled with gratitude also those Irish missionaries who, among others, participated in the work of the first evangelization of the country that extends East and West from the Vistula.

One of my closest friends, a famous Professor of History in Cracow, having learned of my intention to visit Ireland, said: 'What a blessing that the Pope goes to Ireland. This country deserves it in a special way.' I too have always thought like this. Thus I thought that the centenary of the Sanctuary of the Mother of God at Knock constitutes, this year, a providential occasion for the Pope's visit to Ireland. So, by this visit, I am expressing my sense of what Ireland 'deserves', and also satisfying deep needs of my own heart. I am paying a great debt to Jesus Christ, who is the Lord of history and the author of our salvation.

Hence I express my joy that I can be with you today, 29 September 1979, Feast of Saint Michael, Saint Gabriel and Saint Raphael, Archangels, and that I can celebrate the Holy Sacrifice of the Mass and give witness before you to Christ and to his Paschal Mystery. Thus I can proclaim the vivifying reality of conversion through the Eucharist and the Sacrament of Penance, in the midst of the present generation of the sons and daughters of Ireland. *Metanoeite*, 'Be converted'! (Mk 1:15). Be converted continually. Be converted every day; because constantly, every day, the Kingdom of God draws closer. On the road of this temporal world, let Christ be the Lord of your souls, for eternal life. Amen.

DROGHEDA, PEACE AND RECONCILIATION

On his first day in Ireland, Pope John
Paul went to Killineer near Drogheda,
in the Archdiocese of Armagh, where
he delivered an address to a
gathering of about 300,000 persons,
many of whom had come from
Northern Ireland. The sun continued
to shine, and the Pope's address was
a stirring appeal for an end to
violence and for peace in Ireland and
the whole world.

Dear brothers and sisters in Jesus Christ,

1   Having greeted the soil of Ireland today on my arrival in Dublin, I make my
first Irish journey to this place, to Drogheda. The cry of centuries sends me here.
    I arrive as a pilgrim of faith. I arrive also as Successor of Peter, to whom Christ
has given a particular care for the universal Church. I desire to visit those places in
Ireland in particular where the power of God and the action of the Holy Spirit have
been specially manifested. I seek first those places which carry in themselves the sign
of the 'beginning'; and 'beginning' is connected with 'firstness', with primacy. Such
a place on Irish soil is Armagh, for centuries the Episcopal See of the Primate of
Ireland.
    The Primate is he who has the first place among the Bishops, Shepherds of the
People of God in this land. This primacy is linked to the 'beginning' of the faith
and of the Church in this country. That is to say, it is linked to the heritage of Saint
Patrick, patron of Ireland.
    Hence I desired to make my first Irish journey a journey towards the
'beginning', the place of the primacy. The Church is built in her entirety on the
foundation of the Apostles and Prophets, Christ Jesus himself being the chief
cornerstone (cf. Eph 2:20). But in each land and nation the Church has her own
particular foundation stone. So it is towards this foundation here in the Primatial
See of Armagh that I first direct my pilgrim steps. The See of Armagh is the
Primatial See because it is the See of Saint Patrick. The Archbishop of Armagh is
Primate of All Ireland today because he is the *Comharba Pádraig*, the successor of
Saint Patrick, the first Bishop of Armagh.

2   Standing for the first time on Irish soil, on Armagh soil, the Successor of Peter
cannot but recall the first coming here, more than one thousand five hundred years
ago, of Saint Patrick. From his days as a shepherd boy at Slemish right up to his
death at Saul, Patrick was a witness to Jesus Christ. Not far from this spot, on the
Hill of Slane, it is said that he lit, for the first time in Ireland, the Paschal Fire so
that the light of Christ might shine forth on all of Ireland and unite all of its people
in the love of the one Jesus Christ. It gives me great joy to stand here with you
today, within sight of Slane, and so proclaim this same Jesus, the Incarnate Word
of God, the Saviour of the world. He is the Lord of history, the Light of the world,
the Hope of the future of all humanity. In the words of the Easter Liturgy,

celebrated for the first time in Ireland by Saint Patrick on the Hill of Slane, we greet Christ today: he is the Alpha and the Omega, the beginning of all things and their end. All time is his and all the ages. To him be glory for ever and ever. *Lumen Christi: Deo Gratias.* The Light of Christ: Thanks be to God. May the light of Christ, the light of faith continue always to shine out from Ireland. May no darkness ever be able to extinguish it.

That he might be faithful to the end of his life to the light of Christ was Saint Patrick's prayer for himself. That the people of Ireland might remain faithful always to the light of Christ was his constant prayer for the Irish. He wrote in his Confession:

> May God never permit it to happen to me that I should lose his people that he purchased in the utmost parts of the world. I pray to God to give me perseverance and to deign that I be a faithful witness to him to the end of my life for God. . . . From the time I came to know him in my youth, the love of God and the fear of him have grown in me, and up to now, thanks to the grace of God, I have kept the faith (*Confession*, 44, 58)

3 'I have kept the faith.' That has been the ambition of the Irish down the centuries. Through persecution and through poverty, in famine and in exile, you have kept the faith. For many it has meant martyrdom. Here at Drogheda, where his relics are honoured, I wish to mention one Irish martyr, Saint Oliver Plunkett, at whose canonization in the Holy Year, 1975, I was happy to assist, as Cardinal of Cracow, on the invitation of my friend, the late Cardinal Conway. Saint Oliver Plunkett, Primate of Ireland for twelve years is for ever an outstanding example of the love of Christ for all men. As Bishop he preached a message of pardon and peace. He was indeed the defender of the oppressed and the advocate of justice, but he would never condone violence. For men of violence, his word was the word of the Apostle Peter: 'Never pay back one wrong with another' (1 Pt 3:9). As a Martyr for the faith, he sealed by his death the same message of reconciliation that he had preached during his life. In his heart there was no rancour, for his strength was the love of Jesus, the love of the Good Shepherd who gives his life for his flock. His dying words were words of forgiveness for all his enemies.

4 Faith and fidelity are the marks of the Church in Ireland, a Church of martyrs, a Church of witnesses; a Church of heroic faith, heroic fidelity. These are the historical signs marking the track of faith on Irish soil. The Gospel and the Church have struck deep roots in the soul of the Irish people. The See of Armagh, the See of Patrick, is the place to see that track, to feel those roots. It is the place in which to meet, from which to address, those other great and faithful dioceses whose people have suffered so much from the events of the past decade, Down and Connor, Derry, Dromore, Clogher, Kilmore.

During the period and preparation of my visit to Ireland, especially precious to me was the invitation of the Primate of All Ireland that I should visit his Cathedral in Armagh. Particularly eloquent also was the fact that the invitation of the Primate was taken up and repeated by the representatives of the Church of Ireland and by leaders and members of the other Churches, including many from Northern Ireland. For all these invitations I am particularly grateful.

These invitations are an indication of the fact that the Second Vatican Council is achieving its work and that we are meeting with our fellow-Christians of other Churches as people who together confess Jesus Christ as Lord, and who are drawing closer to one another in him as we search for unity and common witness.

15

This truly fraternal and ecumenical act on the part of representatives of the Churches is also a testimony that the tragic events taking place in Northern Ireland do not have their source in the fact of belonging to different Churches and Confessions; that this is not – despite what is so often repeated before world opinion – a religious war, a struggle between Catholics and Protestants. On the contrary, Catholics and Protestants, as people who confess Christ, taking inspiration from their faith and the Gospel, are seeking to draw closer to one another in unity and peace. When they recall the greatest commandment of Christ, the commandment of love, they cannot behave otherwise.

5 But Christianity does not command us to close our eyes to difficult human problems. It does not permit us to neglect and refuse to see unjust social or international situations. What Christianity does forbid is to seek solutions to these situations by the ways of hatred, by the murdering of defenceless people, by the methods of terrorism. Let me say more: Christianity understands and recognizes the noble and just struggle for justice; but Christianity is decisively opposed to fomenting hatred and to promoting or provoking violence or struggle for the sake of 'struggle'. The command, 'Thou shalt not kill', must be binding on the conscience of humanity, if the terrible tragedy and destiny of Cain is not to be repeated.

6 For this reason it was fitting for me to come here before going to America, where I hope to address the United Nations Organization on these same problems of peace and war, justice and human rights. We have decided together, the Cardinal Primate and I, that it would be better for me to come here, to Drogheda, and that it should be from here that I would render homage to the 'beginning' of the faith and to the primacy in your homeland; and from here that I should reflect with all of you, before God, before your splendid Christian history, on this most urgent problem, the problem of peace and reconciliation.

We must, above all, clearly realize where the causes of this dramatic struggle are found. We must call by name those systems and ideologies that are responsible for this struggle. We must also reflect whether the ideology of subversion is for the true good of your people, for the true good of man. Is it possible to construct the good of individuals and peoples on hatred, on war? Is it right to push the young generations into the pit of fratricide? Is it not necessary to seek solutions to our problems by a different way? Does not the fratricidal struggle make it even more urgent for us to seek peaceful solutions with all our energies? These questions I shall be discussing before the United Nations Assembly in a few days. Here today, in this beloved land of Ireland, from which so many before me have departed for America, I wish to discuss them with you.

7 My message to you today cannot be different from what Saint Patrick and Saint Oliver Plunkett taught you. I preach what they preach: Christ, who is the 'Prince of Peace' (Is 9:5); who reconciled us to God and to each other (cf. 2 Cor 5:18); who is the source of all unity.

The Gospel reading tells us of Jesus as 'the Good Shepherd', whose one desire is to bring all together into one flock. I come to you in his name, in the name of Jesus Christ, who died in order 'to gather into one the children of God who are scattered abroad' (Jn 11:52). This is my mission, my message to you: Jesus Christ who is our peace. Christ 'is our peace' (Eph 2:11). And today and for ever he

4

repeats to us: 'My peace I give to you, my peace I leave with you' (Jn 14:27). Never before in the history of mankind has peace been so much talked about and so ardently desired as in our day. The growing interdependence of peoples and nations makes almost everyone subscribe – at least in principle – to the ideal of universal human brotherhood. Great international institutions debate humanity's peaceful coexistence. Public opinion is growing in consciousness of the absurdity of war as a means to resolve differences. More and more, peace is seen as a necessary condition for fraternal relations among nations, and among peoples. Peace is more and more clearly seen as the only way to justice; peace is itself the work of justice. And yet, again and again, one can see how peace is undermined and destroyed. Why is it then that our convictions do not always match our behaviour and our attitudes? Why is it that we do not seem to be able to banish all conflicts from our lives?

8   Peace is the result of many converging attitudes and realities; it is the product of moral concerns of ethical principles based on the Gospel message and fortified by it.

I want to mention here in the first place: justice. In his Message for the 1971 Day of Peace, my revered Predecessor, that Pilgrim for peace, Paul VI said: 'True peace must be founded upon justice, upon a sense of the untouchable dignity of man, upon the recognition of an indelible and happy equality between men, upon the basic principle of human brotherhood, that is, of the respect and love due to each man, because he is man.' This same message I affirmed in Mexico and in Poland. I reaffirm it here in Ireland. Every human being has inalienable rights that must be respected. Each human community – ethnic, historical, cultural or religious – has rights which must be respected. Peace is threatened every time one of these rights is violated. The moral law, guardian of human rights, protector of the dignity of man, cannot be set aside by any person or group, or by the State itself, for any cause, not even for security or in the interests of law and order. The law of God stands in judgment over all reasons of State. As long as injustices exist in any of the areas that touch upon the dignity of the human person, be it in the political, social or economic field, be it in the cultural or religious sphere, true peace will not exist. The causes of inequalities must be identified through a courageous and objective evaluation, and they must be eliminated so that every person can develop and grow in the full measure of his or her humanity.

9   Secondly, peace cannot be established by violence, peace can never flourish in a climate of terror, intimidation and death. It is Jesus himself who said: 'All who take the sword will perish by the sword' (Mt 26:52). This is the word of God, and it commands this generation of violent men to desist from hatred and violence and to repent.

I join my voice today to the voice of Paul VI and my other predecessors, to the voices of your religious leaders, to the voices of all men and women of reason, and I proclaim, with the conviction of my faith in Christ and with an awareness of my mission, that violence is evil, that violence is unacceptable as a solution to problems, that violence is unworthy of man. Violence is a lie, for it goes against the truth of our faith, the truth of our humanity. Violence destroys what it claims to defend: the dignity, the life, the freedom of human beings. Violence is a crime against humanity, for it destroys the very fabric of society. I pray with you that the moral sense and Christian conviction of Irish men and women may never become obscured and blunted by the lie of violence, that nobody may ever call murder by any other name than murder, that the spiral of violence may never be given the distinction of unavoidable logic or necessary retaliation. Let us remember that the word remains for ever: 'All who take the sword will perish by the sword.'

10   There is another word that must be part of the vocabulary of every Christian, especially when barriers of hate and mistrust have been constructed. This word is reconciliation. 'So if you are offering your gift at the altar, and there remember that your brother has something against you, leave your gift there before the altar and go; be reconciled with your brother, and then come and offer your gift' (Mt 5:23–24). This command of Jesus is stronger than any barrier that human inadequacy or malice can build. Even when our belief in the fundamental goodness of every human being has been shaken or undermined, even if long-held convictions and attitudes have hardened our hearts, there is one source of power that is stronger than every disappointment, bitterness or ingrained mistrust, and that power is Jesus Christ, who brought forgiveness and reconciliation to the world.

I appeal to all who listen to me; to all who are discouraged after the many years of strife, violence and alienation – that they attempt the seemingly impossible to put an end to the intolerable. I pay homage to the many efforts that have been made by countless men and women in Northern Ireland to walk the path of reconciliation and peace. The courage, the patience, the indomitable hope for the men and women of peace have lighted up the darkness of these years of trial. The spirit of Christian forgiveness shown by so many who have suffered in their persons or through their loved ones have given inspiration to multitudes. In the years to come, when the words of hatred and the deeds of violence are forgotten, it is the words of love and the acts of peace and forgiveness which will be remembered. It is these which will inspire the generations to come.

To all of you who are listening I say: do not believe in violence; do not support violence. It is not the Christian way. It is not the way of the Catholic Church. Believe in peace and forgiveness and love; for they are of Christ.

Communities who stand together in their acceptance of Jesus' supreme message of love, expressed in peace and reconciliation, and in their rejection of all violence, constitute an irresistible force for achieving what many have come to accept as impossible and destined to remain so.

11   Now I wish to speak to all men and women engaged in violence. I appeal to you, in language of passionate pleading. On my knees I beg you to turn away from the paths of violence and to return to the ways of peace. You may claim to seek justice. I too believe in justice and seek justice. But violence only delays the day of justice. Violence destroys the work of justice. Further violence in Ireland will only drag down to ruin the land you claim to love and the values you claim to cherish. In the name of God I beg you: return to Christ, who died so that men might live in forgiveness and peace. He is waiting for you, longing for each one of you to come to him so that he may say to each of you: your sins are forgiven; go in peace.

12   I appeal to young people who may have become caught up in organizations engaged in violence. I say to you, with all the love I have for you, with all the trust I have in young people: do not listen to voices which speak the language of hatred, revenge, retaliation. Do not follow any leaders who train you in the ways of inflicting death. Love life, respect life; in yourselves and in others. Give yourselves to the service of life, not the work of death. Do not think that courage and strength are proved by killing and destruction. The true courage lies in working for

peace. The true strength lies in joining with the young men and women of your generation everywhere in building up a just and human and Christian society by the ways of peace. Violence is the enemy of justice. Only peace can lead the way to true justice.

My dear young people; if you have been caught up in the ways of violence, even if you have done deeds of violence, come back to Christ, whose parting gift to the world was peace. Only when you come back to Christ will you find peace for your troubled consciences, and rest for your disturbed souls.

And to you Fathers and Mothers I say: teach your children how to forgive, make your homes places of love and forgiveness; make your streets and neighbourhoods centres of peace and reconciliation. It would be a crime against youth and their future to let even one child grow up with nothing but the experience of violence and hate.

13 Now I wish to speak to all the people in positions of leadership, to all who can influence public opinion, to all members of political parties and to all who support them. I say to you:

Never think you are betraying your own community by seeking to understand and respect and accept those of a different tradition. You will serve your own tradition best by working for reconciliation with the others. Each of the historical communities in Ireland can only harm itself by seeking to harm the other. Continued violence can only endanger everything that is most precious in the traditions and aspirations of both communities.

Let no one concerned with Ireland have any illusions about the nature and the menace of political violence. The ideology and the methods of violence have become an international problem of the utmost gravity. The longer the violence continues in Ireland, the more the danger will grow that this beloved land could become yet another theatre for international terrorism.

14 To all who bear political responsibility for the affairs of Ireland, I want to speak with the same urgency and intensity with which I have spoken to the men of violence. Do not cause or condone or tolerate conditions which give excuse or pretext to men of violence. Those who resort to violence always claim that only violence brings about change. They claim that political action cannot achieve justice. You politicians must prove them to be wrong. You must show that there is a peaceful political way to justice. You must show that peace achieves the works of justice, and violence does not.

I urge you who are called to the noble vocation of politics to have the courage to face up to your responsibility, to be leaders in the cause of peace, reconciliation and justice. If politicians do not decide and act for just change, then the field is left open to the men of violence. Violence thrives best when there is political vacuum and a refusal of political movement. Paul VI, writing to Cardinal Conway in March 1972, said: 'Everyone must play his part. Obstacles which stand in the way of justice must be removed: obstacles such as civil inequity, social and political discrimination, and misunderstanding between individuals and groups. There must be a mutual and abiding respect for others: for their persons, their rights and their lawful aspirations.' I make these words of my revered predecessor my own today.

15 I came to Drogheda today on a great mission of peace and reconciliation. I come as a pilgrim of peace, Christ's peace. To Catholics, to Protestants, my message is peace and love. May no Irish Protestant think that the Pope is an enemy, a danger

or a threat. My desire is that instead Protestants would see in me a friend and a brother in Christ. Do not lose trust that this visit of mine may be fruitful, that this voice of mine may be listened to. And even if it were not listened to, let history record that at a difficult moment in the experience of the people of Ireland, the Bishop of Rome set foot in your land, that he was with you and prayed with you for peace and reconciliation, for the victory of justice and love over hatred and violence. Yes, this our witness finally becomes a prayer, a prayer from the heart for peace for the peoples who live on this earth, peace for all the people of Ireland.

Let this fervent prayer for peace penetrate with light all consciences. Let it purify them and take hold of them.

Christ, Prince of Peace;
Mary, Mother of Peace, Queen of Ireland;
Saint Patrick, Saint Oliver, and all saints of Ireland;
I, together with all those gathered here and with all who join with me, invoke you, Watch over Ireland. Protect humanity. Amen.

DUBLIN, GREETING TO THE PRESIDENT

Returning to Dublin after his visit to Drogheda, Pope John Paul visited Dr Patrick J. Hillery, President of Ireland. The meeting took place in the President's residence, Aras an Uachtarain. The following is the text of the Pope's address:

Mr President,

I wish to express my gratitude for the warm welcome that I have received on my arrival in Ireland from the people of Ireland, as well as from their distinguished Representatives. I express my sincere thanks to you, Mr President, for the kind words that you addressed to me, with which you have wished to honour not only my person but the Head of the Roman Catholic Church.

It was fitting, after my visit to Latin America and to my beloved homeland, that I should accept the invitation of the Irish Episcopate to come to your Emerald Isle and meet your people. Many are indeed the bonds that unite your country to the See of Peter in Rome. From the earliest beginnings of Christianity in this land, all through the centuries until the present day, never has the love of the Irish for the Vicar of Christ been weakened, but it has flourished as an example for all to witness. In receiving the faith from Saint Patrick, the Irish Catholic people have also accepted that the Church of Christ is built on the Rock that is Peter, and they have established that loving relationship with the successors of Saint Peter that has always been a guarantee for the preservation of their faith. It gives me pleasure to state here that this unfailing loyalty has been matched only by their profound devotion to our Blessed Lady and by their steadfast fidelity to the duties of religion.

The history of Ireland has certainly not been without its share of suffering and pain. Economic and social conditions have induced many of her sons and daughters in the past to leave home and family and to seek elsewhere the opportunities for life in dignity that were not to be found here. Their loss for Ireland has been a gain for the countries where they settled. Those who remained have not always enjoyed a progress without setbacks. But through it all, the Irish have displayed an uncommon courage and perseverance inspired by their faith. May I be allowed, Mr President, to quote here from your last Saint Patrick's Day Message, where you credit your Patron Saint for 'the moral fibre and spiritual wealth that sustained our nation in times of trial'.

My fervent wish for you and your fellow Irish men and women is that those same qualities – heritage of a living faith preserved and deepened through the centuries – may enable this country to move towards the Third Millennium and to achieve a wellbeing that constitutes a true human advancement for all your people, a wellbeing that brings honour to the name and the history of Ireland. The vitality that draws its strength from over fifteen centuries of uninterrupted Christian tradition will enable you to tackle the many problems of a modern and still young Republic.

The elimination of poverty, the uplifting of the deprived, the finding of full employment for all and especially for the very large number of splendid young people with whom God has blessed your country at this time, the creation of social and economic wellbeing for all classes of society remain real challenges. Reaching the goals of justice in the economic and social fields will require that religious convictions and fervour be not separated from a moral and social conscience, especially for those who plan and control the economic process, be they legislators, government officials, industrialists, trade unionists, office workers and manual workers.

The part that your nation has played with prominence and distinction in the history of Europe, on the spiritual and cultural level, will inspire you also in the future, to make your own distinctive contribution to the growing unity of the European continent, preserving at the same time the values that characterize your community, and witnessing for them in the midst of the political, economic, social and cultural currents that flow through Europe in these days.

It is my fervent wish that this same Ireland will also continue, as it has in the past, to be a force for understanding, brotherhood and collaboration among all the nations of the world. Many of your fellow men and women are working already in every part of the world – and I mention here with special gratitude your many missionaries – bringing through their labours and their zeal, through their unpretentious and unselfish dedication, the assistance that so many of our brothers and sisters in other parts of the world need to advance in their own development and to be able to satisfy their basic needs.

Irish exiles and Irish missionaries have gone all over the world, and wherever they have gone they have made the name of Ireland loved and honoured. The history of Ireland has been and is a source of human and spiritual inspiration to people everywhere. Ireland has inherited a noble Christian and human mission and her contribution to the wellbeing of the world and to the shaping of a new Europe can be as great today as it was in the greatest days of Ireland's history. That is the mission, that is the challenge facing Ireland in this generation.

Finally, Mr President, I want to make a plea for peace and harmony for all the people of this island. Your sadness for the continued unrest, injustice, and violence in Northern Ireland is also my personal sadness and sorrow. On the occasion of the Feast of Saint Patrick in 1972, my beloved and revered predecessor Pope Paul VI, whose love for Ireland will always be remembered with gratitude, wrote to the late Cardinal William Conway: 'The Christian faith must convince all concerned that violence is not an acceptable solution to the problems of Ireland. But at the same time, the Christian sense of values convinces man that lasting peace can be built only on the firm foundation of justice.' Those words retain their full meaning today.

I thank you once again for your courteous and warm reception. I lovingly bless you, your land and your people.

Dia agus Muire libh
Beannacht Dé is Muire libh.
May God and Mary be with you.
May the blessing of God and the blessing of Mary be with you and with the people of Ireland always.

DUBLIN, TO THE IRISH GOVERNMENT

On Saturday evening, 29 September, the Holy Father received the members of the Irish government led by the Prime Minister, Mr Jack Lynch, and members of the Council of State in the Apostolic Nunciature. The Holy Father addressed the group as follows:

Taoiseach,

I am very pleased that I can meet here with the Members of the Irish Government. You represent the aspirations, needs and future of the Irish people, but also their potential and the promises of the future that are contained in the past history of your country. The people of Ireland have had a long history of suffering and struggle to achieve their own cohesion as a modern State and to attain the measure of wellbeing that is due to every nation.

It is your privilege to serve the people, in their name and for their progress, through the mandate that the people have conferred on you. But there are also principles and imperatives that are of a higher order and without which no society can ever hope to foster the true common good. I do not need to spell out before you the demands of justice, of peaceful living in society, of respect and protection for the dignity that derives from the very nature and destiny of every human being as a creature of God's love. It is your task to embody in concrete and practical measures the collaboration of all the citizens towards these lofty goals.

An Ireland that is prosperous, peaceful and committed to the ideal of fraternal relations among its people is also a factor that will contribute to the peaceful and just future of Europe and the whole family of nations. Today at Drogheda, I have made a solemn and passionate plea for justice, for peace and for reconciliation, particularly with regard to the situation in Northern Ireland that can leave no Irishman, no Christian and certainly not the Pope indifferent. It is my fervent prayer that all the people of this island will display the courage and find the ways for resolving a problem that is not religious in nature, but that finds its origin in a variety of historical, social, economic and political reasons.

I desire to renew once again my cordial thanks to you for your kind welcome and for all that the public authorities have done to facilitate my pastoral visit to your country. I express my esteem for you and your colleagues in the Government. May each one, according to the office and the dignity that he holds, discharge his duties inspired by a true desire to foster peace, justice and the respect of the human person.

DUBLIN, TO THE DIPLOMATIC CORPS

The Pope was already well behind schedule by the time he came to address the members of the Diplomatic Corps gathered at the Nunciature. He spoke to them in French.

Your Excellencies, Members of the Diplomatic Corps,

It gives me great pleasure to have this meeting with you on my first day in Ireland. I greatly appreciate your warm welcome.

The pastoral journey that I began today has a deep meaning for me for several reasons, which I would like to share with you. As Successor of Peter in the See of Rome, I have been entrusted with a particular care for the universal Church and for all her members. After my visit to Mexico, where the Third General Assembly of the Bishops of Latin America called me, and after my participation in the ceremonies in Poland commemorating Saint Stanislaus, it was fitting for me to come also to this island, where the Christian faith and the bond of unity with the See of Peter have been kept unbroken from the very first moment of evangelization to this day.

Saint Patrick not only was the first Primate of Ireland, but he was also the one who succeeded in implanting a religious tradition in the Irish soul, in such a way that all Irish Christians can rightly glory in the heritage of Saint Patrick. He was truly Irish, he was truly Christian; and the Irish people have preserved this same heritage of his through many centuries of challenges, suffering, and social and political upheavals, thereby setting an example, for all who believe that the message of Christ enhances and strengthens the most profound aspirations of people for dignity, fraternal unity and truth. I have come to encourage the Irish people in their adherence to the message of Christ.

I intend by my visit to pay homage also to the role which the Church in Ireland has played in the evangelization of the whole European continent. Christianity in Europe cannot be contemplated without reference to the wonderful work of the Irish missionaries and monks. This work is at the basis of many flourishing Christian communities all over the continent. I believe that the values which are so deeply embedded in the history and the culture of this people constitute a lasting force for the building up of a Europe where the spiritual dimension of man and of society remains the only guarantee for unity and progress.

As visible head of the Catholic Church and servant of humanity, I have come to an island that is marked by profound problems in relation to the situation in Northern Ireland. As I had the opportunity to state earlier today at Drogheda, it was my sincere and firm desire to proclaim personally a message of peace and reconciliation to the people in Northern Ireland, but circumstances have not permitted this. I have therefore spoken to them from Drogheda, reaffirming that the Christian sense of values must convince everyone that violence is never an acceptable solution for human problems and that true peace must be built on justice. I have called for reconciliation in the name of Christ.

I am also on my way to the United Nations, where I have been invited to address the General Assembly. My predecessors in the See of Peter have consistently expressed their esteem and encouragement for this Organization which constitutes the appropriate forum where all nations can meet in order to seek together the answers to the many problems of today's world. I go there as a messenger of peace, justice and truth, and I wish to express gratitude to all who devote themselves to international collaboration in order to create a secure and peaceful future for humanity.

The international visit which I begin today in Ireland and which I shall conclude on 7 October in the capital of the United States of America, will, I hope, be accompanied by the prayers of all believers and by the support of all men and women of good will.

Once again I express my gratitude for your presence here, and I pray that Almighty God will bless you and your families with abundant grace, and sustain you in your important work for humanity.

DUBLIN, ECUMENICAL MEETING

On the evening of his first day in Ireland, Pope John Paul II went to the Dominican Convent in Cabra, not far from the Nunciature, where he met about forty representatives of other Christian Churches. Among them were the Anglican Archbishops of Armagh and Dublin. The Holy Father spoke to the group as follows:

My dear brothers in Christ,

Permit me to greet you in the love of our common Lord and Saviour, and with the words of his servant and apostle Paul: 'Grace to you and peace from God our Father and the Lord Jesus Christ' (Eph 1:2).

I am happy to have the opportunity to come together with you in the holy name of Jesus and pray with you. For all of us here today the great promise contained in the Gospel is truly encouraging and uplifting: 'For where two or three are gathered in my name, there am I in the midst of them' (Mt 18:20). And so we rejoice exceedingly to know that Jesus Christ is with us.

We know that he is near to us with the power of his Paschal Mystery, and that from his Paschal Mystery we draw light and strength to walk in what Saint Paul calls 'the newness of life' (Rom 6:4).

What a great grace it is for the entire Christian world, that, in this our day, the Holy Spirit has powerfully stirred up in human hearts a real desire for this 'newness of life'. And what a great gift of God it is that there exists today among Christians a deeper realization of the need to be perfectly one in Christ and in his Church: to be one, in accordance with Christ's own prayer, even as he and his Father are one (cf. Jn 17:11).

Our desire for Christian unity springs from a need to be faithful to the will of God, as revealed in Christ. Our unity in Christ, moreover, conditions the effectiveness of our evangelization; it determines the credibility of our witness before the world. Christ prayed for the unity of his disciples, precisely 'so that the world may believe . . .' (Jn 17:21).

Today has indeed been a memorable day in my life: to have embraced in the love of Christ my separated Christian brethren and to confess with them 'that Jesus Christ is the Son of God' (1 Jn 4:15); that he is 'the Saviour of all men' (1 Tim 5:10); that he is 'the one Mediator between God and men, the man Christ Jesus' (1 Tim 2:5). From Drogheda this morning I appealed for peace and reconciliation according to the supreme will of Christ, who alone can unify the hearts of men in brotherhood and common witness.

Let no one ever doubt the commitment of the Catholic Church and of the Apostolic See of Rome to the pursuit of the unity of Christians. Last November, when I met the members of the Secretariat for Promoting Christian Unity, I spoke of the 'intolerable scandal of division between Christians'. I said that the movement towards unity must not stop until it has reached its goal; and I called for an energetic commitment by Catholic Bishops, priests and people to forward this movement. I said on that occasion: 'The Catholic Church, faithful to the direction taken at the Council, not only wants to go forward on the way that leads to the restoration of unity, but is anxious, according to its means and in full submission to the promptings of the Holy Spirit . . . , to strengthen at every level its contribution to this great movement of all Christians' (Address of 18 November 1978). I renew that commitment and that pledge today here in Ireland, where reconciliation between Christians takes on a special urgency, but where it also has special resources in the tradition of Christian faith and fidelity to religion which marks both the Catholic and the Protestant communities.

The work of reconciliation, the road to unity, may be long and difficult. But, as on the way to Emmaus, the Lord himself is with us on the way, always making 'as if to go on' (Lk 24:28). He will stay with us until the longed-for moment comes, when we can join together in recognizing him in the Holy Scriptures and 'in the breaking of the bread' (Lk 24:35).

Meanwhile, the internal renewal of the Catholic Church, in total fidelity to the Second Vatican Council, to which I pledged all my energies at the beginning of my papal ministry, must continue with undiminished vigour. This renewal is itself an indispensable contribution to the work of unity between Christians. As we each, in our respective Churches, grow in our searching of the Holy Scriptures, in our fidelity to and continuity with the age-old tradition of the Christian Church, in our search for holiness and for authenticity of Christian living, we shall also be coming closer to Christ, and therefore closer to one another in Christ.

It is he alone, through the action of his Holy Spirit, who can bring our hopes to fulfilment. In him we place all our trust: in 'Jesus Christ our hope' (1 Tim 1:2). Despite our human weakness and our sins, despite all obstacles, we accept in humility and faith the great principle enunciated by our Saviour: 'What is impossible with men is possible with God' (Lk 18:27).

May this day truly mark, for all of us and for those whom we serve in Christ, the occasion for ever greater fidelity, in prayer and penance, to the cause of Jesus Christ, and to his message of truth and love, of justice and peace. May our common esteem and love for the holy and inspired word of God unite us ever more, as we continue to study and examine together the important issues affecting ecclesial unity in all its aspects, as well as the necessity for a united service to a world in need.

Ireland, dear brothers in Christ, has special and urgent need for the united service of Christians. All Irish Christians must stand together to defend spiritual and moral values against the inroads of materialism and moral permissiveness. Christians must unite together to promote justice and defend the rights and dignity of every human person. All Christians in Ireland must join together in opposing all violence and all assaults against the human person – from whatever quarter they come – and in finding Christian answers to the grave problems of Northern Ireland. We must all be ministers of reconciliation. We must by example as well as by word try to move citizens, communities and politicians towards the ways of tolerance, cooperation and love. No fear of criticism, no risk of resentment, must deter us from this task. The charity of Christ compels us. Precisely because we have one common Lord, Jesus Christ, we must accept together the responsibility of the vocation we have received from him.

Dear brothers: with a conviction linked to our faith, we realize that the destiny of the world is at stake, because the credibility of the Gospel has been challenged. Only in perfect unity can we Christians adequately give witness to the truth. And so our fidelity to Jesus Christ urges us to do more, to pray more, to love more.

May Christ the Good Shepherd show us how to lead our people along the path of love to the goal of perfect unity: for the praise and glory of the Father, and of the Son, and of the Holy Spirit. Amen.

DUBLIN, TO THE JOURNALISTS

Later that same evening, Pope John Paul met the representatives of the press in the hall of the Dominican Convent at Cabra. Since he was behind schedule, he contented himself with distributing his speech rather than reading it. The press corps sang 'For he's a jolly good fellow'. The text of the prepared speech is given below.

My friends of the communications media,

During my visit to Ireland, I wish to leave a special thought for all of you, a special word for each of you, so that in time to come you will remember: the Pope said many things to many people during his pastoral visit to Ireland, but this was his message to me.

That message is the second of the two great commandments of Jesus: 'Love your neighbour as yourself.' That message and that mandate should have a special meaning to you because your work makes you an honoured guest in millions of homes throughout the world.

Wherever the sounds of transmit are heard, wherever the images you capture are seen, wherever the words you report are read, there is your neighbour. There is a person you must love, someone for whose total wellbeing you must work – and even sometimes go without sleep and miss your meals. You are the instruments through whom that person – and millions of others – enjoy a wider experience and is helped to become a more effective member of the world community, a true neighbour to others.

Your profession, by its very nature, makes you servants, willing servants, of the community. Many of the members of that community will differ from you in political views, in material prospects, in religious conviction or in moral performance. As good communicators, you serve them all just the same – with love and with truth; indeed with a love of truth. As good communicators, you build bridges to unite, not walls to divide. As good communicators, you work out of the conviction that love and service of neighbour are the most important business in your lives.

All your concern, then, will be for the community's good. You will feed it on the truth. You will enlighten its conscience and serve as its peacemaker. You will set before the community standards that will keep it stretching for a way of life and a mode of behaviour worthy of its potential, worthy of human dignity.

You will inspire the community, fire its ideals, stimulate its imagination – if necessary, taunt it – into getting the best out of itself, the human best, the Christian best. You will neither yield to any inducement nor bend before any threat which might seek to deflect you from total integrity in your professional service of those who are not only your neighbours, but your brothers and sisters in the family of God, the Father of us all.

You think of yourselves as hard-headed realists, and I am well aware of the realities with which you must contend. Yet this is the Pope's word to you. It is no small thing he asks, no mean challenge he leaves with you. What he challenges you to do is to build, here in the Irish community and in the world community, the kingdom of God, the kingdom of love and of peace.

I thank you all sincerely for the work you are doing in the coverage of this visit. I ask you to bring my thanks and my love to your families, as I pray for you and for them in the beautiful Irish formula: 'May God hold you in the hollow of his hand. May he keep you and your dear ones in his peace.'

DUBLIN, GREETINGS TO THE VISITING BISHOPS

The last meeting of the Pope's first
day in Ireland took place once more
in the Dominican Convent in Cabra,
where he met the Catholic Bishops
who had come to Ireland for his visit.
He spoke to them as follows:

Dear Brothers in our Lord Jesus Christ,

That so many of you have come from different countries, to share with me the various moments of my visit, is a tribute both to Ireland and to yourselves, for it proves that you feel united with the Bishop of Rome in his 'solicitude for all the Churches' (2 Cor 11:28), and at the same time it shows that you want to honour the faith of the Church in Ireland.

For is it not true that the Christian communities you represent have to discharge a duty of gratitude to the Church of Ireland? You who come from other European nations feel a particular relationship with the people that brought forth so many and so great missionaries, who in centuries past travelled untiringly across the mountains and rivers and through the plains of Europe to support the faith when it was flagging, to revive the Christian communities, and preach the word of the Lord. The vitality of the Church in Ireland made the establishing of many of your own communities possible. *Peregrinari pro Christo*: to be a voyager, a pilgrim for Christ was their reason for leaving their dear native land; and the Church in Europe was given new life by their journeyings.

Outside the continent, Irish immigrants, priests and missionaries were again the founders of new dioceses and parishes, the builders of churches and schools, and their faith succeeded, sometimes against overwhelming odds, to bring Christ to new regions, and to imbue new communities with the same undivided love for Jesus and his Mother, and with the same loyalty and affection for the Apostolic See in Rome as they had known in their homeland.

As we reflect on these historical realities, and as we witness together, during this visit, the piety, the faith and the vitality of the Irish Church, we cannot but feel blessed for these moments. Your presence here will in turn be an encouragement for

28

the Irish Episcopate and for the Irish Christians, since in seeing you gathered around the Bishop of Rome, they will see that it is the whole *Collegium Episcopale* that offers support to the local Pastors and assumes its share of responsibility for the Church that is in Ireland. Let your love for Ireland and your appreciation of Ireland's place in the Church be expressed in prayer for a speedy return to peace in this beautiful island. Lead your faithful people in this earnest and untiring prayer to the Prince of Peace, through the intercession of Mary, Queen of Peace.

When the people of this beloved country see you, gathered together with the Irish Bishops around the Bishop of Rome, they witness that special union that constitutes a core of the episcopal collegiality, a union of mind and heart, a union of commitment and dedication in the building up of the Body of Christ, that is the Church. It is this profound union, this sincere 'communion' that confers depth and meaning to the concept of collegiality and that carries it beyond a mere practical collaboration or a sharing of insights. It then becomes a bond that truly unites the Bishops of the whole world with the Successor of Peter and among themselves, in order to carry out *cum Petro et sub Petro* the apostolic ministry which the Lord entrusted to the Twelve. Knowing that such are the sentiments that animate your presence here with me not only gives me satisfaction but also supports me in my own unique and universal pastoral ministry.

From this union among all the Bishops will flow forth for each ecclesial community, and for the Church as a whole, abundant fruits of unity and communion among all the faithful and with their Bishops, as well as with the visible Head of the universal Church.

Thank you for sharing with me the privilege and the supernatural grace of this visit. May the Lord Jesus bless you and your dioceses with ever more abundant fruits of union in mind and heart. And may every Christian everywhere, and the whole Church of God as one, increasingly become a sign and a presence of hope for all of humanity.

DUBLIN, TO THE POLISH COMMUNITY

Having visited a group of handicapped children at the Dominican Convent in Cabra on Sunday morning, 30 September, the Holy Father returned to the Nunciature and in the garden there met a group of about 400 Polish emigrants led by Cardinal Franciszek Macharski, Archbishop of Cracow. The Pope spoke to the group in Polish:

Beloved fellow-countrymen!

I would like to greet all of you who have come from all over Ireland to this meeting of ours that has been included in the programme of my visit to Ireland. The first year of my Pontificate urges me for the third time to leave Rome – this time to go to Ireland and to the United States of America. The special motive for my journey is the invitation of the Secretary General of the United Nations Organization in New York, which I could not have left unanswered.

My visit to Ireland at the beginning of this responsible journey has a special meaning. I wish to express my thanks to all here present for your fraternal solidarity with the Pope, whose homeland is also yours. I am aware that this solidarity has been proved by your constant prayer and other spiritual acts supporting me in all my services. For my high mission I need this support immensely.

At the same time I would like to wish you all God's blessings in the lives that you live in Ireland, while being still deeply rooted in Polish soil, in Polish culture and in Polish traditions. It is from Poland that you have brought over your faith – a bond of spiritual unity with the Bishop of Rome and with the whole Catholic Church. May this unity support you – not only to achieve your own salvation and that of your neighbours but also to maintain this spiritual profile that decides our national identity, our presence in European history and our contribution to the struggle for peace, justice and freedom.

I will repeat here the wish I expressed on May 16, when addressing more than six thousand Poles during a special audience in Rome:

'At this exceptional meeting today we must hope – with the help of God's grace and through the intercession of Mary, Mother of the Church, who is our Lady of Jasna Góra, Queen of Poland, with the intercession of Saint Stanislaus, Saint Wojciech (Adalbert) and all the Polish Saints and Blesseds up to Blessed Maximilian Kolbe and Blessed Mary Teresa Ledochowska – that all of us, wherever we may be, may succeed in bearing witness to the maturity of Poland, in strengthening our right of citizenship among all the nations of Europe and of the world, and in serving this noble purpose: to bear witness to Christian universalism.'

That is my heartfelt wish for you and in this spirit I bless you all, as well as your families, your Pastors, priests, and the whole Polonia.

Sunday, 30 September

CLONMACNOIS

On his way to Galway, the Pope's helicopter stopped at Clonmacnois, the seat of an ancient Irish monastery.

While there he spoke to those gathered as follows:

Dear brothers and sisters,

This visit to Clonmacnois gives me the opportunity to render homage to the traditions of faith and Christian living in Ireland.

In particular, I wish to recall and honour the great monastic contribution to Ireland that was made here on this revered spot for one thousand years, and whose influence was carried all over Europe by missionary monks and by students of this monastic school of Clonmacnois.

When we look at the works of faith, we must give thanks to God. Thanks to God for the origins of this apostolic faith in Ireland. Thanks to God for the saints and apostles and all who were the instruments for implanting and keeping alive this faith, and who 'have done God's will throughout the ages'. Thanks to God for the generosity of faith that brought forth fruits of justice and holiness of life. Thanks to God for the preservation of the faith in integrity and purity of teaching. Thanks to God for the continuity of the message of the Apostles handed down intact to this day.

Never forget the wonderful boast and commitment made by Saint Columban to Boniface IV in Rome: 'We Irish . . . are disciples of Saints Peter and Paul . . . ; we hold unbroken that Catholic faith which we first received from you.'

And in Ireland today, this Catholic faith is unbroken, alive and active. By the merits of our Lord Jesus Christ and by the power of his grace, it can, and must, always be this way in Ireland.

Clonmacnois was long the centre of a renowned school of sacred art. The Shrine of Saint Manchan, standing on the altar today, is one outstanding example of its work. This is therefore a fitting place for me to express my gratitude for the works of Irish sacred art, several pieces of which have been presented to me on the occasion of my visit.

Irish art embodies in many instances the deep faith and devotion of the Irish people as expressed in the personal sensitivity of its artists. Every piece of art, be it religious or secular, be it a painting, a sculpture, a poem or any form of handicraft made by loving skill, is a sign and a symbol of the inscrutable secret of human existence, of man's origin and destiny, of the meaning of his life and work. It speaks to us of the meaning of birth and death, of the greatness of man.

Praised be Jesus Christ!

ARRIVAL AT GALWAY

Awaiting the arrival of the Holy Father at Ballybrit racecourse in Galway, where his Holiness would shortly celebrate Mass for 300,000 youth of Ireland on Sunday, 30 September, were the Bishop of Galway, Dr Eamon Casey and the Mayor of the city. In response to their warm welcome, the Pope spoke as follows:

I thank the Bishop of Galway and Kilmacduagh and the esteemed Mayor of the city of Galway for this warm welcome. It is a special pleasure for me to be able to come West today across the width of Ireland to beautiful Galway Bay.

To you, dear Brother, pastor of this Western See which in Saint Patrick's time was 'beyond the confines of the inhabited earth', but which now is at the meeting place of Europe and the Americas – to you and to your priests, religious and laity I extend a word of special greeting. It honours your Diocese and your City that you invited me to meet with representatives of all the youth of Ireland. Among you I shall meet the future of Ireland, those who will carry the torch of the Christian faith into the twenty-first century.

On this first visit of the Vicar of Christ on earth to the people of the West of Ireland, I wish to ask your prayerful support for my universal mission as Bishop of Rome. I count in a special way on your daily prayers for me in your families, when parents and children together invoke the help of the Lord Jesus and of his Mother Mary.

May God bless this City and all its inhabitants, and grant his strength to the weak and the sick, his courage to those who struggle, and his peace and joy to all.

GALWAY, MASS FOR THE YOUTH OF IRELAND

At Galway, an Irish city on the West coast, the Pope met a large gathering of young people who came from all parts of Ireland. Many had camped out overnight and remained cheerful despite the rain which was now falling. After an enthusiastic welcome, with songs in English and in Irish, the Holy Father delivered the following homily during the Mass. It was interrupted for twelve minutes with songs and cheers when he reached the phrase, 'Young people of Ireland, I love you'.

Dear young people, brothers and sisters of our Lord Jesus Christ,

1   This is a very special occasion, a very important one. This morning, the Pope belongs to the youth of Ireland! I have looked forward to this moment; I have

prayed that I may touch your hearts with the words of Jesus. Here I wish to recall what I said so often before as Archbishop of Cracow and what I have repeated as Successor of Saint Peter: I believe in youth. I believe in youth with all my heart and with all the strength of my conviction. And today I say: I believe in the youth of Ireland! I believe in you who stand here before me, in every one of you.

When I look at you, I see the Ireland of the future. Tomorrow, you will be the living force of your country; you will decide what Ireland will be. Tomorrow, as technicians or teachers, nurses or secretaries, farmers or tradesmen, doctors or engineers, priests or religious – tomorrow you will have the power to make dreams come true. Tomorrow, Ireland will depend on you.

When I look at you assembled around this altar and listen to your praying voices, your singing voices, I see the future of the Church. God has his plan for the Church in Ireland, but he needs you to carry it out. What the Church will be in the future depends on your free cooperation with God's grace.

When I look at the thousands of young people here before me, I also see the challenges that you face. You have come from the parishes of Ireland as the representatives of those that could not be here. You carry in your hearts the rich heritage that you have received from your parents, your teachers and your priests. You carry in your hearts the treasures which Irish history and culture have given you, but you also share in the problems that Ireland faces.

2   Today, for the first time since Saint Patrick preached the faith to the Irish, the Successor of Peter comes from Rome and sets foot on Irish soil. You rightly ask yourselves what message he brings and what words he will speak to Ireland's youth. My message can be none other than the message of Christ himself; my words can be none other than the word of God.

I did not come here to give you an answer to all your individual questions. You have your Bishops, who know your local circumstances and local problems; you have your priests, especially those who devote themselves to the demanding but rewarding pastoral care of youth. They know you personally and will help you to find the right answers. But, I too feel that I know you, for I know and understand young people. And I know that you, like other young people of your age in other countries, are affected by what is happening in society around you. Although you still live in an atmosphere where true religious and moral principles are held in honour, you have to realize that your fidelity to these principles will be tested in many ways. The religious and moral traditions of Ireland, the very soul of Ireland, will be challenged by the temptations that spare no society in our age. Like so many other young people in various parts of the world, you will be told that changes must be made, that you must have more freedom, that you should be different from your parents, and that the decisions about your lives depend on you, and you alone.

The prospect of growing economic progress, and the chance of obtaining a greater share of the goods that modern society has to offer, will appear to you as an opportunity to achieve greater freedom. The more you possess – you may be tempted to think – the more you will feel liberated from every type of confinement. In order to make more money and to possess more, in order to eliminate effort and worry, you may be tempted to take moral shortcuts where honesty, truth and work are concerned. The progress of science and technology seems inevitable and you may be enticed to look towards the technological society for the answers to all your problems.

3   The lure of pleasure, to be had whenever and wherever it can be found, will be strong and it may be presented to you as part of progress towards greater autonomy and freedom from rules. The desire to be free from external restraints may manifest itself very strongly in the sexual domain, since this is an area that is so closely tied to a human personality. The moral standards that the Church and society have held up to you for so long a time, will be presented as obsolete and a hindrance to the full development of your own personality. Mass media, entertainment, and literature will present a model for living where all too often it is every man for himself, and where the unrestrained affirmation of self leaves no room for concern for others.

You will hear people tell you that your religious practices are hopelessly out of date, that they hamper your style and your future, that with everything that social and scientific progress has to offer, you will be able to organize your own lives, and that God has played out his role. Even many religious persons will adopt such attitudes, breathing them in from the surrounding atmosphere, without attending to the practical atheism that is at their origin.

A society that, in this way, has lost its higher religious and moral principles will become an easy prey for manipulation and for domination by the forces, which, under the pretext of greater freedom, will enslave it ever more.

Yes, dear young people, do not close your eyes to the moral sickness that stalks your society today, and from which your youth alone will not protect you. How many young people have already warped their consciences and have substituted the true joy of life with drugs, sex, alcohol, vandalism and the empty pursuit of mere material possessions.

4   Something else is needed: something that you will find only in Christ, for he alone is the measure and the scale that you must use to evaluate your own life. In Christ you will discover the true greatness of your own humanity; he will make you understand your own dignity as human beings 'created to the image and likeness of God' (Gen 1:26). Christ has the answers to your questions and the key to history; he has the power to uplift hearts. He keeps calling you, he keeps inviting you, he who is 'the way, and the truth, and the life' (Jn 14:6). Yes, Christ calls you, but he calls you in truth. His call is demanding, because he invites you to let yourselves be 'captured' by him completely, so that your whole lives will be seen in a different light. He is the Son of God, who reveals to you the loving face of the Father. He is the Teacher, the only one whose teaching does not pass away, the only one who teaches with authority. He is the friend who said to his disciples, 'No longer do I call you servants . . . but I have called you friends' (Jn 15:15). And he proved his friendship by laying down his life for you.

His call is demanding for he taught us what it means to be truly human. Without heeding the call of Jesus, it will not be possible to realize the fullness of your own humanity. You must build on the foundation which is Christ (cf. 1 Cor 3:11); only with him your life will be meaningful and worthwhile.

You come from Catholic families; you go regularly and meet Christ in Holy Communion on Sundays or even during the week. Many of you pray with your families every day; and I hope you all will continue to do so throughout later life. And yet it can happen that you will be tempted to walk away from Christ. This can happen especially if you see the contradiction in the life of some of your fellow men between the faith they profess and their way of living. But I wish to insist and to plead that you always heed the call of Christ, for he alone can teach you the true meaning of life and of all temporal realities.

5 Permit me, in this context, to recall still another phrase of the Gospel, a phrase that we must remember even when its consequences are particularly difficult for us to accept. It is the phrase that Christ pronounced in the Sermon on the Mount: 'Love your enemies, do good to those who hate you' (Lk 6:27). You have guessed already that even by my reference to these words of the Saviour, I have before my mind the painful events that for over ten years have been taking place in Northern Ireland. I am sure that all young people are living these events very deeply and very painfully, for they are tracing deep furrows in your young hearts. These events, painful as they are, must also be an incitement to reflection. They demand that you form an interior judgment of conscience to determine where you, as young Catholics, stand on the matter.

You heard the words of Jesus: 'Love your enemies.' The command of Jesus does not mean that we are not bound by love for our native land; it means that we can remain indifferent before injustice in its various temporal and historical aspects. These words of Jesus take away only hate. I beg you to reflect deeply: what would human life be if Jesus had never spoken such words? What would the world be if in our mutual relations we were to give primacy to hatred among people, between classes, between nations? What would the future of humanity be if we were to base on this hatred the future of individuals and of nations?

Sometimes, one could have the feeling that, before the experiences of history and before concrete situations, love has lost its power and that it is impossible to practise it. And yet, in the long run, love always brings victory, love is never defeated. And, I could add, the history of Ireland proves that. If it were not so, humanity would only be condemned to destruction.

6 Dear young friends, this is the message I entrust to you today, asking you to take it with you and share it with your family at home and with your friends in school and at work. On returning home, tell your parents, and everyone who wants to listen, that the Pope believes in you and that he counts on you. Say that the young are the strength of the Pope, who wishes to share with them his hope for the future and his encouragement.

I have given you the words of my heart. Now let me also ask you for something in return. You know that from Ireland I am going to the United Nations. The truth which I have proclaimed before you is the same that I shall present, in a different way, before that supreme forum of the nations. I hope that your prayers – the prayers of the youth of Ireland – will accompany me and support me in this important mission. I count on you, because the future of human life on this earth is at stake, in every country and in the whole world. The future of all peoples and nations, the future of humanity itself depends on this: whether the words of Jesus in the Sermon on the Mount, whether the message of the Gospel will be listened to once again.

May the Lord Jesus be always with you! With his truth that makes you free (cf. Jn 8:32); with his word that unlocks the mystery of man and reveals to man his own humanity; with his death and Resurrection that makes you new and strong.

Let us place this intention at the feet of Mary, Mother of God and Queen of Ireland, example of generous love and dedication to the service of others.

Young people of Ireland, I love you! Young people of Ireland, I bless you! I bless you in the name of our Lord Jesus Christ.

KNOCK, HOMILY

After visiting 2,500 sick people in the
Basilica of Knock ('I have come to
bear witness to Christ's love for you'
said the Pope), the Holy Father
concelebrated Mass in the open
before an estimated crowd of
500,000. His voice echoed over the
hillsides as the evening mist came
down. After the Gospel, the Pope
preached the following homily:

Dear brothers and sisters in Christ, faithful sons and daughters of Mary,

1   Here I am at the goal of my journey to Ireland: the Shrine of Our Lady at
Knock. Since I first learnt of the centenary of this Shrine, which is being celebrated
this year, I have felt a strong desire to come here, the desire to make yet another
pilgrimage to the Shrine of the Mother of Christ, the Mother of the Church, the
Queen of Peace. Do not be surprised at this desire of mine. It has been my custom
to make pilgrimages to the shrines of our Lady, starting with my earliest youth and
in my own country. I made such pilgrimages also as a Bishop and as a Cardinal. I
know very well that every people, every country, indeed every diocese, has its holy
places in which the heart of the whole people of God beats, one could say, in more
lively fashion: places of special encounter between God and human beings; places in
which Christ dwells in a special way in our midst. If these places are so often
dedicated to his Mother, it reveals all the more fully to us the nature of his Church.
Since the Second Vatican Council, which concluded its Constitution on the Church
with the chapter on 'The Blessed Virgin Mary, Mother of God, in the Mystery of
Christ and of the Church', this fact is more evident for us today than ever – yes, for
all of us, for all Christians. Do we not confess with all our brethren, even with those
with whom we are not yet linked in full unity, that we are a pilgrim people. As once
this people travelled on its pilgrimage under the guidance of Moses, so we, the
People of God of the New Covenant, are travelling on our pilgrim way under the
guidance of Christ.
    I am here then as a pilgrim, a sign of the pilgrim Church throughout the world
participating, through my presence as Peter's Successor, in a very special way in the
centenary celebration of this Irish Shrine at Knock.
    The Liturgy of the Word of today's Mass gives me my pilgrim's salutation to
Mary, as now I come before her in Ireland's Marian Shrine at Cnoc Mhuire, the Hill
of Mary.

2   'Blessed are you among women, and blessed is the fruit of your womb' (Lk
1:42). These are the words with which Elizabeth, filled with the Holy Spirit,
greeted Mary, her kinswoman from Nazareth.
    'Blessed are you among women, and blessed is the fruit of your womb'! This is
also my greeting to Muire Máthair Dé, Mary the Mother of God, Queen of Ireland,
at this Shrine of Knock. With these words, I want to express the immense joy and

gratitude that fills my heart today in this place. I could not have wanted it any differently. Highlights of my recent pastoral journeys have been the visits to the Shrines of Mary: to our Lady of Guadalupe in Mexico, to the Black Madonna of Jasna Góra in my homeland, and three weeks ago to our Lady of Loreto in Italy. Today I come here because I want all of you to know that my devotion to Mary unites me, in a very special way, with the people of Ireland.

3 Yours is a long spiritual tradition of devotion to our Lady. Mary can truly say of Ireland what we have just heard in the first reading: 'So I took root in an honoured people' (Sir 24:12). Your veneration of Mary is so deeply interwoven in your faith that its origins are lost in the early centuries of the evangelization of your country. I have been told that, in Irish speech, the names of God and Jesus and Mary are linked with one another, and that God is seldom named in prayer or in blessing without Mary's name being mentioned also. I also know that you have an eighth-century Irish poem that calls Mary 'Sun of our race', and that a litany from that same period honours her as 'Mother of the heavenly and earthly Church'. But better than any literary source, it is the constant and deeply rooted devotion to Mary that testifies to the success of evangelization by Saint Patrick, who brought you the Catholic faith in all its fullness.

It is fitting then, and it gives me great happiness to see, that the Irish people maintain this traditional devotion to the Mother of God in their homes and their parishes, and in a special way at this Shrine of Cnoc Mhuire. For a whole century now, you have sanctified this place of pilgrimage through your prayers, through your sacrifices, through your penance. All those who have come here have received blessings through the intercession of Mary. From that day of grace, 21 August 1879, until this very day, the sick and suffering, people handicapped in body or mind, troubled in their faith or their conscience, all have been healed, comforted and confirmed in their faith because they trusted that the Mother of God would lead them to her Son Jesus. Every time a pilgrim comes up to what was once an obscure bogside village in County Mayo, every time a man, woman or child comes up to the Old Church with the Apparition Gable or to the new Shrine of Mary Queen of Ireland, it is to renew his or her faith in the salvation that comes through Jesus, who made us all children of God and heirs of the kingdom of heaven. By entrusting yourselves to Mary, you receive Christ. In Mary, 'the Word was made flesh'; in her the Son of God became man, so that all of us might know how great our human dignity is. Standing on this hallowed ground, we look up to the Mother of God and say 'Blessed are you among women, and blessed is the fruit of your womb'.

The present time is an important moment in the history of the universal Church, and, in particular, of the Church in Ireland. So many things have changed. So many valuable new insights have been gained in what it means to be Christian. So many new problems have to be faced by the faithful, either because of the increased pace of change in society, or because of the new demands that are made on the People of God – demands to live to the fullest the mission of evangelization. The Second Vatican Council and the Synod of Bishops have brought new pastoral vitality to the whole Church. My revered predecessor Paul VI laid down wise guidelines for renewal and gave the whole people of God inspiration and enthusiasm for the task. In everything he said and did, Paul VI taught the Church to be open to the needs of humanity and at the same time to be unfailingly faithful to the unchanging message of Christ. Loyal to the teaching of the College of Bishops together with the Pope, the Church in Ireland has gratefully accepted the riches of the Council and the Synods. The Irish Catholic people have clung faithfully, sometimes in spite of pressures to the contrary, to the rich expressions of faith, to the fervent sacramental practices, and to that dedication to charity, which have always been a special mark of your Church. But the task of renewal in Christ is never finished. Every generation, with its own mentality and characteristics, is like a new continent to be won for Christ. The Church must constantly look for new ways that will enable her to understand more profoundly and to carry out with renewed vigour the mission received from her Founder. In this arduous task, like so many times before when the Church was faced with a new challenge, we turn to Mary, the Mother of God and the Seat of Wisdom, trusting that she will show us again the way to her Son. A very old Irish homily for the feast of the Epiphany (from the *Leabhar Breac*) says that as the Wise Men found Jesus on the lap of his Mother, so we today find Christ on the lap of the Church.

4   Mary was truly united with Jesus. Not many of her own words have been preserved in the Gospels; but those that have been recorded refer us again to her Son and to his word. At Cana in Galilee, she turned from her Son to the servants and said 'Do whatever he tells you' (Jn 2:5). This same message, she still speaks to us today.

5   'Do whatever he tells you.' What Jesus tells us – through his life and by his word – has been preserved for us in the Gospels, and in the letters of the Apostles and of Saint Paul and transmitted to us by the Church. We must make ourselves familiar with his words. We do this by listening to the readings from Sacred Scripture in the liturgy of the word, which introduce us to the Eucharistic Sacrifice; by reading the Scriptures on our own; in the family, or together with friends, by reflecting on what the Lord tells us when we recite the Rosary and combine our devotion to the Mother of God with prayerful meditation on the mysteries of her Son's life. Whenever we have questions, whenever we are burdened, whenever we are faced with the choices that our faith imposes on us, the word of the Lord will comfort and guide us.

   Christ has not left his followers without guidance in the task of understanding and living the Gospel. Before returning to his Father, he promised to send his Holy Spirit to the Church: 'But the Counsellor, the Holy Spirit whom the Father will send in my name, he will teach you all things, and bring to your remembrance all I have said to you' (Jn 14:26).

   This same Spirit guides the Successors of the Apostles, your Bishops, united with the Bishop of Rome, to whom it was entrusted to preserve the faith and to 'preach the Gospel to the whole creation' (Mk 16:14). Listen to their voices, for they bring you the word of the Lord.

6   'Do whatever he tells you.' So many different voices assail the Christian in today's wonderful but complicated and demanding world. So many false voices are heard that conflict with the word of the Lord. They are the voices that tell you that truth is less important than personal gain; that comfort, wealth, and pleasure are the true aims of life; that the refusal of new life is better than generosity of spirit and the taking up of responsibility; that justice must be achieved but without any personal involvement by the Christian; that violence can be a means to a good end; that unity can be built without giving up hate.

   And now let us return in thought from Cana in Galilee to the Shrine of Knock. Do we not hear the Mother of Christ pointing him out to us here too and speaking to us the same words that she used at Cana: 'Do whatever he tells you'? She is saying it to all of us. Her voice is heard more expressly by my Brothers in the Episcopate, the pastors of the Church in Ireland, who by inviting me here have asked me to respond to an invitation from the Mother of the Church. And so, Venerable Brothers, I am responding, as I enter in thought into the whole of your country's past and as I feel also the force of its eloquent present, so joyful and yet at the same time so anxious and at times so sorrowful. I am responding, as I did at Guadalupe in Mexico and at Jasna Góra in Poland. In my own name and on your behalf and in the name of all the Catholic People of Ireland, I pronounce, at the close of this homily, the following words of trust and consecration:

Mother, in this shrine you gather the People of God of all Ireland and constantly point out to them Christ in the Eucharist and in the Church. At this solemn moment we listen with particular attention to your words: 'Do whatever my Son tells you.' And we wish to respond to your words with all our heart. We wish to do what your Son tells us, what he commands us, for he has the words of eternal life. We wish to carry out and fulfil all that comes from him, all that is contained in the Good News, as our forefathers did for many centuries. Their fidelity to Christ and to his Church, and their heroic attachment to the Apostolic See, have in a way stamped on all of us an indelible mark that we all share. Their fidelity has, over the centuries, borne fruit in Christian heroism and in a virtuous tradition of living in accordance with God's law, especially in accordance with the holiest commandment of the Gospel – the commandment of love. We have received this splendid heritage from their hands at the beginning of a new age, as we approach the close of the second millennium since the Son of God was born of you, our *alma Mater*, and we intend to carry this heritage into the future with the same fidelity with which our forefathers bore witness to it.

Today therefore, on the occasion of the first visit of a Pope to Ireland, we entrust and consecrate to you, Mother of Christ and Mother of the Church, our hearts, our consciences, and our works, in order that they may be in keeping with the faith we profess. We entrust and consecrate to you each and every one of those who make up both the community of the Irish people and the community of the People of God living in this land.

We entrust and consecrate to you the Bishops of Ireland, the clergy, the religious men and women, the contemplative monks and sisters, the seminarians, the novices. We entrust and consecrate to you the mothers and fathers, the youth, the children. We entrust and consecrate to you the teachers, the catechists, the students; the writers, the poets, the actors, the artists, the workers and their leaders, the employers and managers, the professional people, the farmers; those engaged in political and public life; those who form public opinion. We entrust and consecrate to you the married and those preparing for marriage; those called to serve you and their fellow-men in single life; the sick, the aged, the mentally ill, the handicapped and all who nurse and care for them. We entrust and consecrate to you the prisoners and all who feel rejected; the exiled, the homesick and the lonely.

We entrust to your motherly care the land of Ireland, where you have been and are so much loved. Help this land to stay true to you and your Son always. May prosperity never cause Irish men and women to forget God or abandon their faith. Keep them faithful in prosperity to the faith they would not surrender in poverty and persecution. Save them from greed, from envy, from seeking selfish or sectional interest. Help them to work together with a sense of Christian purpose and a common Christian goal, to build a just and peaceful and loving society where the poor are never neglected and the rights of all, especially the weak, are respected. Queen of Ireland, Mary Mother of the heavenly and earthly Church, Máthair Dé, keep Ireland true to her spiritual tradition and her Christian heritage. Help her to respond to her historic mission of bringing the light of Christ to the nations, and so making the glory of God be the honour of Ireland.

Mother, can we keep silent about what we find most painful, what leaves us many a time so helpless? In a very special way we entrust to you this great wound now afflicting our people, hoping that your hands will be able to cure and heal it. Great is our concern for those young souls who are caught up in bloody acts of vengeance and hatred. Mother, do not abandon these youthful hearts. Mother, be with them in their most dreadful hours, when we can neither counsel nor assist them. Mother, protect all of us and especially the youth of Ireland from being overcome by hostility and hatred. Teach us to distinguish clearly what proceeds from love for our country from what bears the mark of destruction and the brand of Cain. Teach us that evil means can never lead to a good end; that all human life is sacred; that murder is murder no matter what the motive or end. Save others, those who view these terrible events, from another danger: that of living a life robbed of Christian ideals or in conflict with the principles of morality.

May our ears constantly hear with the proper clarity your motherly voice: 'Do whatever my Son tells you.' Enable us to persevere with Christ. Enable us, Mother of the Church, to build up his Mystical Body by living with the life that he alone can grant us from his fullness, which is both divine and human.

At the close of this solemn celebration at the Shrine of Knock in honour of Mary, Queen of Ireland and Mother of the Church, I wish to express a special word of greeting to the President of Ireland, who is here present. In greeting him I greet and thank the entire Irish nation for the demonstration of faith shown to the world during this my visit to Ireland and, in particular, during my pilgrimage to the Shrine of Mary at Knock.

I greet also the Taoiseach and the civil authorities present.

And now it gives me great pleasure to announce that, to honour our Blessed Lady in this her centenary year at Knock, the new church, recently built in her honour, will, from this day forward, be known under the title of the Basilica of Our Lady, Queen of Ireland.

And finally I am happy to offer as my personal tribute and gift to the Shrine of Knock a Rose in gold which will remain as my testimony of gratitude to Mary, 'the Mother of the heavenly and the earthly Church'.

Praised be Jesus Christ!

KNOCK, TO THE SICK

The papal helicopter circled over Knock for an extra wave, descended, and the Pope alighted. His first act was to salute the crowds gathered in the valley and on the hillside but then he went inside the modern Basilica to meet the 2,500 sick who had been waiting patiently in their beds and wheelchairs. He spoke to them as follows:

Dear brothers and sisters,

The Gospels are filled with instances where our Lord shows his particular love and concern for the sick and for all those in pain. Jesus loved those who suffered, and this attitude has been passed on to his Church. To love the sick is something that the Church has learned from Christ.

Today I am happy to be with the sick and the handicapped. I have come to give witness to Christ's love for you, and to tell you that the Church and the Pope love you too. They reverence and esteem you. They are convinced that there is something very special about your mission in the Church.

By his suffering and death Jesus took on himself all human suffering, and he gave it a new value. As a matter of fact, he calls upon the sick, upon everyone who suffers, to collaborate with him in the salvation of the world.

Because of this, pain and sorrow are not endured alone or in vain. Although it remains difficult to understand suffering, Jesus has made it clear that its value is linked to his own suffering and death, to his own sacrifice. In other words, by your suffering you help Jesus in his work of salvation. This great truth is difficult to express accurately, but Saint Paul puts it this way: '. . . in my flesh I complete what is lacking in Christ's afflictions for the sake of his body, that is, the Church' (Col 1:24).

Your call to suffering requires strong faith and patience. Yes, it means that you are called to love with a special intensity. But remember that our Blessed Mother Mary is close to you, just as she was close to Jesus at the foot of the Cross. And she will never leave you all alone.

KNOCK, TO THE HANDMAIDS AND HELPERS OF THE SHRINE AND TO THE DIRECTORS OF PILGRIMAGE

Before leaving the Basilica, the Pope spoke to the handmaids and helpers who have made Knock a place where the sick are cared for in a special way. He said:

Dear brothers and sisters in the Lord,

As a pastor I feel in my heart a special joy in addressing a few words also to the handmaids and stewards of the Knock Shrine Society and to the Directors of Pilgrimages of Cnoc Mhuire, the Mountain of Mary.

The Eucharistic celebration of this afternoon brings back happy memories of the many pilgrimages in which I took part in my homeland at the Shrine of Jasna Góra, the Bright Mountain, in Czestochowa and at the other sites throughout Poland; it also recalls my visit to the Shrine of Our Lady of Guadalupe in Mexico.

I know from first hand experience the value of the services you render to make every pilgrim feel at home at this Shrine, and to help them to make every visit a loving and prayerful encounter with Mary, the Mother of Divine Grace. In a special way, you are the servants of the Mother of Jesus. You help people to approach her, to receive her message of love and dedication, and to entrust to her their whole life so that they may be true witnesses to the love of her Son.

You are also servants of your brothers and sisters. In helping and guiding the many pilgrims and especially the sick and handicapped, you perform not only a work of charity but also a task of evangelization. May this insight be your inspiration and your strength in order that all the tasks that you so generously accept to perform may become a living witness for the Word of God and for the good tidings of salvation.

I pray for you, I thank you, and I invoke upon you abundant graces of goodness and holiness of life. Receive the blessing which I cordially extend to you and all your loved ones.

DUBLIN, MEETING WITH THE IRISH BISHOPS

In the late evening of 30 September,
Pope John Paul met the Irish
Bishops led by the President of the
Irish Episcopal Conference, Cardinal
Tomas O Fiaich, Archbishop of
Armagh and Primate of All Ireland.
The Holy Father spoke to them as
follows:

My dear Brothers,

1   Once again I want you to know how profoundly grateful I am to you for your invitation to come to Ireland. For me this visit is the fulfilment of a deep desire of my heart: to come as a servant of the Gospel and as a pilgrim to the Shrine of Our Lady at Knock, on the occasion of its centenary.

I come also as your Brother Bishop from Rome, and I have greatly looked forward to this day: so that we may celebrate together the unity of the Episcopate of our Lord Jesus Christ, so that we may give public expression to a dimension of our Episcopal Collegiality, and so that we may reflect together on the role of pastoral leadership in the Church, particularly in regard to our own common responsibility for the wellbeing of the People of God in Ireland.

We are deeply conscious of the special charge that has been laid upon us as Bishops. For 'by virtue of sacramental consecration and by hierarchical communion' (*Lumen Gentium*, 22) we are constituted members of the College charged with the pastoral mission of our Lord Jesus Christ.

2   The Episcopal collegiality in which we share is manifested in different ways. Today it is expressed in a very important way: the Successor of Peter is present with you, in order personally to confirm you in your faith and apostolic ministry, and, together with you, to exercise the pastoral care of the faithful in Ireland. Thus,

my pilgrimage as Pastor of the universal Church is seen in its deep dimension of ecclesial and hierarchical communion. And through the action of the Holy Spirit the teaching on collegiality finds expression and actuation here and now.

In my first discourse to the College of Cardinals and to the world after my election to the See of Peter, I urged 'a deeper reflection on the implications of the collegial bond' (17 October 1978). I am also convinced that my meeting with the Episcopal Conference today leads to a better understanding of the nature of the Church, viewed as People of God, 'which takes its citizens from every race, making them citizens of a kingdom which is of a heavenly and not an earthly nature' (*Lumen Gentium*, 13).

3   In our present meeting, we are living the experience of the People of God in Ireland, first in the 'vertical' dimension, climbing up, as it were, through all the generations to the very beginnings of Christianity here. At the same time we are mindful of the 'horizonal' dimension, realizing how the People of God in Ireland are joined in the unity and the universality of the Church with all peoples on the earth, how they share in the mystery of the universal Church and in her great mission of salvation. The Bishops of Ireland have, moreover, their own sharing in this dimension of the life of the whole Church because they share in the tasks of the College of Bishops: *cum Petro et sub Petro*. Hence this meeting of the Pope and the Bishops of Ireland is highly important and marvellously eloquent, for Ireland and for the universal Church.

4   The basis of our personal identity, of our common bond and of our ministry is found in Jesus Christ, the Son of God and High Priest of the New Testament. For this reason, Brethren, my first exhortation as I come among you today is this: 'Let us keep our eyes fixed on Jesus, who inspires and perfects our faith' (Heb 12:2). Since we are pastors of this flock, we must indeed look to him who is the chief Shepherd – *Princeps Pastorum* (1 Pt 5:4) – to enlighten us, to sustain us, and to give us joy as we serve the flock, leading it 'in paths of righteousness for his name's sake' (Ps 23:3).

But the effectiveness of our service to Ireland and to the whole Church is linked with our personal relationship to him whom Saint Peter also called 'the Shepherd and Bishop of your souls' (1 Pt 2:25). The secure basis of our pastoral leadership is then a deep personal relationship of faith and love with Jesus Christ our Lord. Like the Twelve, we too were appointed to be with him, to be his companions (cf. Mk 3:14). We can present ourselves as religious leaders of our people in the situations that deeply affect their daily lives only after we have been in prayerful communion with the Teacher, only after we have discovered in faith that God has made Christ to be 'our wisdom, our righteousness and sanctification and redemption' (1 Cor 1:30). In our own lives we are called to *hear* and *guard* and *do* the word of God. In the Sacred Scriptures, and especially in the Gospels, we meet Christ constantly; and through the power of the Holy Spirit his words become light and strength for us and for our people. His words themselves contain a power for conversion, and we learn by his example.

Through prayerful contact with the Jesus of the Gospels, we, his servants and apostles, increasingly absorb his serenity and we assume his attitudes. Above all we take on that fundamental attitude of love for his Father, so much so that each one of us finds deep joy and fulfilment in the truth of our filial relationship: *Diligo Patrem* (Jn 14:31) – *Pater diligit Filium* (Jn 3:35). Our relationship with Christ and in Christ finds its supreme and unique expression in the Eucharistic Sacrifice, in which we act to the full: *in persona Christi*.

Our personal relationship with Jesus is then a guarantee of confidence for us and for our ministry. In our faith we find the victory that overcomes the world. Because we are united with Jesus and sustained by him, there is no challenge we cannot meet, no difficulty we cannot sustain, no obstacle we cannot overcome for the Gospel. Indeed, Christ himself guarantees that 'he who believes in me will also do the works that I do; and greater works than these will he do . . .' (Jn 14:12). Yes, Brethren, the answer to so many problems is found only in faith – a faith manifested and sustained in prayer.

5   Our relationship with Jesus will be the fruitful basis of our relationship with our priests, as we strive to be their brother, father, friend and guide. In the charity of Christ we are called to listen to and to understand them; to exchange views regarding evangelization and the pastoral mission they share with us as co-workers with the Order of Bishops. For the entire Church – but especially for the priests – we must be a human sign of the love of Christ and the fidelity of the Church. Thus we sustain our priests with the Gospel message, supporting them by the certainty of the Magisterium, and fortifying them against the pressures that they must resist. By word and example we must constantly invite our priests to prayer.

We are called to show generously to our priests that human concern, personal interest and sincere esteem whereby they will readily perceive our love. Despite the multiplicity of our commitments, our priests must recognize in us the faithful reflection of the Shepherd and Bishop of their souls (cf. 1 Pt 2:25).

Our priests have made many sacrifices, including the renunciation of marriage for the sake of the Kingdom of Heaven; and they must be firmly encouraged to persevere. Fidelity to Christ and the demands of human dignity and freedom require them to maintain constancy in their commitment.

The pastoral solicitude we have for priests must also be shown to our seminarians. Let us exercise personally also our responsibility for their training in the word of God, and for all the formation they receive in Ireland, and abroad, including Rome. In my letter to the Bishops of the Church on Holy Thursday, I wrote: 'The full reconstitution of the life of the seminaries throughout the Church will be the best proof of the achievement of the renewal to which the Council directed the Church.'

6   Like Christ, the Bishop comes among the laity as one who serves. The laity are the vast majority of the flock of Jesus Christ. Through Baptism and Confirmation, Christ himself gives them a sharing in his own mission of salvation. Together with the clergy and the religious, the laity make up the one communion of the Church: 'a chosen race, a royal priesthood, a holy nation, God's own people' (1 Pt 2:9).

The greatest expression of the Bishop's service to the laity is his personal proclamation of the word of God, which reaches its summit in the Eucharist (cf. *Presbyterorum Ordinis*, 5). As a faithful steward of the Gospel message, each Bishop is called to expound to his people 'the whole mystery of Christ' (*Christus Dominus*, 12).

As the Bishop proclaims the dignity of the laity, it is also his role to do everything possible to promote their contribution to evangelization, urging them to assume every responsibility that is theirs in temporal realities. In the words of Paul VI 'Their own field of evangelizing activity is the vast and complicated world of politics, society and economics, the world of culture, of the sciences and the arts, of international life, of mass media' (*Evangelii Nuntiandi*, 70). And there are other spheres of activities in which they can effectively work for the transformation of society.

In accordance with the will of God, the Christian family is an evangelizing agent of immense importance. In all the moral issues of authentic Christian living, the laity look to the Bishops as their leaders, their pastors and their fathers. The Bishops must constantly reply to the great cry of humanity, usually not articulated in words, but very real: 'We wish to see Jesus' (Jn 12:21). And in this the Bishops have a role of great importance: to show Jesus to the world; to present him authentically and convincingly: Jesus Christ, true God and true man – Jesus Christ, the way and the truth and the life – Jesus Christ the man of prayer.

7   Bishops are called to be true fathers of all their people, excelling in the spirit of love and solicitude for all (cf. *Christus Dominus*, 16). They should have a special care for those who live on the margin of society. Among those most needing pastoral care from Bishops are prisoners. My dear Brothers, do not neglect to provide for their spiritual needs and to concern yourselves also about their material conditions and their families.

Try to bring the prisoners such spiritual care and guidance as may help to turn them from the ways of violence and crime, and make their detention instead be an occasion of true conversion to Christ and personal experience of love. Have a special care for young offenders. So often their wayward lives are due to society's neglect more than to their own sinfulness. Detention should be especially for them a school of rehabilitation.

8   In the light of our commitment to Jesus, and to his Gospel, in the light also of our collegial responsibility, our meeting here today assumes a special importance because of the present difficult time for Ireland, on account of the whole situation relating to Northern Ireland. These circumstances impelled some people to advise me against making a pilgrimage to Ireland. These very difficulties, however, made it all the more important to be here, to share closely with all of you these uncommon trials, and to seek in union with you the aid of God and good human counsel. These reasons for coming here gain in eloquence if they are placed in the framework of my visit to the United Nations, where it will be my privilege and duty to seek out ways of living in peace and reconciliation throughout the world.

I am sure that the pastors of the Church in Ireland have a better understanding and deeper feeling for the painful problems of the present moment. Their duty, as I pointed out already, is to guide and sustain the flock, the People of God, but they can perform this duty in no other way than by suffering with those who suffer, and by weeping with those who weep (cf. Rom 12:15).

On this point, I draw my conviction both from the Gospel and from the personal and historical experience that I had in the Church and nation from which I come. During the last two centuries, the Church in Poland has struck root in a special way in the soul of the nation. Part of the reason for this is that its pastors – its bishops and priests – did not hesitate to share in the trials and sufferings of their fellow countrymen. They were found among those deported to Siberia in the time of the Czars. They were found in the concentration camps at the time of the unleashing of Nazi terrorism during the last war. This self-sacrifice and dedication confirmed more fully the truth about the priest, that he is 'chosen from among men . . . to act on behalf of men' (Heb 5:1).

9   Because of this faithfulness to their brothers and sisters, to their fellow countrymen, the sons and daughters of the same homeland, pastors, and especially Bishops, must reflect beforehand on how to prevent bloodshed, hatred and terror,

on how to strengthen peace, and on how to spare the people from these terrible sufferings. This was the message that Paul VI repeated over thirty times, in appealing for peace and justice in relation to Northern Ireland. He never ceased to condemn violence and to appeal for justice. 'We earnestly beg' – he wrote to Cardinal Conway on the solemnity of Pentecost 1974 – 'that all violence should cease, from whatever side it may come, for it is contrary to the law of God and to the Christian and civilized way of life; that, in response to the common Christian conscience and the voice of reason, a climate of mutual trust and dialogue be re-established in justice and charity; that the real deep-seated causes of social unrest – which are not to be reduced to differences of a religious nature – be identified and eliminated.'

These efforts, venerable and dear Brothers, must be continued. Faith and social ethics demand from us respect for the established State authorities. But this respect also finds its expression in individual acts of mediation, in persuasion, in moral influence, and indeed in firm requests. For while it is true, as Saint Paul says, that he who is in authority bears the sword (cf. Rom 13:4), which we renounce in accordance with the clear recommendation of Christ to Peter in the Garden of Gethsemane (cf. Mt 26:52), nevertheless, precisely because we are defenceless, we have a special right and duty to influence those who wield the sword of authority. For it is well known that, in the field of political action, as elsewhere, not everything can be obtained by means of the sword. There are deeper reasons and stronger laws to which men, nations and peoples are subject. It is for us to discern these reasons and in their light to become, before those in authority, spokesmen for the moral order. This order is superior to force and violence. In this superiority of the moral order is expressed all the dignity of men and nations.

10   I recall with deep satisfaction a significant feature in the series of events connected with my journey to Ireland. It is highly significant that the invitation from the Episcopate, through its four Archbishops, was followed by invitations from other Churches, especially from Irish Anglicans. I take the opportunity to stress this once again and to express my renewed thanks and appreciation to them. I see in this circumstance a very promising sign of hope. In view of the reasons with which you are all familiar, I have been unable to accept this truly ecumenical invitation by visiting Armagh in Northern Ireland, and have been able to go no further than Drogheda. Nonetheless, the eloquence of this ecumenical readiness fully corresponds to what was expressed in my first Encyclical: 'In the present historical situation of Christianity and the world, the only possibility we see of fulfilling the Church's universal mission, with regard to ecumenical questions, is that of seeking sincerely, perseveringly, humbly and also courageously the ways of drawing closer and of union. . . . We must seek unity without being discouraged at the difficulties that can appear or accumulate along that road; otherwise we would be unfaithful to the word of Christ, we would fail to accomplish his testament. Have we the right to run this risk?' (*Redemptor Hominis*, 6).

The witness to faith in Christ which we share with our brethren must continue to find expression not only in prayer for full unity but also in prayer and sustained effort for reconciliation and peace in this beloved land. This union of endeavour must lead us to take into consideration the whole mechanism of strife, cruelty, and growing hatred, in order to 'overcome evil with good' (Rom 12:12).

What are we to do? I earnestly hope that, in a continued effort, you and our brothers in the faith will become spokesmen for the just reasons of peace and reconciliation before those who wield the sword and those who perish by the sword.

How sad it is to think of all the lives that have been lost, especially the lives of young people. What a terrible loss for their country, for the Church, for the whole of humanity!

11   Venerable Pastors of the Church in Ireland: this service to justice and social love that is yours to perform in this present moment is difficult. It is difficult, but it is your duty! Do not fear: Christ is with you! He will give you his Holy Spirit: the Spirit of counsel and fortitude. And although this Spirit of God is frequently resisted, in the heart of man and in the history of humanity, by 'the spirit of this world' and by 'the spirit of darkness', nevertheless the final victory can only be that of love and truth. Continue steadfast in the difficult service that is yours, doing everything 'in the name of the Lord Jesus' (Col 3:17). Be assured that in your ministry you have my support and that of the universal Church. And all men and women of good will stand by you in the quest for peace, justice and human dignity.

Dear Brothers: In the name of Jesus Christ and his Church I thank you – and through you, all Ireland. I thank you for your fidelity to the Gospel, for your everlasting contribution to the spread of the Catholic faith, for your authentic and irreplaceable service to the world.

As far as the future goes, Brethren, courage and trust!

Walk in the illumination of the Paschal Mystery – in that light which must never be extinguished in your land! Go forward in the power of the Holy Spirit, in the merits of Jesus Christ!

And rejoice with a great joy in the unfailing intercession and protection of Mary, Great Mary, Mother of God, Queen of the Apostles, Queen of Ireland, Queen of Peace!

Brethren, let us go forward together, for the good of Ireland and for the glory of the Most Holy Trinity. And therefore 'Let us keep our eyes fixed on Jesus, who inspires and perfects our faith'.

Monday, 1 October

The Holy Father met the seminarians
in the chapel of St Patrick's College
in Maynooth. The following is the
text of his address:

Dear brothers and sons in our Lord Jesus Christ,

You have a very special place in my heart and in the heart of the Church. During
my visit to Maynooth I wanted to be alone with you, even though it could be for
only a few moments.

I have many things that I would tell you – things that I have been saying about
the life of seminarians and about seminaries all during the first year of my
pontificate.

In particular I would like to speak again about the word of God: about how you
are called to hear and guard and do the word of God. And about how you are to
base your entire lives and ministry upon the word of God, just as it is transmitted
by the Church, just as it is expounded by the Magisterium, just as it has been
understood throughout the history of the Church by the faithful guided by the Holy
Spirit: *semper et ubique et ab omnibus*. The word of God is the great treasure of your
lives. Through the word of God you will come to a deep knowledge of the
mystery of Jesus Christ, Son of God and Son of Mary; Jesus Christ, the High
Priest of the New Testament and the Saviour of the world.

The word of God is worthy of all your efforts. To embrace it in its purity and
integrity, and to spread it by word and example is a great mission. And this is your
mission, today and tomorrow and for the rest of your lives.

As you pursue your vocation – a vocation so intimately related to the word of
God, I wish to recall to you one simple but important lesson taken from the life of
Saint Patrick; and it is this: In the history of evangelization, the destiny of an entire
people – your people – was radically affected for time and eternity because of the
fidelity with which Saint Patrick embraced and proclaimed the word of God, and by
reason of the fidelity with which Saint Patrick pursued his call to the end.

What I really want you to realize is this: that God counts on you; that he makes
his plans, in a way, depend on your free collaboration, on the oblation of your lives,
and on the generosity with which you follow the inspirations of the Holy Spirit in
the depths of your hearts.

The Catholic faith of Ireland today was linked, in God's plan to the fidelity of
Saint Patrick. And tomorrow? Yes, tomorrow some part of God's plan will be
linked to your fidelity – to the fervour with which you say *yes* to God's word in
your lives.

Today Jesus Christ is making this appeal to you through me: the appeal for
fidelity. In prayer you will see more and more every day what I mean and what the

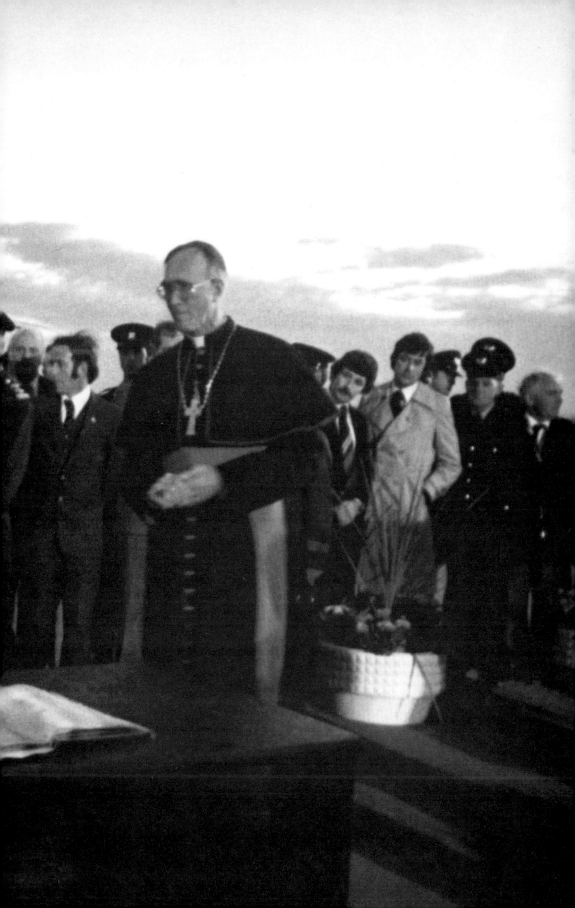

implications of this call are. By God's grace you will understand more and more every day how God requires and accepts your fidelity as a condition for the supernatural effectiveness of all your activity. The supreme expression of fidelity will come with your irrevocable and total self-giving in union with Jesus Christ to his Father. And may our Blessed Mother Mary help you to make this gift acceptable.

Remember Saint Patrick. Remember what the fidelity of just one man has meant for Ireland and the world. Yes, dear sons and brothers, fidelity to Jesus Christ and to his word makes all the difference in the world. Let us therefore look up to Jesus, who is for all time the Faithful Witness of the Father.

MAYNOOTH, ADDRESS TO PRIESTS, MISSIONARIES, RELIGIOUS BROTHERS AND SISTERS, SEMINARIANS

To the vast gathering of priests,
religious men and women,
missionaries and seminarians in St
Patrick's College, Maynooth, the
Holy Father delivered the following
address:

My dear brothers and sisters in Christ,

1   The name of Maynooth is respected all over the Catholic world. It recalls what is noblest in the Catholic priesthood in Ireland. Here come seminarists from every Irish diocese, sons of Catholic homes which were themselves true 'seminaries', true seedbeds of priestly or religious vocations. From here have gone out priests to every Irish diocese and to the dioceses of the far-flung Irish diaspora. Maynooth has, in this century, given birth to two new Missionary Societies, one initially directed towards China, the other towards Africa; and it has sent out hundreds of alumni as volunteers to the mission fields. Maynooth is a school of priestly holiness, an academy of theological learning, a university of Catholic inspiration. Saint Patrick's College is a place of rich achievement, which promises a future just as great.

Therefore Maynooth is a fitting place in which to meet and talk with priests, diocesan and religious, with religious brothers, religious sisters, missionaries and seminarians. Having, as a priest-student in Paris, lived for a time in the atmosphere of an Irish Seminary – the Collège Irlandais in Paris, now loaned by the Irish Bishops to the Hierarchy of Poland – I have profound joy in meeting with you all here in Ireland's National Seminary.

2   My first words go to the priests, diocesan and religious. I say to you what Saint Paul said to Timothy. I ask you 'to fan into a flame the gift that God gave you when (the Bishop) laid (his) hands on you' (2 Tim 1:6). Jesus Christ himself, the one High Priest said: 'I have come to bring fire to the earth, and how I wish it were blazing already!' (Lk 12:49). You share in his priesthood; you carry on his work in

the world. His work cannot be done by lukewarm or half-hearted priests. His fire of love for the Father and for men must burn in you. His longing to save mankind must consume you.

You are called by Christ as the apostles were. You are appointed like them, to be with Christ. You are sent, as they were, to go out in his name, and by his authority, to 'make disciples of all the nations' (cf. Mt 10:1, 28:19, Mk 3:13–16).

Your first duty is to be *with Christ*. You are each called to be 'a witness to his Resurrection' (Acts 1:22). A constant danger with priests, even zealous priests, is that they become so immersed in the work of the Lord that they neglect the Lord of the work.

We must find time, we must make time, to be with the Lord in prayer. Following the example of the Lord Jesus himself, we must 'always go off to some place where (we can) be alone and pray' (cf. Lk 5:16). It is only if we spend time with the Lord that our sending out to others will be also a bringing of him to others.

3   To be with the Lord is always also to be sent by him to do his work. A priest is *called* by Christ; a priest is *with* Christ; a priest is *sent* by Christ. A priest is sent in the power of the same Holy Spirit which drove Jesus untiringly along the roads of life, the roads of history. Whatever the difficulties, the disappointments, the setbacks, we priests find in Christ and in the power of his Spirit the strength to 'struggle wearily on, helped only by his power driving (us) irresistibly' (cf. Col 1:29).

As priests, you are privileged to be pastors of a faithful people, who continue to respond generously to your ministry, and who are a strong support to your own priestly vocation through their faith and their prayer. If you keep striving to be the kind of priest your people expect and wish you to be, then you will be holy priests. The degree of religious practice in Ireland is high. For this we must be constantly thanking God. But will this high level of religious practice continue? Will the next generation of young Irishmen and Irish women still be as faithful as their fathers were? After my two days in Ireland, after my meeting with Ireland's youth in Galway, I am confident that they will. But this will require both unremitting work and untiring prayer on your part. You must work for the Lord with a sense of urgency. You must work with the conviction that this generation, this decade of the 1980s which we are about to enter, could be crucial and decisive for the future of the faith in Ireland. Let there be no complacency. As Saint Paul said: 'Be awake to all the dangers; stay firm in the faith; be brave and be strong' (1 Cor 16:13). Work with confidence; work with joy. You are witnesses to the Resurrection of Christ.

4   What the people expect from you, more than anything else, is faithfulness to the priesthood. This is what speaks to them of the faithfulness of God. This is what strengthens them to be faithful to Christ through all the difficulties of their lives, of their marriages. In a world so marked by instability as our world today, we need more signs and witnesses to God's fidelity to us, and to the fidelity we owe to him. This is what causes such great sadness to the Church, such great but often silent anguish among the people of God, when priests fail in their fidelity to their priestly commitment. That countersign, that counterwitness, has been one of the setbacks to the great hopes for renewal aroused throughout the Church by the Second Vatican Council. Yet this has also driven priests, and the whole Church, to more intense and fervent prayer; for it has taught us all that without Christ we can do nothing (cf. Jn 15:5). And the fidelity of the immense majority of priests has shone with even

greater clarity and is all the more manifest and glorious a witness to the faithful God, and to Christ, the Faithful Witness (cf. Rev 1:5).

5 In a centre of theological learning, which is also a seminary, like Maynooth, this witness of fidelity has the added importance and the special value of impressing on candidates for the priesthood the strength and the grandeur of priestly fidelity. Here in Maynooth, theological learning, being part of formation for the priesthood, is preserved from ever being an academic pursuit of the intellect only. Here theological scholarship is linked with liturgy, with prayer, with the building of a community of faith and love, and thus with the building up, the 'edifying', of the priesthood of Ireland, and the edifying of the Church. My call today is a call to prayer. Only in prayer will we meet the challenges of our ministry and fulfil the hopes of tomorrow. All our appeals for peace and reconciliation can be effective only through prayer.

This theological learning, here as everywhere throughout the Church, is a reflection on faith, a reflection in faith. A theology which did not deepen faith and lead to prayer might be a discourse on words about God; it could not be a discourse about God, the Living God, the God who *is* and whose being is *Love*. It follows that theology can only be authentic in the Church, the community of faith. Only when the teaching of theologians is in conformity with the teaching of the College of Bishops, united with the Pope, can the people of God know with certitude that that teaching is 'the faith which has been once and for all entrusted to the Saints' (Jude 3). This is not a limitation for theologians, but a liberation; for it preserves them from subservience to changing fashions and binds them securely to the unchanging truth of Christ, the truth which makes us free (Jn 7:32).

6 In Maynooth, in Ireland, to speak of priesthood is to speak of mission. Ireland has never forgotten that 'the pilgrim Church is missionary by her very nature; for it is from the mission of the Son and the mission of the Holy Spirit that she takes her origin, in accordance with the decree of God the Father' (*Ad Gentes*, 2). In the ninth and tenth centuries, Irish monks rekindled the light of faith in regions where it had burnt low or been extinguished by the collapse of the Roman Empire, and evangelized new nations not yet evangelized, including areas of my own native Poland. How can I forget that there was an Irish monastery as far east as Kiev, even up to the thirteenth century; and that there was even an Irish college for a short time in my own city of Cracow, during the persecution of Cromwell. In the eighteenth and nineteenth centuries, Irish priests followed their exiles all over the English-speaking world. In the twentieth century, new missionary institutes of men and women sprang up in Ireland, which, together with the Irish branches of international missionary institutes and with existing Irish religious congregations, gave a new missionary impetus to the Church.

May that missionary spirit never decline in the hearts of Irish priests, whether members of missionary institutes or of the diocesan clergy or of religious congregations devoted to other apostolates. May this spirit be actively fostered by all of you among the laity, already so devoted in their prayer, so generous in their support for the missions. May a spirit of partnership grow between the home dioceses and the home religious congregations in the total mission of the Church, until each local diocesan church and each religious congregation and community is fully seen to be 'missionary of its very nature', entering into the eager missionary movement of the universal Church.

I have learned with much pleasure that the Irish Missionary Union plans to establish a National Missionary Centre, which will both serve as a focus for missionary renewal by missionaries themselves and foster the missionary awareness of the clergy, religious and faithful of the Irish Church. May its work be blessed by God. May it contribute to a great new upsurge of missionary fervour and a new wave of missionary vocations from this great motherland of faith which is Ireland.

7   I wish to speak a special word to religious Brothers. The past decade has brought great changes, and with them problems and trials unprecedented in all your previous experience. I ask you not to be discouraged. Be men of great truth, of great and unbounded hope. 'May the God of Hope bring you such joy and peace in your faith that the power of the Holy Spirit will remove all bounds to hope' (Rom 15:13). The past decade has also brought a great renewal in your understanding of your holy vocation, a great deepening of your liturgical lives and your prayer, a great extension of the field of your apostolic influence. I ask God to bless you with renewed fidelity in vocation among your members, and with increased vocations to your Institutes. The Church in Ireland and on the missions owes much to all the Institutes of Brothers. Your call to holiness is a precious adornment of the Church. Believe in your vocation. Be faithful to it. 'God has called you and he will not fail you' (1 Thess 5:23).

8   The Sisters too have known years of searching, sometimes perhaps of uncertainty or of unrest. These have also been years of purification. I pray that we are now entering a period of consolidation and of construction. Many of you are engaged in the apostolate of education and the pastoral care of youth. Do not doubt the continuing relevance of that apostolate, particularly in modern Ireland, where youth are such a large and important part of the population. The Church has repeatedly, in many solemn recent documents, reminded religious of the primary importance of education, and has invited congregations of men and women with the tradition and the charism of education to persevere in that vocation and to redouble their commitment to it. The same is true of the traditional apostolates of care of the sick, nursing, care of the aged, the handicapped, the poor. These must not be neglected while new apostolates are being undertaken. In the words of the Gospel, you must 'bring out from (your) storeroom things both new and old' (cf. Mt 13:52). You must be courageous in your apostolic undertakings, not letting difficulties, shortage of personnel, insecurity for the future, deter or depress you.

But remember always that your field of apostolate is your own personal lives. Here is where the message of the Gospel has first to be preached and lived. Your first apostolic duty is your own sanctification. No change in religious life has any importance unless it be also conversion of yourselves to Christ. No movement in religious life has any value unless it be also movement inwards to the 'still centre' of your existence, where Christ is. It is not what you *do* that matters most; but what you *are*, as women consecrated to God. For you, Christ has consecrated himself, so that you too 'may be consecrated in truth' (cf. Jn 17:19).

9   To you and to priests, diocesan and religious, I say: Rejoice to be witnesses to Christ in the modern world. Do not hesitate to be recognizable, identifiable, in the streets as men and women who have consecrated their lives to God and who have given up everything worldly to follow Christ. Believe in the value for contemporary men and women of the visible signs of your consecrated lives. People need signs and reminders of God in the modern secular city, which has few reminders of God left. Do not help the trend towards 'taking God off the streets' by adopting secular modes of dress and behaviour yourselves!

10   My special blessing and greeting goes to the cloistered Sisters and contemplatives, men as well as women. I express to you my gratitude for what you have done for me by your lives of prayer and sacrifice since my papal ministry began. I express the Pope's need for you, the Church's need for you. You are foremost in that 'great, intense and growing prayer' for which I called in *Redemptor Hominis*. Never was the contemplative vocation more precious or more relevant than in our modern restless world. May there be many Irish boys and girls called to the contemplative life, at this time when the future of the Church and the future of humanity depends on prayer.

Gladly do I repeat to all contemplatives, on this feast of Saint Theresa of Lisieux, the words I used in addressing the Sisters of Rome: 'I commend to you the Church; I commend mankind and the world to you. To you, to your prayers, to your "holocaust" I commend also myself, Bishop of Rome. Be with me, close to me, you who are in the heart of the Church! May there be fulfilled in each of you that which was the programme of life for Saint Theresa of the Child Jesus: "*in corde Ecclesiae amor ero*" – "I will be love in the heart of the Church"!'

Much of what I have been saying has been intended also for the seminarians. You are preparing for the total giving of yourselves to Christ and to the service of his Kingdom. You bring to Christ the gift of your youthful enthusiasm and vitality. In you Christ is eternally youthful; and through you he gives youth to the Church. Do not disappoint him. Do not disappoint the people who are waiting for you to bring Christ to them. Do not fail your generation of young Irish men and women. Bring Christ to the young people of your generation as the only answer to their longings. Christ looks on you and loves you. Do not, like the young man in the Gospel, go away sad, 'because he had great possessions' (cf. Mt 19:22). Instead, bring all your possessions of mind and hand and heart to Christ, that he may use them to 'draw all men to himself' (cf. Jn 12:32).

To all of you I say: this is a wonderful time in the history of the Church. This is a wonderful time to be a priest, to be a religious, to be a missionary for Christ. Rejoice in the Lord always. Rejoice in your vocation. I repeat to you the words of Saint Paul: 'I want you to be happy, always happy in the Lord; I repeat, what I want is your happiness. There is no need to worry; but if there is anything you need, pray for it, asking God for it with prayer and thanksgiving, and that peace of God which is so much greater than we can understand, will guard your hearts and your thoughts, in Christ Jesus' (Phil 4:4–7).

Mary, Mother of Christ, the Eternal Priest, Mother of priests and of religious, will keep you from all anxiety, as you 'wait in joyful hope for the coming of our Lord and Saviour, Jesus Christ'. Entrust yourselves to her, as I commend you to her, to Mary, Mother of Jesus and Mother of his Church.

LIMERICK, HOMILY AT THE MASS FOR THE PEOPLE OF GOD

The last religious celebration of the
Pope during his pilgrimage to
Ireland was a Mass at Greenpark
Racecourse, Limerick. An estimated
250,000 people were present. After
the Gospel, the Holy Father
delivered the following homily:

Dear brothers and sisters in Christ,

1   On this last day of my visit to Ireland I come to you to celebrate with you the
Holy Eucharist. I wish to seal once more, in the love of Christ Jesus, the bond that
links the Successor of Peter in the See of Rome with the Church that is in Ireland.
In you I greet once more all the People of Ireland, who have taken their place in the
mystery of the Church through the preaching of Saint Patrick and through the
Sacraments of Baptism and Confirmation. I invite you to make this last Mass, which
I offer with you and for you, into a special hymn of thanksgiving to the Most Holy
Trinity for the days that I have been able to spend in your midst.
    I come in the name of Christ to preach to you his own message. The liturgy of
the word today speaks of a building, of the cornerstone that supports and gives
strength to the house, of the city that is built on the hill for security and protection.
These images contain an invitation for all of us, for all Christians, to come close to
Christ, the cornerstone, so that he may become our support and the unifying
principle which gives meaning and coherence to our lives. It is the same Christ who
gives dignity to all the members of the Church and who assigns to each one his
mission.

2   Today, I would like to speak to you about that special dignity and mission
entrusted to the lay people in the Church. Saint Peter says that Christians are 'a
royal priesthood, a holy nation' (1 Pt 2:9). All Christians, incorporated into Christ
and his Church by baptism, are consecrated to God. They are called to profess the
faith which they have received. By the sacrament of Confirmation, they are further
endowed by the Holy Spirit with special strength to be witnesses of Christ and
sharers in his mission of salvation. Every lay Christian is therefore an extraordinary
work of God's grace and is called to the heights of holiness. Sometimes, lay men
and women do not seem to appreciate to the full the dignity and the vocation that is
theirs as lay people. No, there is no such thing as an 'ordinary layman', for all of you
have been called to conversion through the death and Resurrection of Jesus Christ.
As God's holy people you are called to fulfil your role in the evangelization of the
world.
    Yes, the laity are 'a chosen race, a holy priesthood', also called to be 'the salt of
the earth' and 'the light of the world'. It is their specific vocation and mission to
express the Gospel in their lives and thereby to insert the Gospel as a leaven into the
reality of the world in which they live and work. The great forces which shape the
world – politics, the mass media, science, technology, culture, education, industry
and work – are precisely the areas where lay people are especially competent to

54

exercise their mission. If these forces are guided by people who are true disciples of Christ, and who are, at the same time, fully competent in the relevant secular knowledge and skill, then indeed will the world be transformed from within by Christ's redeeming power.

3   Lay people today are called to a strong Christian commitment: to permeate society with the leaven of the Gospel, for Ireland is at a point of decision in her history. The Irish people have to choose today their way forward. Will it be the transformation of all strata of humanity into a new creation, or the way that many nations have gone, giving excessive importance to economic growth and material possessions while neglecting the things of the spirit? The way of substituting a new ethic of temporal enjoyment for the law of God? The way of false freedom which is only slavery to decadence? Will it be the way of subjugating the dignity of the human person to the totalitarian domination of the State? The way of violent struggle between classes? The way of extolling revolution over God?

Ireland must choose. You the present generation of Irish people must decide; your choice must be clear and your decision firm. Let the voice of your forefathers, who suffered so much to maintain their faith in Christ and thus to preserve Ireland's soul, resound today in your ears through the voice of the Pope when he repeats the words of Christ: 'What will it profit a man, if he gains the whole world, and forfeits his life?' (Mt 16:26). What would it profit Ireland to go the easy way of the world and suffer the loss of her own soul?

Your country seems in a sense to be living again the temptations of Christ: Ireland is being asked to prefer the 'kingdoms of the world and their splendour' to the Kingdom of God (cf. Mt 4:8). Satan, the Tempter, the Adversary of Christ, will use all his might and all his deceptions to win Ireland for the way of the world. What a victory he would gain, what a blow he would inflict on the Body of Christ in the world, if he could seduce Irish men and women away from Christ. Now is the time of testing for Ireland. This generation is once more a generation of decision.

Dear sons and daughters of Ireland, pray, pray not to be led into temptation. I asked in my first Encyclical for a 'great, intense and growing prayer for all the Church'. I ask you today for a great, intense and growing prayer for all the people of Ireland, for the Church in Ireland, for all the Church which owes so much to Ireland. Pray that Ireland may not fail in the test. Pray as Jesus taught us to pray: 'Lead us not into temptation, but deliver us from evil.'

Above all, have an immense confidence in the merits of our Lord Jesus Christ and in the power of his death and Resurrection. It is precisely because of the strength of his Paschal Mystery that each of us and all Ireland can say: 'I can do all things in him who strengthens me' (Phil 4:13).

4   Ireland in the past displayed a remarkable interpenetration of her whole culture, speech and way of life by the things of God and the life of grace. Life was in a sense organized around religious events. The task of this generation of Irish men and women is to transform the more complex world of modern industry and urban life by the same Gospel spirit. Today, you must keep the city and the factory for God, as you have always kept the farm and the village community for him in the past. Material progress has in so many places led to decline of faith and growth in Christ, growth in love and in justice.

To accomplish this you must have, as I said in Phoenix Park, consistency between your faith and your daily life. You cannot be a genuine Christian on Sunday, unless you try to be true to Christ's spirit also in your work, your commercial dealings, at your trade union or your employers' or professional meetings. How can you be a true community in Christ at Mass unless you try to think of the welfare of the whole national community when decisions are being taken by your particular sector or group? How can you be ready to meet Christ in judgment unless you remember how the poor are affected by the behaviour of your group or by your personal life style? For Christ will say to us all: 'In so far as you did this to one of the least of these brothers of mine, you did it to me' (Mt 25:40).

I have learned with great joy and gratitude of the wonderful spirit of work and cooperation with which you all joined in the material preparations as well as the spiritual preparation for my visit. How much more wonderful still it would be if you could have the same spirit of work and cooperation always 'for the glory of God and the honour of Ireland'!

5   Here in Limerick, I am in a largely rural area and many of you are people of the land. I feel at home with you as I did with the rural and mountain people of my native Poland, and I repeat here to you what I told them: Love the land; love the work of the fields for it keeps you close to God, the Creator, in a special way.

To those who have gone to the cities, here or abroad, I say: Keep in contact with your roots in the soil of Ireland, with your families and your culture. Keep true to the faith, to the prayers and the values you learned here; and pass on that heritage to your children, for it is rich and good.

To all I say, revere and protect your family and your family life, for the family is the primary field of Christian action for the Irish laity, the place where your 'royal priesthood' is chiefly exercised. The Christian family has been in the past Ireland's greatest spiritual resource. Modern conditions and social changes have created new patterns and new difficulties for family life and for Christian marriage. I want to say to you: do not be discouraged, do not follow the trends where a close-knit family is seen as outdated; the Christian family is more important for the Church and for society today than ever before.

It is true that the stability and sanctity of marriage are being threatened by new ideas and by the aspirations of some. Divorce, for whatever reason it is introduced, inevitably becomes easier and easier to obtain and it gradually comes to be accepted as a normal part of life. The very possibility of divorce in the sphere of civil law makes stable and permanent marriages more difficult for everyone. May Ireland always continue to give witness before the modern world to her traditional commitment to the sanctity and the indissolubility of the marriage bond. May the Irish always support marriage, through personal commitment and through positive social and legal action.

Above all, hold high the esteem for the wonderful dignity and grace of the Sacrament of marriage. Prepare earnestly for it. Believe in the spiritual power which this Sacrament of Jesus Christ gives to strengthen the marriage union, and to overcome all the crises and problems of life together. Married people must believe in the power of the Sacrament to make them holy; they must believe in their vocation to witness through their marriage to the power of Christ's love. True love and the grace of God can never let marriage become a self-centred relationship of two individuals, living side by side for their own interests.

6   And here, I want to say a very special word to all Irish parents. Marriage must include openness to the gift of children. Generous openness to accept children from God as the gift to their love is the mark of the Christian couple. Respect the God-given cycle of life, for this respect is part of our respect for God himself, who created male and female, who created them in his own image, reflecting his own

life-giving love in the patterns of their sexual being.

And so I say to all, have an absolute and holy respect for the sacredness of human life from the first moment of its conception. Abortion, as the Vatican Council stated, is one of the 'abominable crimes' (*Gaudium et Spes*, 51). To attack unborn life at any moment from its conception is to undermine the whole moral order which is the true guardian of the wellbeing of man. The defence of the absolute inviolability of unborn life is part of the defence of human rights and human dignity. May Ireland never weaken in her witness, before Europe and before the whole world, to the dignity and sacredness of all human life, from conception until death.

Dear fathers and mothers of Ireland, believe in your vocation, that beautiful vocation of marriage and parenthood which God has given to you. Believe that God is with you – for all parenthood in heaven and on earth takes its name from him. Do not think that anything you will do in life is more important than to be a good Christian father and mother. May Irish mothers, young women and girls not listen to those who tell them that working at a secular job, succeeding in a secular profession, is more important than the vocation of giving life and caring for this life as a mother. The future of the Church, the future of humanity depend in great part on parents and on the family life that they build in their homes. The family is the true measure of the greatness of a nation, just as the dignity of man is the true measure of civilization.

7   Your homes should always remain homes of prayer. As I leave today this island which is so dear to my heart, this land and its people which is such a consolation and strength to the Pope, may I express a wish: that every home in Ireland may remain, or may begin again to be, a home of daily family prayer. That you would promise me to do this would be the greatest gift you could give me as I leave your hospitable shores.

I know that your Bishops are preparing a pastoral programme designed to encourage greater sharing by parents in the religious education of their children under the motto 'handing on the faith in the home'. I am confident that you will all join in this programme with enthusiasm and generosity. To hand on to your children the faith you received from your parents is your first duty and your greatest privilege as parents. The home should be the first school of religion, as it must be the first school of prayer. The great spiritual influence of Ireland in the history of the world was due in great degree to the religion of the homes of Ireland, for here is where evangelization begins, here is where vocations are nurtured. I appeal therefore to Irish parents to continue fostering vocations to the priesthood and the religious life in their homes, among their sons and daughters. It was, for generations, the greatest desire of every Irish parent to have a son a priest or religious, to have a daughter consecrated to God. May it continue to be your desire and your prayer. May increased opportunities for boys and girls never lessen your esteem for the privilege of having a son or daughter of yours selected by Christ and called by him to give up all things and follow him.

I entrust all this to Mary, bright 'Sun of the Irish race'. May her prayers help all Irish homes to be like the holy house of Nazareth. From them may young Christians go forth, as Jesus did from Nazareth. May they go forth in the power of the Spirit to continue Christ's work and to follow in his footsteps towards the end of the millennium, into the twenty-first century. Mary will keep you all close to him, who is 'Father of the world to come' (Is 9:6).

Dia agus Muire libh!

May God and Mary be with you and with the families of Ireland, always!

SHANNON, DEPARTURE FROM IRELAND

Before boarding the plane at Shannon Airport, the Holy Father, after receiving a loving farewell in music and song from a large gathering of Irish people, delivered a farewell address as follows:

Dear brothers and sisters,

The time has come for me to leave Ireland, to continue my pastoral mission, my apostolic journey.

I came here to proclaim peace and love, to speak to you about the Son of God made man, about your life in Christ. Yes, as Successor of the Apostle Peter I came to confirm my brethren in the faith, and to ask all Ireland to lift up its heart to a new vision of hope – in the words of Saint Paul: to 'Christ Jesus our hope' (1 Tim 1:1).

I began my pilgrimage under the protection of our Blessed Lady, and on the feast of the Archangels. And I take leave of you on the feast of Theresa of the Child Jesus, splendid example of joyful simplicity, and proof of the extraordinary effectiveness of generous Christian love.

I am deeply grateful for all the kindnesses shown me by the civil and religious authorities of this land. I also thank those who worked so hard and with such great skill here in Ireland to organize the many details of this visit. I thank all the people for the warm and loving reception in which they manifested their keen sense of humanity and their lively faith.

With the Apostle Paul, I now beg you for ever 'to lead a life worthy of the calling to which you have been called . . . eager to maintain the unity of the Spirit in the bond of peace' (Eph 4:1, 3).

In the name of the Lord I exhort you to preserve the great treasure of your fidelity to Jesus Christ and to his Church. Like the early Christian community described in the Acts of the Apostles, Ireland is called to be 'faithful to the teaching of the apostles, to the brotherhood, to the breaking of bread and to the prayers' (Acts 2:42).

Ireland: *semper fidelis*, always faithful!

Ireland: always faithful!

UNITED STATES

1 October – 7 October

Monday, 1 October

ARRIVAL AT BOSTON

A large crowd, along with many American Cardinals, Mrs Rosalynn Carter, wife of the President of the United States, and the authorities of the state of Massachusetts, were waiting for Pope John Paul II at Logan Airport, Boston in the late afternoon of 1 October. After an address of welcome from Mrs Carter, the Pope replied:

Praised be Jesus Christ!

It is a great joy for me to be in the United States of America, to begin my pastoral visit to the Catholic Church in this land, and at the same time to greet all the American people, of every race, colour and creed.

I am grateful for the cordial welcome given me on behalf of President Carter, whom I thank most sincerely for his invitation to the United States. I am looking forward to meeting the President after my visit to the United Nations.

My thanks go also to the Cardinal Archbishop of Boston, who in this historic city offers me the first hospitality of this country. I am grateful to the Episcopal Conference and to all the individual Bishops who have so kindly asked me to come. My only regret is that I cannot accept all the invitations extended to me by religious and civil officials, by individuals, families and groups.

From so many quarters – Catholics, Protestants and Jews – America has opened her heart to me. And on my part I come to you – America – with sentiments of friendship, reverence and esteem. I come as one who already knows you and loves you, as one who wishes you to fulfil completely your noble destiny of service to the world. Once again I can now admire firsthand the beauty of this vast land stretching between two oceans; once again I am experiencing the warm hospitality of the American people.

Although it is not possible for me to enter into every home, to greet personally every man and woman, to caress every child in whose eyes is reflected the innocence of love – still, I feel close to all of you, and you are all in my prayers.

Permit me to express my sentiments in the lyrics of your own song: 'America! America! God shed His grace on thee, And crown thy good with brotherhood, From sea to shining sea.'

And may the peace of the Lord be with you always – America!

BOSTON, IN HOLY CROSS CATHEDRAL

An estimated two million people
watched the motorcade of the Pope
from Logan Airport to Holy Cross
Cathedral, Boston. There the Pope
met priests and religious from the
archdiocese of Boston and other New
England dioceses. Cardinal Humberto
S. Medeiros, Archbishop of Boston,
gave a speech of welcome, and after
a brief liturgy of the Word, the Holy
Father pronounced the following
discourse:

Dear Cardinal Medeiros, dear brothers and sisters in Christ,

On the first day of my pastoral visit to the United States of America, it is a great joy
for me to come to this city of Boston, and in this Cathedral, and later tonight on
the Common, to be able to meet with the Catholic community. It is the first time in
history that a Successor of Peter is received in your midst. On this wonderful
occasion I wish to render homage to the Most Holy Trinity, in whose name I have
come. And I make my own the greeting of the Apostle Paul to the Corinthians: 'To
you who have been consecrated in Christ Jesus and called to be a holy people, and
to all those who, wherever they may be, call on the name of our Lord Jesus Christ,
their Lord and ours. Grace and peace from God our Father and the Lord Jesus
Christ' (1 Cor 1:2-3).
    My cordial thanks go to you, Cardinal Medeiros, Archbishop of Boston, for
your welcome today. In your Cathedral Church, I am happy to renew to you the
expression of my deep esteem and friendship. Warm greetings also to the Auxiliary
Bishops and to all the clergy, both diocesan and religious: you who are my brother
priests in virtue of the Sacrament of Holy Orders. Through your priesthood, you
are also God's gift to the Christian community. Because you are servants of the
Gospel, you will always be close to the people and their problems. Because you
share in the Priesthood of Christ, your presence in the world shall always be marked
by Christ's zeal, for he set you apart so that you might build up his Body, the
Church (cf. Eph 4:12).
    I wish to extend a special blessing to you religious, both Religious Brothers and
Sisters, who have consecrated your lives to Jesus Christ. May you always find joy in
his love. And to all of you, the laity of this Diocese, who are united with the
Cardinal and the clergy in a common mission, I open my heart in love and trust.
You are the workers for evangelization in the realities of daily life, and you give
witness to the love of Christ in the service that you give to all your fellow men and
women, beginning with your own families.
    To all I want to say how happy I am to be in your midst. I pray for each one of
you, asking you to remain always united in Jesus Christ and his Church, so that
together we may 'display to the world our unity in proclaiming the mystery of
Christ, in revealing the divine dimension and also the human dimension of the
Redemption, and in struggling with unwearying perseverance for the dignity that

each human being has reached and can continually reach in Christ' (*Redemptor Hominis*, 11). May this Cathedral, dedicated to the Holy Cross of Jesus, always be a reminder of our calling to greatness, for through the mystery of the Incarnation and of the redeeming Sacrifice of Jesus on the Cross we share in 'the unsearchable riches of Christ' (Eph 3:8).

From this Cathedral I send my greeting to all the people of this city of Boston: to those in particular who are, in one way or another, burdened by suffering; to the sick and the bedridden; to those whom society seems to have left by the wayside, and those who have lost faith in God and in their fellow human beings. To all, I have come with a message of hope and peace – the hope and peace of Jesus Christ, for whom every human being is of immense value and dignity, and in whom are found all the treasures of justice and love.

In the city of Boston I am greeting a community that through the many upheavals of history has always been able to change and yet to remain true to itself – a community where people of all backgrounds, creeds, races and convictions have provided workable solutions to problems and have created a home where all people can be respected in their human dignity. For the honour of all the citizens of Boston, who have inherited a tradition of fraternal love and concern, may I recall what one of the founders of this city told his fellow-settlers as they were aboard ship en route to their new home in America: 'We must love one another with a pure heart fervently, we must bear one another's burdens.' These simple words explain so much of the meaning of life – our life as brothers and sisters in our Lord Jesus Christ.

May God's peace descend on this City of Boston, and bring joy to every conscience and joy to every heart!

BOSTON, HOMILY AT BOSTON COMMON

Half a million people were present in the rain at the first Mass celebrated by Pope John Paul on Boston Common. The Mass was celebrated with the Bishops of New England and Canada and with Cardinal Agostino Casaroli, Secretary of State, who accompanied the Pope throughout his journey to the United States. After the Gospel, the Holy Father gave the following homily:

Dear brothers and sisters, dear young people of America,

1   Earlier today, I set foot on the soil of the United States of America. In the name of Christ I begin a pastoral journey that will take me to several of your cities. At the beginning of this year, I had the occasion to greet this continent and its people from a place where Christopher Columbus landed; today I stand at this gateway to the United States, and again I greet all of America. For its people, wherever they are, have a special place in the love of the Pope.

I come to the United States of America as Successor of Peter and as a pilgrim of faith. It gives me great joy to be able to make this visit. And so, my esteem and affection go out to all the people of this land. I greet all Americans without distinction; I want to meet you and tell you all – men and women of all creeds and ethnic origins, children and youth, fathers and mothers, the sick and the elderly – that God loves you, that he has given you a dignity as human beings that is beyond compare. I want to tell everyone that the Pope is your friend and a servant of your humanity. On this first day of my visit, I wish to express my esteem and love for America itself, for the experience that began two centuries ago and that carries the name 'United States of America'; for the past achievements of this land and for its dedication to a more just and human future; for the generosity with which this country has offered shelter, freedom and a chance for betterment to all who have come to its shores; and for the human solidarity that impels you to collaborate with all other nations so that freedom may be safeguarded and full human advancement made possible. I greet you, America the beautiful!

2   I am here because I wanted to respond to the invitation which the Secretary General of the United Nations Organization first addressed to me. Tomorrow I shall have the honour, as guest of the United Nations, to go to this supreme international forum of nations, and to deliver an address to the General Assembly: to make a plea to the whole world for justice and peace – a plea in defence of the unique dignity of every human being. I feel highly honoured by the invitation of the United Nations Secretary General. At the same time I am conscious of the greatness and importance of the challenge that this invitation brings with it. I have been convinced from the very first that this invitation by the United Nations should be accepted by me as Bishop of Rome and pastor of the universal Church of Christ. And so, I express my deep gratitude also to the Hierarchy of the Church in the United States, who joined in the initiative of the United Nations. I have received many invitations from individual dioceses, and from different regions of this country, as well as from Canada. I deeply regret that I am unable to accept all the invitations; I would willingly make a pastoral visit everywhere, if it were possible. My pilgrimage to Ireland on the occasion of the centenary of the Shrine of our Lady at Knock constituted a fitting introduction to my visit with you. I sincerely hope that my whole visit in the United States will be seen in the light of the Second Vatican Council's Constitution on the Church in the Modern World.

And tonight I am deeply pleased to be with you on Boston Common. In you I greet the City of Boston and all its people, as well as the Commonwealth of Massachusetts and all its civil authorities. With special warmth, I greet here Cardinal Medeiros and the whole Archdiocese of Boston. A special remembrance links me with the city, for three years ago, at the invitation of its Divinity School, I had the opportunity to speak at the University of Harvard. As I recall this memorable event, I wish to express once again my gratitude to the authorities of Harvard and to the Dean of the Divinity School for that exceptionally valuable opportunity.

3   During my first visit to the United States as Pope, on the eve of my visit to the United Nations Organization, I now wish to speak a special word to the young people that are gathered here.

Tonight, in a very special way, I hold out my hands to the youth of America. In Mexico City and Guadalajara I met the youth of Latin America. In Warsaw and Cracow I met the youth of Poland. In Rome I meet frequently groups of young people from Italy and from all over the world. Yesterday I met the youth of

31

Ireland in Galway. And now with great joy I meet you. For me, each one of these meetings is a new discovery. Again and again I find in young people the joy and enthusiasm of life, a searching for truth and for the deeper meaning of the existence that unfolds before them in all its attraction and potential.

4   Tonight, I want to repeat what I keep telling youth: you are the future of the world, and 'the day of tomorrow belongs to you'. I want to remind you of the encounters that Jesus himself had with the youth of his day. The Gospels preserve for us a striking account of a conversation Jesus had with a young man. We read there that the young man put to Christ one of the fundamental questions that youth everywhere ask: 'What must I do . . . ?' (Mk 10:17), and he received a precise and penetrating answer. 'Then, Jesus looked at him with love and told him. . . . Come and follow me' (Mk 10:21). But see what happens: the young man, who had shown such interest in the fundamental question 'went away sad, for he had many possessions' (Mk 10:22). Yes, he went away, and – as can be deduced from the context – he refused to accept the call of Christ.

This deeply penetrating event, in its concise eloquence, expresses a great lesson in a few words: it touches upon substantial problems and basic questions that have in no way lost their relevance. Everywhere young people are asking important questions – questions on the meaning of life, on the right way to live, on the true scale of values: 'What must I do . . . ?' 'What must I do to share in everlasting life?' This questioning bears witness to your thoughts, your consciences, your hearts and wills. This questioning tells the world that you, young people, carry within yourselves a special openness with regard to what is good and what is true. This openness is, in a sense, a 'revelation' of the human spirit. And in this openness to truth, to goodness and to beauty, each one of you can find yourself; indeed, in this openness you can all experience in some measure what the young man in the Gospel experienced: 'Jesus looked at him with love' (Mk 10:21).

5   To each one of you I say therefore: heed the call of Christ when you hear him saying to you: 'Follow me!' Walk in my path! Stand by my side! Remain in my love! There is a choice to be made: a choice for Christ and his way of life, and his commandment of love.

The message of love that Christ brought is always important, always relevant. It is not difficult to see how today's world, despite its beauty and grandeur, despite the conquests of science and technology, despite the refined and abundant material goods that it offers, is yearning for more truth, for more love, for more joy. And all of this is found in Christ and in his way of life.

Do I then make a mistake when I tell you, Catholic youth, that it is part of your task in the world and the Church to reveal the true meaning of life where hatred, neglect or selfishness threaten to take over the world? Faced with problems and disappointments, many people will try to escape from their responsibility: escape in selfishness, escape in sexual pleasure, escape in drugs, escape in violence, escape in indifference and cynical attitudes. But today, I propose to you the option of love, which is the opposite of escape. If you really accept that love from Christ, it will lead you to God. Perhaps in the priesthood or religious life; perhaps in some special service to your brothers and sisters: especially to the needy, the poor, the lonely, the abandoned, those whose rights have been trampled upon, or those whose basic needs have not been provided for. Whatever you make of your life, let it be something that reflects the love of Christ. The whole People of God will be all the richer because of the diversity of your commitments. In whatever you do, remember that Christ is calling you, in one way or another, to the service of love: the love of God and your neighbour.

6   And now coming back to the story of the young man in the Gospels, we see that he heard the call – 'Follow me' – but that he 'went away sad, for he had many possessions'.

The sadness of the young man makes us reflect. We could be tempted to think that many possessions, many of the goods of this world, can bring happiness. We see instead in the case of the young man in the Gospel that his many possessions had become an obstacle to accepting the call of Jesus to follow him. He was not ready to say *yes* to Jesus, and *no* to self, to say *yes* to love and *no* to escape.

Real love is demanding. I would fail in my mission if I did not clearly tell you so. For it was Jesus – our Jesus himself – who said: 'You are my friends if you do what I command you' (Jn 15:14). Love demands effort and a personal commitment to the will of God. It means discipline and sacrifice, but it also means joy and human fulfilment.

Dear young people: do not be afraid of honest effort and honest work; do not be afraid of the truth. With Christ's help, and through prayer, you can answer his call, resisting temptations and fads, and every form of mass manipulation. Open your hearts to the Christ of the Gospels – to his love and his truth and his joy. Do not go away sad!

And, as a last word to all of you who listen to me tonight, I would say this: the reason for my mission, for my journey, through the United States is to tell you, to tell everyone – young and old alike – to say to everyone in the name of Christ: 'Come and follow me!'

Follow Christ! You who are married: share your love and your burdens with each other; respect the human dignity of your spouse; accept joyfully the life that God gives through you; make your marriage stable and secure for your children's sake.

Follow Christ! You who are single or who are preparing for marriage. Follow Christ! You who are young or old. Follow Christ! You who are sick or ageing; who are suffering or in pain. You who feel the need for healing, the need for love, the need for a friend – follow Christ!

To all of you I extend – in the name of Christ – the call, the invitation, the plea: 'Come and follow Me.' This is why I have come to America, and why I have come to Boston tonight: to call you to Christ – to call all of you and each of you to live in his love, today and forever. Amen!

Tuesday, 2 October

NEW YORK, ARRIVAL AT LA GUARDIA AIRPORT

On 2 October, the Holy Father was met at La Guardia Airport, New York, by Kurt Waldheim, Secretary General of the United Nations, who gave an address of welcome. Present also were the highest authorities of the city and state of New York. In response to Dr Waldheim's address of welcome, the Pope spoke as follows:

Mr Secretary General,
Ladies and Gentlemen,

I reply with deep gratitude to the greetings of the Secretary General of the United Nations Organization. I have looked forward to this moment since the day he extended to me, immediately after the beginning of my pontificate, the invitation to address the thirty-fourth General Assembly. Your kind initiative, that honours me greatly, was thus at the basis of the journey that has taken me first to Ireland and that I shall continue in the United States of America.

Your Organization has a special significance for the whole world, for in it the needs and the aspirations of all the people of our planet come together. The supreme international forum that it is brings together the efforts and the determination of all men and women of good will, who have resolved to honour the pledge that the Founders of the United Nations made thirty-four years ago and inscribed in the first Article of the Charter: to work together harmonize the actions of the nations in the attainment of international peace and security, to develop friendly relations among nations, to achieve international cooperation, and to promote respect for human rights and for fundamental freedoms for all, without distinction as to race, sex, language or religion.

The very first day after the solemn beginning of my ministry as Supreme Pastor of the Catholic Church, in addressing the representatives of the States and the International Organizations, I took the opportunity to express my esteem for the important role of the International Organizations, and of the United Nations in particular. Here I wish to state again how greatly I value your Institution. For as I stated on that other occasion: 'You are the first to be convinced that there can be no true human progress or lasting peace without the courageous, loyal and disinterested pursuit of growing cooperation and unity among peoples' (23 October 1978).

Yes, the conviction that unites us in this common service of humanity is that, at the basis of all efforts, there must be 'the dignity and worth of the human person' (Charter, Preamble). It is likewise the human person – every individual – who must make the aims of your Organization come true in the concrete realities of friendly relations, of tolerance, of freedom and harmony for all. Decisions and resolutions can be adopted by the representatives of the nations, but their true embodiment will have to be brought about by the people.

Through you then, Mr Secretary General and distinguished Ladies and

Gentlemen, at the beginning of my visit to the United Nations, I greet all the men, women and children of the countries that are represented at the United Nations. May the hopes that they place in the efforts and in the solidarity that link us all never be disappointed. May they experience in the achievements of the United Nations the fact that there is only one world, and that it is the home of all.

Thank you, and may God sustain you in your high ideals.

NEW YORK, AT THE GENERAL ASSEMBLY OF THE UNITED NATIONS

At the General Assembly of the United Nations on 2 October John Paul II delivered his appeal for peace and human rights to the representatives of 151 nations, and through them to all the inhabitants of the earth. After addresses of welcome by Mr Salim Ahmed Salim, President of the General Assembly, and Dr Kurt Waldheim, Secretary General of the United Nations, Pope John Paul delivered the following address:

Mr President,

1   I desire to express my gratitude to the General Assembly of the United Nations, which I am permitted today to participate in and to address. My thanks go in the first place to the Secretary General of the United Nations Organization, Dr Kurt Waldheim. Last autumn, soon after my election to the Chair of Saint Peter, he invited me to make this visit, and he renewed his invitation in the course of our meeting in Rome last May. From the first moment I felt greatly honoured and deeply obliged. And today, before this distinguished Assembly, I also thank you, Mr President, who have so kindly welcomed me and invited me to speak.

2   The formal reason for my intervention today is, without any question, the special bond of cooperation that links the Apostolic See with the United Nations Organization, as is shown by the presence of the Holy See's Permanent Observer to this Organization. The existence of this bond, which is held in high esteem by the Holy See, rests on the sovereignty with which the Apostolic See has been endowed for many centuries. The territorial extent of that sovereignty is limited to the small State of Vatican City, but the sovereignty itself is warranted by the need of the papacy to exercise its mission in full freedom, and to be able to deal with any

interlocutor, whether a government or an international organization, without dependence on other sovereignties. Of course the nature and aims of the spiritual mission of the Apostolic See and the Church make their participation in the tasks and activities of the United Nations Organization very different from that of the States, which are communities in the political and temporal sense.

3 Besides attaching great importance to its collaboration with the United Nations Organization, the Apostolic See has always, since the foundation of your Organization, expressed its esteem and its agreement with the historic significance of this supreme forum for the international life of humanity today. It also never ceases to support your Organization's functions and initiatives, which are aimed at peaceful coexistence and collaboration between nations. There are many proofs of this. In the more than thirty years of the existence of the United Nations Organization, it has received much attention in papal messages and encyclicals, in documents of the Catholic episcopate, and likewise in the Second Vatican Council. Pope John XXIII and Pope Paul VI looked with confidence on your important institution as an eloquent and promising sign of our times. He who is now addressing you has, since the first months of his pontificate, several times expressed the same confidence and conviction as his predecessors.

4 This confidence and conviction on the part of the Apostolic See is the result, as I have said, not of merely political reasons but of the religious and moral character of the mission of the Roman Catholic Church. As a universal community embracing faithful belonging to almost all countries and continents, nations, peoples, races, languages and cultures, the Church is deeply interested in the existence and activity of the Organization whose very name tells us that it unites and associates nations and States. It unites and associates: it does not divide and oppose. It seeks out the ways for understanding and peaceful collaboration, and endeavours with the means at its disposal and the methods in its power to exclude war, division and mutual destruction within the great family of humanity today.

5 This is the real reason, the essential reason, for my presence among you, and I wish to thank this distinguished Assembly for giving consideration to this reason, which can make my presence among you in some way useful. It is certainly a highly significant fact that among the representatives of the States, whose raison d'être is the sovereignty of powers linked with territory and people, there is also today the representative of the Apostolic See and the Catholic Church. This Church is the Church of Jesus Christ, who declared before the tribunal of the Roman judge Pilate that he was a king, but with a kingdom not of this world (cf. Jn 18:36–37). When he was then asked about the reason for the existence of his kingdom among men, he explained: 'For this I was born, and for this I have come into the world, to bear witness to the truth' (Jn 18:37). Here, before the representatives of the States, I wish not only to thank you but also to offer my special congratulations, since the invitation extended to the Pope to speak in your Assembly shows that the United Nations Organization accepts and respects the religious and moral dimension of those human problems that the Church attends to, in view of the message of truth and love that it is her duty to bring to the world. The questions that concern your functions and receive your attention – as is indicated by the vast organic complex of institutions and activities that are part of or collaborate with the United Nations, especially in the fields of culture, health, food, labour, and the peaceful uses of nuclear energy – certainly make it essential for us to meet in the name of man in his

wholeness, in all the fullness and manifold riches of his spiritual and material existence, as I have stated in my encyclical *Redemptor Hominis*, the first of my pontificate.

6   Now, availing myself of the solemn occasion of my greeting with the representatives of the nations of the earth, I wish above all to send my greetings to all the men and women living on this planet. To every man and every woman, without any exception whatever. Every human being living on earth is a member of a civil society, of a nation, many of them represented here. Each one of you, distinguished ladies and gentlemen, represents a particular State, system and political structure, but what you represent above all are individual human beings; you are all representatives of men and women, of practically all the people of the world, individual men and women, communities and peoples who are living the present phase of their own history and who are also part of the history of humanity as a whole, each of them a subject endowed with dignity as a human person, with his or her own culture, experiences and aspirations, tensions and sufferings, and legitimate expectations. This relationship is what provides the reason for all political activity, whether national or international, for in the final analysis this activity comes *from man*, is exercised *by man* and is *for man*. And if political activity is cut off from this fundamental relationship and finality, if it becomes in a way its own end, it loses much of its reason to exist. Even more, it can also give rise to a specific alienation; it can become extraneous to man; it can come to contradict humanity itself. In reality, what justifies the existence of any political activity is service to man, concerned and responsible attention to the essential problems and duties of his earthly existence in its social dimension and significance, on which also the good of each person depends.

7   I ask you, ladies and gentlemen, to excuse me for speaking of questions that are certainly self-evident for you. But it does not seem pointless to speak of them, since the most frequent pitfall for human activities is the possibility of losing sight, while performing them, of the clearest truths, the most elementary principles.

I would like to express the wish that, in view of its universal character, the United Nations Organization will never cease to be the forum, the high tribune from which all man's problems are appraised in truth and justice. It was in the name of this inspiration, it was through this historic stimulus, that on 26 June 1945, towards the end of the terrible Second World War, the Charter of the United Nations was signed and on the following 24 October your Organization began its life. Soon after, on 10 December 1948, came its fundamental document, the *Universal Declaration of Human Rights*, the rights of the human being as a concrete individual and of the human being in his universal value. This document is a milestone on the long and difficult path of the human race. The progress of humanity must be measured not only by the progress of science and technology, which shows man's uniqueness with regard to nature, but also and chiefly by the primacy given to spiritual values and by the progress of moral life. In this field is manifested the full dominion of reason, through truth, in the behaviour of the individual and of society, and also the control of reason over nature; and thus human conscience quietly triumphs, as was expressed in the ancient saying: '*Genus humanum arte et ratione vivit*'.

It was when technology was being directed in its one-sided progress towards goals of war, hegemony and conquest, so that man might kill man and nation destroy nation by depriving it of its liberty and the right to exist – and I still have before my mind the image of the Second World War in Europe, which began forty years ago on 1 September 1939 with the invasion of Poland and ended on 9 May 1945 – it was precisely then that the United Nations Organization arose. And three years later the document appeared which, as I have said, must be considered a real milestone on the path of the moral progress of humanity – the *Universal Declaration of Human Rights*. The governments and States of the world have understood that, if they are not to attack and destroy each other, they must unite. The real way, the fundamental way to this is through each human being, through the definition and recognition of and respect for the inalienable rights of individuals and of the communities of peoples.

8   Today, forty years after the outbreak of the Second World War, I wish to recall the whole of the experiences by individuals and nations that were sustained by a generation that is largely still alive. I had occasion not long ago to reflect again on some of those experiences, in one of the places that are most distressing and overflowing with contempt for man and his fundamental rights – the extermination camp of Oświecim (Auschwitz), which I visited during my pilgrimage to Poland last June. This infamous place is unfortunately only one of the many scattered over the continent of Europe. But the memory of even one should be a warning sign on the path of humanity today, in order that every kind of concentration camp anywhere on earth may once and for all be done away with. And everything that recalls those horrible experiences should also disappear for ever from the lives of nations and States, everything that is a continuation of those experiences under different forms, namely the various kinds of torture and oppression, either physical or moral, carried out under any system, in any land; this phenomenon is all the more distressing if it occurs under the pretext of internal 'security' or the need to preserve an apparent peace.

9   You will forgive me, ladies and gentlemen, for evoking this memory. But I would be untrue to the history of this century, I would be dishonest with regard to the great cause of man, which we all wish to serve, if I should keep silent, I who come from the country on whose living body Oświecim was at one time constructed. But my purpose in evoking this memory is above all to show what painful experiences and sufferings by millions of people gave rise to the *Universal Declaration of Human Rights*, which has been placed as the basic inspiration and cornerstone of the United Nations Organization. This Declaration was paid for by millions of our brothers and sisters at the cost of their suffering and sacrifice, brought about by the brutalization that darkened and made insensitive the human consciences of their oppressors and of those who carried out a real genocide. This price cannot have been paid in vain! The *Universal Declaration of Human Rights* – with its train of many declarations and conventions on highly important aspects of human rights, in favour of children, of women, of equality between races, and especially the two international covenants on economic, social and cultural rights and on civil and political rights – must remain the basic value in the United Nations Organization with which the consciences of its members must be confronted and from which they must draw continual inspiration. If the truths and principles contained in this document were to be forgotten or ignored and were thus to lose the genuine self-evidence that distinguished them at the time they were brought painfully to birth, then the noble purpose of the United Nations Organization could be faced with the threat of a new destruction. This is what would happen if the simple yet powerful eloquence of the *Universal Declaration of Human Rights* were

decisively subjugated by what is wrongly called political interest, but often really means no more than one-sided gain and advantage to the detriment of others, or a thirst for power regardless of the needs of others – everything which by its nature is opposed to the spirit of the Declaration. 'Political interest' understood in this sense, if you will pardon me, ladies and gentlemen, dishonours the noble and difficult mission of your service for the good of your countries and of all humanity.

10 Fourteen years ago my great predecessor Pope Paul VI spoke from this podium. He spoke memorable words, which I desire to repeat today: 'No more war, war never again! Never one against the other', or even 'one above the other', but always, on every occasion, 'with each other'.

Paul VI was a tireless servant of the cause of peace. I wish to follow him with all my strength and continue his service. The Catholic Church in every place on earth proclaims a message of peace, prays for peace, educates for peace. This purpose is also shared by the representatives and followers of other Churches and Communities and of other religions of the world, and they have pledged themselves to it. In union with efforts by all people of good will, this work is certainly bearing fruit. Nevertheless we are continually troubled by the armed conflicts that break out from time to time. How grateful we are to the Lord when a direct intervention succeeds in avoiding such a conflict, as in the case of the tension that last year threatened Argentina and Chile.

It is my fervent hope that a solution also to the Middle East crises may draw nearer. While being prepared to recognize the value of any concrete step or attempt made to settle the conflict, I want to recall that it would have no value if it did not truly represent the 'first stone' of a general overall peace in the area, a peace that, being necessarily based on equitable recognition of the rights of all, cannot fail to include the consideration and just settlement of the Palestinian question. Connected with this question is that of the tranquility, independence and territorial integrity of Lebanon within the formula that has made it an example of peaceful and mutually fruitful coexistence between distinct communities, a formula that I hope will, in the common interest, be maintained, with the adjustments required by the developments of the situation. I also hope for a special statute that, under international guarantees – as my predecessor Paul VI indicated – would respect the particular nature of Jerusalem, a heritage sacred to the veneration of millions of believers of the three great monotheistic religions, Judaism, Christianity and Islam.

We are troubled also by reports of the development of weaponry exceeding in quality and size the means of war and destruction ever known before. In this field also we applaud the decisions and agreements aimed at reducing the arms race. Nevertheless, the life of humanity today is seriously endangered by the threat of destruction and by the risk arising even from accepting certain 'tranquillizing' reports. And the resistance to actual concrete proposals of real disarmament, such as those called for by this Assembly in a special session last year, shows that together with the will for peace that all profess and that most desire there is also in existence – perhaps in latent or conditional form but nonetheless real – the contrary and the negation of this will. The continual preparations for war demonstrated by the production of ever more numerous, powerful and sophisticated weapons in various countries show that there is a desire to be ready for war, and being ready means being able to start it; it also means taking the risk that sometime, somewhere, somehow, someone can set in motion the terrible mechanism of general destruction.

11   It is therefore necessary to make a continuing and even more energetic effort to do away with the very possibility of provoking war, and to make such catastrophes impossible by influencing the attitudes and convictions, the very intentions and aspirations of governments and peoples. This duty, kept constantly in mind by the United Nations Organization and each of its institutions, must also be a duty for every society, every regime, every government. This task is certainly served by initiatives aimed at international cooperation for the fostering of development. As Paul VI said at the end of his encyclical *Populorum Progressio*, 'If the new name for peace is development, who would not wish to labour for it with all his powers?' However, this task must also be served by constant reflection and activity aimed at discovering the very roots of hatred, destructiveness and contempt – the roots of everything that produces the temptation to war, not so much in the hearts of the nations as in the inner determination of the systems that decide the history of whole societies. In this titanic labour of building up the peaceful future of our planet the United Nations Organization has undoubtedly a key function and guiding role, for which it must refer to the just ideals contained in the Universal Declaration of Human Rights. For this Declaration has struck a real blow against the many deep roots of war, since the spirit of war, in its basic primordial meaning, springs up and grows to maturity where the inalienable rights of man are violated.

This is a new and deeply relevant vision of the cause of peace, one that goes deeper is more radical. It is a vision that sees the genesis, and in a sense the substance, of war in the more complex forms emanating from injustice viewed in all its various aspects: this injustice first attacks human rights and thereby destroys the organic unity of the social order and it then affects the whole system of international relations. Within the Church's doctrine, the encyclical *Pacem in Terris* by John XXIII provides in synthetic form a view of this matter that is very close to the ideological foundation of the United Nations Organization. This must therefore form the basis to which one must loyally and perseveringly adhere in order to establish true 'peace on earth'.

12   By applying this criterion we must diligently examine which principal tensions in connection with the inalienable rights of man can weaken the construction of this peace which we all desire so ardently and which is the essential goal of the efforts of the United Nations Organization. It is not easy, but it must be done. Anyone who undertakes it must take up a totally objective position and be guided by sincerity, readiness to acknowledge one's prejudices and mistakes and readiness even to renounce one's own particular interests, including political interests. Peace is something greater and more important than any of these interests. It is by sacrificing these interests for the sake of peace that we serve them best. After all, in whose 'political interest' can it ever be to have another war?

Every analysis must necessarily start from the premise that – although each person lives in a particular concrete social and historical context – every human being is endowed with a dignity that must never be lessened, impaired or destroyed but must instead be respected and safeguarded, if peace is really to be built up.

13   In a movement that one hopes will be progressive and continuous, the *Universal Declaration of Human Rights* and the other international and national juridical instruments are endeavouring to create general awareness of the dignity of the human being, and to define at least some of the inalienable rights of man. Permit me to enumerate some of the most important human rights that are universally recognized: the right to life, liberty and security of person; the right to

food, clothing, housing, sufficient health care, rest and leisure; the right to freedom of expression, education and culture; the right to freedom of thought, conscience and religion, and the right to manifest one's religion either individually or in community, in public or in private; the right to choose a state of life, to found a family and to enjoy all conditions necessary for family life; the right to property and work, to adequate working conditions and a just wage; the right of assembly and association; the right to freedom of movement, to internal and external migration; the right to nationality and residence; the right to political participation and the right to participate in the free choice of the political system of the people to which one belongs. All these human rights taken together are in keeping with the substance of the dignity of the human being, understood in his entirety, not as reduced to one dimension only. These rights concern the satisfaction of man's essential needs, the exercise of his freedoms, and his relationships with others; but always and everywhere they concern man, they concern man's full human dimension.

14   Man lives at the same time both in the world of material values and in that of spiritual values. For the individual living and hoping man, his needs, freedoms and relationships with others never concern one sphere of values alone, but belong to both. Material and spiritual realities may be viewed separately in order to understand better that in the concrete human being they are inseparable, and to see that any threat to human rights, whether in the field of material realities or in that of spiritual realities, is equally dangerous for peace, since in every instance it concerns man in his entirety. Permit me, distinguished ladies and gentlemen, to recall a constant rule of the history of humanity, a rule that is implicitly contained in all that I have already stated with regard to integral development and human rights. The rule is based on the relationship between spiritual values and material or economic values. In this relationship, it is the spiritual values that are pre-eminent, both on account of the nature of these values and also for reasons concerning the good of man. The pre-eminence of the values of the spirit defines the proper sense of earthly material goods and the way to use them. This pre-eminence is therefore at the basis of a just peace. It is also a contributing factor to ensuring that material development, technical development and the development of civilization are at the service of what constitutes man. This means enabling man to have full access to truth, to moral development, and to the complete possibility of enjoying the goods of culture which he has inherited, and of increasing them by his own creativity. It is easy to see that material goods do not have unlimited capacity for satisfying the needs of man: they are not in themselves easily distributed and, in the relationship between those who possess and enjoy them and those who are without them, they give rise to tension, dissension and division that will often even turn into open conflict. Spiritual goods, on the other hand, are open to unlimited enjoyment by many at the same time, without diminution of the goods themselves. Indeed, the more people share in such goods, the more they are enjoyed and drawn upon, the more then do those goods show their indestructible and immortal worth. This truth is confirmed, for example, by the works of creativity – I mean by the works of thought, poetry, music, and the figurative arts, fruits of man's spirit.

15   A critical analysis of our modern civilization shows that in the last hundred years it has contributed as never before to the development of material goods, but that it has also given rise, both in theory and still more in practice, to a series of attitudes in which sensitivity to the spiritual dimension of human existence is

74

diminished to a greater or less extent, as a result of certain premises which reduce the meaning of human life chiefly to the many different material and economic factors – I mean to the demands of production, the market, consumption, the accumulation of riches or of the growing bureaucracy with which an attempt is made to regulate these very processes. Is this not the result of having subordinated man to one single conception and sphere of values?

16   What is the link between these reflections and the cause of peace and war? Since, as I have already stated, material goods by their very nature provoke conditionings and divisions, the struggle to obtain these goods becomes inevitable in the history of humanity. If we cultivate this onesided subordination of man to material goods alone, we shall be incapable of overcoming this state of need. We shall be able to attenuate it and avoid it in particular cases, but we shall not succeed in eliminating it systematically and radically, unless we emphasize more and pay greater honour, before everyone's eyes, in the sight of every society, to the second dimension of the goods of man: the dimension that does not divide people but puts them into communication with each other, associates them and unites them.

I consider that the famous opening words of the Charter of the United Nations, in which 'the peoples of the United Nations, determined to save succeeding generations from the scourge of war' solemnly reaffirmed 'faith in fundamental human rights, in the dignity and worth of the human person, in the equal rights of men and women and of nations large and small', are meant to stress this dimension.

Indeed, the fight against incipient wars cannot be carried out on a merely superficial level, by treating the symptoms. It must be done in a radical way, by attacking the causes. The reason I have called attention to the dimensions constituted by spiritual realities is my concern for the cause of peace, peace which is built up by men and women uniting around what is most fully and profoundly human, around what raises them above the world about them and determines their indestructible grandeur – indestructible in spite of the death to which everyone on earth is subject. I would like to add that the Catholic Church and, I think I can say, the whole of Christianity sees in this very domain its own particular task. The Second Vatican Council helped to establish what the Christian faith has in common with the various non-Christian religions in this aspiration. The Church is therefore grateful to all who show respect and good will with regard to this mission of hers and do not impede it or make it difficult. An analysis of the history of mankind, especially at its present stage, shows how important is the duty of revealing more fully the range of the goods that are linked with the spiritual dimension of human existence. It shows how important this task is for building peace and how serious is any threat to human rights. Any violation of them, even in a 'peace situation', is a form of warfare against humanity.

It seems that in the modern world there are two main threats. Both concern human rights in the field of international relations and human rights within the individual States or societies.

17   The first of these systematic threats against human rights is linked in an overall sense with the distribution of material goods. This distribution is frequently unjust both within individual societies and on the planet as a whole. Everyone knows that these goods are given to man not only as nature's bounty: they are enjoyed by him chiefly as the fruit of his many activities, ranging from the simplest manual and physical labour to the most complicated forms of industrial production, and to the

highly qualified and specialized research and study. Various forms of inequality in the possession of material goods, and in the enjoyment of them, can often be explained by different historical and cultural causes and circumstances. But, while these circumstances can diminish the moral responsibility of people today, they do not prevent the situations of inequality from being marked by injustice and social injury.

People must become aware that economic tensions within countries and in the relationship between States and even between entire continents contain within themselves substantial elements that restrict or violate human rights. Such elements are the exploitation of labour and many other abuses that affect the dignity of the human person. It follows that the fundamental criterion for comparing social, economic and political systems is not, and cannot be, the criterion of hegemony and imperialism: it can be, and indeed it must be, the humanistic criterion, namely the measure in which each system is really capable of reducing, restraining and eliminating as far as possible the various forms of exploitation of man and of ensuring for him, through work, not only the just distribution of the indispensable material goods, but also a participation, in keeping with his dignity, in the whole process of production and in the social life that grows up around that process. Let us not forget that, although man depends on the resources of the material world for his life, he cannot be their slave, but he must be their master. The words of the book of Genesis, 'Fill the earth and subdue it' (Gen: 1:28), are in a sense a primary and essential directive in the field of economy and of labour policy.

18 Humanity as a whole, and the individual nations, have certainly made remarkable progress in this field during the last hundred years. But it is a field in which there is never any lack of systematic threats and violations of human rights. Disturbing factors are frequently present in the form of the frightful disparities between excessively rich individuals and groups on the one hand, and on the other hand the majority made up of the poor or indeed of the destitute, who lack food and opportunities for work and education and are in great numbers condemned to hunger and disease. And concern is also caused at times by the radical separation of work from property, by man's indifference to the production enterprise to which he is linked only by a work obligation, without feeling that he is working for a good that will be his or for himself.

It is no secret that the abyss separating the minority of the excessively rich from the multitude of the destitute is a very grave symptom in the life of any society. This must also be said with even greater insistence with regard to the abyss separating countries and regions of the earth. Surely the only way to overcome this serious disparity between areas of satiety and areas of hunger and depression is through coordinated cooperation by all countries. This requires above all else a unity inspired by an authentic perspective of peace. Everything will depend on whether these differences and contrasts in the sphere of the 'possession' of goods will be systematically reduced through truly effective means, on whether the belts of hunger, malnutrition, destitution, underdevelopment, disease and illiteracy will disappear from the economic map of the earth, and on whether peaceful cooperation will avoid imposing conditions of exploitation and economic or political dependence, which would only be a form of neocolonialism.

19 I would now like to draw attention to a second systematic threat to man in his inalienable rights in the modern world, a threat which constitutes no less a danger

than the first to the cause of peace. I refer to the various forms of injustice in the field of the spirit.

Man can indeed be wounded in his inner relationship with truth, in his conscience, in his most personal belief, in his view of the world, in his religious faith, and in the sphere of what are known as civil liberties. Decisive for these last is equality of rights without discrimination on grounds of origin, race, sex, nationality, religion, political convictions and the like. Equality of rights means the exclusion of the various forms of privilege for some and discrimination against others, whether they are people born in the same country or people from different backgrounds of history, nationality, race and ideology. For centuries the thrust of civilization has been in one direction: that of giving the life of individual political societies a form in which there can be fully safeguarded the objective rights of the spirit, of human conscience and of human creativity, including man's relationship with God. Yet in spite of this we still see in this field recurring threats and violations, often with no possibility of appealing to a higher authority or of obtaining an effective remedy.

Besides the acceptance of legal formulas safeguarding the principle of the freedom of the human spirit, such as freedom of thought and expression, religious freedom, and freedom of conscience, structures of social life often exist in which the practical exercise of these freedoms condemns man, in fact if not formally, to become a second-class or third-class citizen, to see compromised his chances of social advancement, his professional career or his access to certain posts of responsibility, and to lose even the possibility of educating his children freely. It is a question of the highest importance that in internal social life, as well as in international life, all human beings in every nation and country should be able to enjoy effectively their full rights under any political regime or system.

Only the safeguarding of this real completeness of rights for every human being without discrimination can ensure peace at its very roots.

20   With regard to religious freedom, which I, as Pope, am bound to have particularly at heart, precisely with a view to safeguarding peace, I would like to repeat here, as a contribution to respect for man's spiritual dimension, some principles contained in the Second Vatican Council's Declaration *Dignitatis Humanae*: 'In accordance with their dignity, all human beings, because they are persons, that is, beings endowed with reasons and free will and therefore bearing personal responsibility, are both impelled by their nature and bound by a moral obligation to seek the truth, especially religious truth. They are also bound to adhere to the truth once they come to know it and to direct their whole lives in accordance with its demands' (*Dignitatis Humanae*, 2).

'The practice of religion of its very nature consists primarily of those voluntary and free internal acts by which a human being directly sets his course towards God. No merely human power can either command or prohibit acts of this kind. But man's social nature itself requires that he give external expression to his internal acts of religion, that he communicate with others in religious matters and that he profess his religion in community' (*Dignitatis Humanae*, 3).

These words touch the very substance of the question. They also show how even the confrontation between the religious view of the world and the agnostic or or even atheistic view, which is one of the 'signs of the times' of the present age, could preserve honest and respectful human dimensions without violating the essential rights of conscience of any man or woman living on earth.

Respect for the dignity of the human person would seem to demand that, when the exact tenor of the exercise of religious freedom is being discussed or determined with a view to national laws or international conventions, the institutions that are by their nature at the service of religion should also be brought in. If this participation is omitted, there is a danger of imposing, in so intimate a field of man's life, rules or restrictions that are opposed to his true religious needs.

21   The United Nations Organization has proclaimed 1979 the Year of the Child. In the presence of the representatives of so many nations of the world gathered here, I wish to express the joy that we all find in children, the springtime of life, the anticipation of the future history of each of our present earthly homelands. No country on earth, no political system can think of its own future otherwise than through the image of these new generations that will receive from their parents the manifold heritage of values, duties and aspirations of the nation to which they belong and of the whole human family. Concern for the child, even before birth, from the first moment of conception and then throughout the years of infancy and youth, is the primary and fundamental test of the relationship of one human being to another.

    And so, what better wish can I express for every nation and the whole of mankind, and for all the children of the world than a better future in which respect for human rights will become a complete reality throughout the third millennium, which is drawing near.

22   But in this perspective we must ask ourselves whether there will continue to accumulate over the heads of this new generation of children the threat of common extermination for which the means are in the hands of the modern States, especially the major world powers. Are the children to receive the arms race from us as a necessary inheritance? How are we to explain this unbridled race?

    The ancients said: *Si vis pacem, para bellum.* But can our age still really believe that the breathtaking spiral of armaments is at the service of world peace? In alleging the threat of a potential enemy, is it really not rather the intention to keep for oneself a means of threat, in order to get the upper hand with the aid of one's own arsenal of destruction? Here too it is the human dimension of peace that tends to vanish in favour of ever new possible forms of imperialism.

    It must be our solemn wish here for our children, for the children of all the nations on earth, that this point will never be reached. And for that reason I do not cease to pray to God each day so that in his mercy he may save us from so terrible a day.

23   At the close of this address, I wish to express once more before all the high representatives of the States who are present a word of esteem and deep love for all the peoples, all the nations of the earth, for all human communities. Each one has its own history and culture. I hope that they will live and grow in the freedom and truth of their own history. For that is the measure of the common good of each one of them. I hope that each person will live and grow strong with the moral force of the community that forms its members as citizens. I hope that the State authorities, while respecting the just rights of each citizen, will enjoy the confidence of all for the common good. I hope that all the nations, even the smallest, even those that do not yet enjoy full sovereignty, and those that have been forcibly robbed of it, will meet in full equality with the others in the United Nations Organization. I hope that the United Nations will ever remain the supreme forum of peace and justice, the authentic seat of freedom of peoples and individuals in their longing for a better future.

NEW YORK, TO THE REPRESENTATIVES OF THE INTERGOVERNMENTAL AND NON-GOVERNMENTAL ORGANIZATIONS AT UN HEADQUARTERS

Having delivered his message to the
UN Assembly, Pope John Paul met
the diplomats to whom he spoke in
French. Following this he met the
directors of the intergovernmental
and non-governmental organizations
at the UN headquarters, and spoke to
them as follows:

Ladies and Gentlemen,

It gives me great pleasure to extend my greetings to the representatives of the Intergovernmental and Non-governmental Organizations who are present here, and to thank you for your cordial welcome.

Your presence at the centre of the United Nations' activities is a consequence of the growing awareness that the problems of today's world can only be solved when all forces are joined together and directed towards the same common aim. The problems that the human family faces today may seem overwhelming. I for my part am convinced that there is immense potential with which to face them. History tells us that the human race is capable of reacting and of changing direction every time it perceives clearly the warning that it is on the wrong course. You are privileged to witness in this building how the representatives of the nations endeavour to chart a common course in order that life on this planet will be lived in peace, order, justice and progress for all. But you are also aware that every individual must work towards the same end. It is individual actions put together which bring about today and tomorrow the total impact which is either beneficial or harmful for humanity.

The various programmes and organizations that exist within the framework of the United Nations Organization, as well as the Specialized Agencies and other intergovernmental bodies, are an important part of that total effort. In the area of its own specialization – be it food, agriculture, trade, environment, development, science, culture, education, health, disaster relief, or the problems of children and refugees – each one of these organizations make a unique contribution not only to providing for people's wants, but also to fostering respect for human dignity and the cause of world peace.

No organization however, not even the United Nations or any of its specialized agencies, can alone solve the global problems which are constantly brought to its attention, if its concerns are not shared by all the people. It is then the privileged task of the non-governmental organizations to help bring these concerns into the communities and the homes of the people, and to bring back to the established agencies the priorities and aspirations of the people, so that all the solutions and projects which are envisaged be truly geared to the needs of the human person.

The Delegates who drafted the Charter of the United Nations had a vision of united and cooperating governments, but behind the nations, they saw also the individual and they wanted every human being to be free and to enjoy his or her fundamental rights. This fundamental inspiration must be preserved.

79

I wish to express my best wishes to all of you here who work together to bring the benefits of concerted action to all parts of the world. My cordial greeting goes to the Representatives of the various Protestant, Jewish and Moslem associations, and in a particular way to the Representatives of the International Catholic Organizations. May your dedication and your moral sense never become blunted by difficulties, may you never lose sight of the ultimate aim of your efforts: to create a world where every human person can live in dignity and loving harmony as a child of God.

UNITED NATIONS, TO THE JOURNALISTS

The Pope also found time for a brief
meeting with journalists — both those
who are accredited to the United
Nations and those who had been
following his visit so far. He spoke to
them as follows:

My dear friends of the communications media,

It would hardly be possible for me to depart from the United Nations without saying 'thank you' from my heart to those who have reported, not only this day's events, but all the activities of this worthy Organization. In this international assembly, you can truly be instruments of peace by being messengers of truth.

You are indeed servants of truth; you are its tireless transmitters, diffusers, defenders. You are dedicated communicators, promoting unity among all nations by sharing truth among all peoples.

If your reporting does not always command the attention you would desire, or if it does not always conclude with the success that you would wish, do not grow discouraged. Be faithful to the truth and to its transmission, for truth endures; truth will not go away. Truth will not pass or change.

And I say to you – take it as my parting word to you – that the service of truth, the service of humanity through the medium of the truth – is something worthy of your best years, your finest talents, your most dedicated efforts. As transmitters of truth, you are instruments of understanding among people and of peace among nations.

May God bless your labours for truth with the fruit of peace. This is my prayer for you, for your families and for those whom you serve as messengers of truth, and as instruments of peace.

UNITED NATIONS, TO THE MEMBERS OF THE STAFF

While visiting the United Nations the
Holy Father met the staff members of
the United Nations and delivered to
them the following discourse:

Ladies and gentlemen, dear friends,

It is with great pleasure that I take this opportunity to greet all the Members of the
Staff of the United Nations Headquarters in New York, and to reiterate before you
my firm belief in the extraordinary value and importance of the role and activities of
this international institution, of all its agencies and programmes.

When you accepted to serve here, either in study or research, in administrative
tasks or in planning, in secretarial or logistical activities, you did so because you
believed that your work, often hidden and unnoticed in the complexity of this
operation, would constitute a valuable contribution to the aims and objectives of
this Organization. And rightly so. For the first time in the history of humanity,
there exists the possibility for all peoples, through their representatives, to meet
constantly with each other in order to exchange views; to confer on and to seek
peaceful solutions, effective solutions to the conflicts and problems that are causing
suffering in all parts of the world to large numbers of men, women and children.
You are part of this great and universal endeavour. You provide the necessary
services, information and help that are indispensable for the success of this exciting
adventure – you guarantee continuity of action and implementation. Each one of
you is a servant of the unity, peace and brotherhood of all men.

Your task is no less important than that of the Representatives of the nations of
the world, provided you are motivated by the great ideal of world peace and
fraternal collaboration between all peoples: what counts is the spirit with which you
perform your tasks. Peace and harmony among the nations, the progress of all
humanity, the possibility for all men and women to live in dignity and happiness
depend on you, on each one of you, and on the tasks that you perform here.

The builders of the pyramids in Egypt and Mexico, of the temples in Asia, of the
cathedrals in Europe were not only the architects who laid out the designs, or those
who provided financing, but also, and in no small way, the carvers of the stones,
many of whom never had the satisfaction of contemplating in its entirety the beauty
of the masterpiece that their hands helped create. And yet, they were producing a
work of art that would be the object of admiration for generations to come.

You are in so many ways the carvers of the stones. Even a lifetime of dedicated
service will not always enable you to see the finished monument of universal peace,
of fraternal collaboration and of true harmony between peoples. Sometimes you will
catch a glimpse of it, in a particularly successful achievement, in a problem solved,
in the smile of a happy and healthy child, in a conflict avoided, in a reconciliation of
minds and hearts achieved. More often, you will experience only the monotony of
your daily labours, or the frustrations of bureaucratic entanglements. But know that
your work is great and that history will judge your achievements with favour.

The challenges that the world community will face in the coming years and
decades will not diminish. The rapidly changing pace of world events, the

tremendous steps forward of science and technology will increase both the potential for development and the complexity of the problems. Be prepared, be capable, but above all have confidence in the ideal you serve.

Look upon your contribution not only in terms of increased industrial production, of enhanced efficiency, of eliminated suffering. Above all look upon it in terms of growing dignity for every human being, of increased possibility for every person to advance to the fullest measure of spiritual, cultural and human completion. Your calling as international servants takes its value from the objectives pursued by the international organizations. These aims transcend the mere material or intellectual spheres; they reach out into the moral and spiritual fields. Through your work, you are able to extend your love to the entire human family, to every person who has received the wondrous gift of life, so that all may live together in peace and harmony, in a just and peaceful world, where all their basic needs – physical, moral and spiritual – may be fulfilled.

You have in the visitor who stands before you someone who admires what you do and who believes in the value of your task.

Thank you for your welcome. I send my heartfelt greetings also to your families. I especially hope that you may experience a deep and never fading joy in the work that you perform for the benefit of all men, women and children on this earth.

UNITED NATIONS, DEPARTURE

Having expressed his thanks to the
representatives of the nations and
the Secretariat of the United Nations,
Pope John Paul spoke his farewell
message in the following discourse:

Mr Secretary General,

As I am about to conclude my all too brief visit at the world headquarters of the United Nations, I wish to express my heartfelt thanks to all who were instrumental in making this visit possible.

My thanks go first of all to you, Mr Secretary General, for your kind invitation, which I considered not only a great honour but also an obligation, since it allowed me by my presence here to attest publicly and solemnly to the commitment of the Holy See to collaborate, to the extent consonant with its own mission, with this worthy Organization.

My gratitude goes also to the distinguished President of the thirty-fourth General Assembly, who honoured me in inviting me to address this unique forum of the delegates of nearly all the nations of the world. By proclaiming the incomparable dignity of every human being and by manifesting my firm belief in the unity and solidarity of all nations, I have been permitted to affirm once again a basic tenet of my Encyclical Letter: 'After all, peace comes down to respect for man's inviolable rights' (*Redemptor Hominis*, 17).

May I also thank all the distinguished delegates of the nations represented here, as well as the whole staff of the United Nations, for the friendly reception which they have given to the representatives of the Holy See, particularly to our Permanent Observer, Archbishop Giovanni Cheli.

The message which I wish to leave with you is a message of certitude and hope: the certitude that peace is possible when it is based on the recognition of the fatherhood of God and the brotherhood of all men; the hope that the sense of moral responsibility which every person must assume will make it possible to create a better world in freedom, in justice and in love.

As one whose ministry is void of meaning except insofar as he is the faithful Vicar of Christ on earth, I now take leave of you with the words of the one whom I represent, of Jesus Christ himself: 'Peace I leave with you, my peace I give to you' (Jn 14:27). My constant prayer for all of you is this: that there may be peace in justice and in love. May the praying voice of all those who believe in God – Christians and non-Christians alike – bring it about that the moral resources present in the hearts of men and women of good will be united for the common good, and call down from heaven that peace which human efforts alone cannot effect.

May God bless the United Nations.

NEW YORK, VISIT TO SAINT PATRICK'S CATHEDRAL

After his visit to the United Nations, Pope John Paul, accompanied by Cardinal Terence Cooke, went to St Patrick's Cathedral. It was filled with representatives from the various wards of the archdiocese, priests, religious and ecumenical repre- sentatives, including rabbis. Having prayed for a moment before the Altar of Our Lady and heard a speech of welcome from Cardinal Cooke, the Pope replied:

Dear Cardinal Cooke, dear brothers and sisters in Christ,

I consider it a special grace to come back to New York – to be back in Saint Patrick's during the Cathedral's centenary year.

Six months ago I wrote a letter to Cardinal Cooke, stating that it was 'my earnest hope that the local ecclesial community, symbolized by this glorious edifice in stone (cf. 1 Pt 2:5), may be renewed in the faith of Peter and Paul – in the faith of our Lord Jesus Christ – and that each one of you will find fresh vigour for authentic Christian living'. And this is my hope for all of you today. This is why I am here: to confirm you in your holy, Catholic and apostolic faith; to invoke upon you the joy and strength that will sustain you in Christian living.

On this occasion I send my greetings to all the people of New York. In a special way my heart is with the poor, with those who suffer, with those who are alone and abandoned in the midst of this teeming metropolis.

I pray for the success of the apostolate in this Archdiocese: may the spires of Saint Patrick's Cathedral always reflect the thrust with which the Church fulfils her fundamental function in every age: 'to direct man's gaze, to point the awareness and experience of the whole of humanity towards the mystery of God, to help all men and women to be familiar with the profundity of the Redemption taking place in Christ Jesus' (*Redemptor Hominis*, 10).

This too is included in the symbolism of Saint Patrick's; this is the mission of the Church in New York – the expression of her vital and distinctive service to humanity: to direct hearts to God, to keep alive hope in the world. And so we repeat with Saint Paul: 'This explains why we work and struggle as we do; our hopes are fixed on the living God' (1 Tim 4:10).

HARLEM, PARISH OF SAINT CHARLES BORROMEO

After a brief pause in the archiopiscopal palace, Pope John Paul set off for the Yankee Stadium where a crowd of 80,000 people awaited him. On his way he stopped in Harlem where he was greeting in characteristic fashion by the black community of the parish of St Charles Borromeo, his patron. After words of greeting from Monsignor Emerson Moore, pastor, who said that Harlem was 'the capital of black America', the Pope spoke as follows:

Dear friends,
Dear brothers and sisters in Christ,

'This is the day the Lord has made; let us be glad and rejoice in it' (Ps 118:24).

I greet you in the joy and peace of our Lord Jesus Christ. I welcome this opportunity to be with you and to speak to you, and through you to extend my greetings to all black Americans.

At Cardinal Cooke's suggestion, I was happy to include in my plans a visit to the Parish of Saint Charles Borromeo in Harlem, and to its black community, which for half a century has nurtured here the cultural, social and religious roots of black people. I have greatly looked forward to being here this evening.

I come to you as a servant of Jesus Christ, and I want to speak to you about him. Christ came to bring joy: joy to children, joy to parents, joy to families and to friends, joy to workers and to scholars, joy to the sick and to the elderly, joy to all humanity. In a true sense, joy is the keynote of the Christian message and the recurring motif of the Gospels. Recall the first words of the angel to Mary: 'Rejoice, O full of grace, the Lord is with you' (Lk 1:28). And at the birth of Jesus, the angels announced to the shepherds: 'Listen, I bring you news of great joy, joy to be shared by all people' (Lk 2:10). Years later as Jesus entered Jerusalem riding on a colt, 'the whole group of disciples joyfully began to praise God at the top of their voices. "Blessed is the King who comes in the name of the Lord"!' (Lk 19:37–38). We are told that some Pharisees in the crowd complained, saying: 'Master, stop your disciples.' But Jesus answered: 'I tell you, if they were silent, the very stones would cry out' (Lk 19:39–40).

Are not those words of Jesus still true today? If we are silent about the joy that comes from knowing Jesus, the very stones of our cities will cry out! For we are an Easter people and 'Alleluia' is our song. With Saint Paul I exhort you: 'Rejoice in the Lord always, I say it again, rejoice' (Phil 4:4).

> Rejoice because Jesus has come into the world!
> Rejoice because Jesus has died upon the cross!
> Rejoice because he rose again from the dead!
> Rejoice because in baptism, he washed away our sins!
> Rejoice because Jesus has come to set us free!
> And rejoice because he is the master of our life!

But how many people have never known this joy? They feed on emptiness and tread the paths of despair. 'They walk in darkness and the shadow of death' (Lk 1:79). And we need not look to the far ends of the earth for them. They live in our neighbourhoods, they walk down our streets, they may even be members of our own families. They live without true joy because they live without hope. They live without hope because they have never heard, really heard the Good News of Jesus Christ, because they have never met a brother or a sister who touched their lives with the love of Jesus and lifted them up from their misery.

We must go to them therefore as messengers of hope. We must bring to them the witness of true joy. We must pledge to them our commitment to work for a just society and city where they feel respected and loved.

And so I encourage you, be men and women of deep and abiding faith. Be heralds of hope. Be messengers of joy. Be true workers for justice. Let the Good News of Christ radiate from your hearts, and the peace he alone gives remain forever in your souls.

My dear brothers and sisters in the black community: 'Rejoice in the Lord always, again I say rejoice.'

Alleluia!

NEW YORK, GREETING TO
THE SPANISH-SPEAKING PEOPLE
OF THE SOUTH BRONX

While still on his way to the Yankee
Stadium, Pope John Paul stopped in
the South Bronx, at the crossroads
between Morris Avenue and 152nd
Street. He blessed the first stone of a
new housing project and addressed a
congregation mostly of Spanish-
speaking immigrants in their own
language.

Dear brothers and sisters and friends,

One of the visits to which I attribute great importance, and to which I would like to
be able to devote more time, is precisely the one that I am now making to South
Bronx, in this immense city of New York, where many immigrants of different
colours, races and peoples live, among them the numerous Spanish-speaking
community, you, to whom I am now addressing myself.

I come here because I know of the difficult conditions of your existence, because
I know that your lives are marked by pain. For this reason you deserve special
attention on the part of the Pope.

My presence in this place is meant to be a sign of gratitude and as an
encouragement for what the Church has done and is continuing to do, through her
parishes, schools, health centres, institutes for assisting youth and the ageing, on
behalf of so many who experience inner anxiety and material deprivation.

I would wish that this flame of hope – sometimes one of the least hopes – should
not only not go out, but that it might increase in strength, so that all who live in the
area and the city may succeed in being able to live with dignity and serenity, as
individual human beings, as families, as sons and daughters of God.

Brothers and sisters and friends, do not give in to despair, but work together,
take the steps possible for you in the task of increasing your dignity, unite your
efforts towards the goals of human and moral advancement. And do not forget that
God has your lives in his care, goes with you, calls you to better things, calls you to
overcome.

But since help from outside is also necessary, I make an insistent call to the
leaders, to those who can do it, that they should give their generous collaboration in
such a praiseworthy and urgent task.

Please God that the house-building project – and other necessary projects – may
soon become a beautiful reality, so that each person and each family may find
suitable housing in which to live in peace beneath the gaze of God.

Friends: I greet you and all those dear to you, I bless you and I encourage you
not to grow faint as you travel the right road.

NEW YORK, HOMILY, YANKEE STADIUM

About 80,000 people were gathered
in the Yankee Stadium. It was there,
in 1965, that Pope Paul VI had
celebrated his only Mass in the
United States during his visit to the
United Nations. In his homily after
the Gospel, Pope John Paul II
emphasized that wealth carried with
it responsibility and made a
contemporary application of the
parable of the rich man and Lazarus.

1   'Peace be with you!'
    These were the first words that Jesus spoke to his Apostles after his Resurrection.
With these words the Risen Christ restored peace to their hearts, at a time when
they were still in a state of shock after the first terrible experience of Good Friday.
Tonight, in the name of our Lord Jesus Christ, in the power of his Spirit, in the
midst of a world that is anxious about its own existence, I repeat these words to
you, for they are words of life: 'Peace be with you!'
    Jesus does not merely give us peace. He gives us *his* Peace accompanied by *his*
Justice. He *is* Peace and Justice. He becomes *our* Peace and *our* Justice.
    What does this mean? It means that Jesus Christ – the Son of God made man,
the perfect man – perfects, restores and manifests in himself the unsurpassable
dignity that God wishes to give to man from the beginning. He is the one who
realizes in himself what man has the vocation to be: the one who is fully reconciled
with the Father, fully one in himself, fully devoted to others. Jesus Christ is living
Peace and living Justice.
    Jesus Christ makes us sharers in what he is. Through his Incarnation, the Son of
God in a certain manner united himself with every human being. In our inmost
being he has recreated us; in our inmost being he has reconciled us with God,
reconciled us with ourselves, reconciled us with our brothers and sisters: he is *our*
Peace.

2   What unfathomable riches we bear within us, and in our Christian communities!
We are bearers of the Justice and Peace of God! We are not primarily painstaking
builders of a justice and peace that are merely human, always wearing out and
always fragile. We are primarily the humble beneficiaries of the very life of God,
who is Justice and Peace in the bond of Charity. During Mass, when the priest
greets us with these words: 'the peace of the Lord be with you always', let us think
primarily of this Peace which is God's gift: Jesus Christ our Peace. And when,
before Communion, the priest invites us to give one another a sign of peace, let us
think primarily of the fact that we are invited to exchange with one another the
Peace of Christ, who dwells within us, who invites us to share in his Body and
Blood, for our joy and for the service of all humanity.
    For God's Justice and Peace cry out to bear fruit in human works of justice and
peace, in all the spheres of actual life. When we Christians make Jesus Christ the
centre of our feelings and thoughts, we do not turn away from people and their

87

needs. On the contrary, we are caught up in the eternal movement of God's love that comes to meet us; we are caught up in the movement of the Son, who came among us, who became one of us; we are caught up in the movement of the Holy Spirit, who visits the poor, calms fevered hearts, binds up wounded hearts, warms cold hearts, and gives us the fullness of his gifts. The reason why man is the primary and fundamental way for the Church is that the Church walks in the footsteps of Jesus: it is Jesus who has shown her this road. This road passes in an unchangeable way through the mystery of the Incarnation and Redemption; it leads from Christ to man. The Church looks at the world through the very eyes of Christ; Jesus is the principle of her solicitude for man (cf. *Redemptor Hominis*, 13–18).

3   The task is immense. And it is an enthralling one. I have just emphasized various aspects of it before the General Assembly of the United Nations, and I shall touch upon others during my apostolic journey across your country. Today, let me just dwell on the spirit and nature of the Church's contribution to the cause of Justice and Peace, and let me also mention certain urgent priorities which your service to humanity ought to concentrate upon today.

Social thinking and social practice inspired by the Gospel must always be marked by a special sensitivity towards those who are most in distress, those who are extremely poor, those suffering from all the physical, mental and moral ills that afflict humanity, including hunger, neglect, unemployment and despair. There are many poor people of this sort around the world. There are many in your own midst. On many occasions, your nation has gained a well deserved reputation for generosity, both public and private. Be faithful to that tradition, in keeping with your vast possibilities and present responsibilities. The network of charitable works of each kind that the Church has succeeded in creating here is a valuable means for effectively mobilizing generous undertakings aimed at relieving the situations of distress that continually arise both at home and elsewhere in the world. Make an effort to ensure that this form of aid keeps its irreplaceable character as a fraternal and personal encounter with those who are in distress; if necessary, re-establish this very character against all the elements that work in the opposite direction. Let this sort of aid be respectful of the freedom and dignity of those being helped, and let it be a means of forming the conscience of the givers.

4   But this is not enough. Without the framework of your national institutions and in cooperation with all your compatriots, you will also want to seek out the structural reasons which foster or cause the different forms of poverty in the world and in your own country, so that you can apply the proper remedies. You will not allow yourselves to be intimidated or discouraged by over-simplified explanations, which are more ideological than scientific – explanations which try to account for a complex evil by some single cause. But neither will you recoil before the reforms – even profound ones – of attitudes and structures that may prove necessary in order to re-create over and over again the conditions needed by the disadvantaged if they are to have a fresh chance in the hard struggle of life. The poor of the United States and of the world are your brothers and sisters in Christ. You must never be content to leave them just the crumbs from the feast. You must take of your substance, and not just of your abundance, in order to help them. And you must treat them like guests at your family table.

5   Catholics of the United States, while developing your own legitimate institutions, you also participate in the nation's affairs within the framework of

institutions and organizations springing from the nation's common history and from your common concern. This you do hand in hand with your fellow citizens of every creed and confession. Unity among you in all such endeavours is essential, under the leadership of your Bishops, for deepening, proclaiming and effectively promoting the truth among man, his dignity and his inalienable rights, the truth such as the Church receives it in Revelation and such as she ceaselessly develops it in her social teaching in the light of the Gospel. These shared convictions, however, are not a ready-made model for society (cf. *Octogesima Adveniens*, 42). It is principally the task of lay people to put them into practice in concrete projects, to define priorities and to develop models that are suitable for promoting man's real good. The Second Vatican Council's Pastoral Constitution *Gaudium et Spes* tells us that 'lay people should seek from priests light and spiritual strength. Let the lay people not imagine that their pastors are always such experts, that to every problem which arises, however complicated, they can readily give a concrete solution, or even that such is their mission. Rather, enlightened by Christian wisdom and giving close attention to the teaching authority of the Church, let the lay people assume their own distinctive role' (*Gaudium et Spes*, 43).

6   In order to bring this undertaking to a successful conclusion, fresh spiritual and moral energy drawn from the inexhaustible divine source is needed. This energy does not develop easily. The life style of many of the members of our rich and permissive societies is easy, and so is the life style of increasing groups inside the poorer countries. As I said last year to the Plenary Assembly of the Pontifical Commission Justice and Peace, 'Christians will want to be in the vanguard in favouring ways of life that decisively break with a frenzy of consumerism, exhausting and joyless' (11 November 1978). It is not a question of slowing down progress, for there is no human progress when everything conspires to give full reign to the instincts of self-interest, sex and power. We must find a simple way of living. For it is not right that the standard of living of the rich countries should seek to maintain itself by draining off a great part of the reserves of energy and raw materials that are meant to serve the whole of humanity. For readiness to create a greater and more equitable solidarity between peoples is the first condition for peace. Catholics of the United States, and all you citizens of the United States, you have such a tradition of spiritual generosity, industry, simplicity and sacrifice that you cannot fail to heed this call today for a new enthusiasm and a fresh determination. It is in the joyful simplicity of a life inspired by the Gospel and the Gospel's spirit of fraternal sharing that you will find the best remedy for sour criticism, paralysing doubt and the temptation to make money the principal means and indeed the very measure of human advancement.

7   On various occasions, I have referred to the Gospel parable of the rich man and Lazarus. 'Once there was a rich man who dressed in purple and linen and feasted splendidly every day. At his gate lay a beggar named Lazarus who was covered with sores. Lazarus longed to eat the scraps that fell from the rich man's table' (Lk 16:19 ff.). Both the rich man and the beggar died and were carried before Abraham, and there judgment was rendered on their conduct. And the Scripture tells us that Lazarus found consolation, but that the rich man found torment. Was the rich man condemned because he had riches, because he abounded in earthly possessions, because he 'dressed in purple and linen and feasted splendidly every day'? No, I would say that it was not for this reason. The rich man was condemned because he did not pay attention to the other man. Because he failed to take notice of Lazarus,

the person who sat at his door and who longed to eat the scraps from his table. Nowhere does Christ condemn the mere possession of earthly goods as such. Instead, he pronounces very harsh words against those who use their possessions in a selfish way, without paying attention to the needs of others. The Sermon on the Mount begins with the words: 'Blessed are the poor in spirit.' And at the end of the account of the last judgment as found in Saint Matthew's Gospel, Jesus speaks the words that we all know so well: 'I was hungry and you gave me no food, I was thirsty and you gave me no drink. I was away from home and you gave me no welcome, naked and you gave me no clothing. I was ill and in prison and you did not come and comfort me' (Mt 25:42–43).

The parable of the rich man and Lazarus must always be present in our memory; it must form our conscience. Christ demands openness to our brothers and sisters in need – openness from the rich, the affluent, the economically advanced; openness to the poor, the underdeveloped and the disadvantaged. Christ demands an openness that is more than benign attention, more than token actions or half-hearted efforts that leave the poor as destitute as before or even more so.

All of humanity must think of the parable of the rich man and the beggar. Humanity must translate it into contemporary terms, in terms of economy and politics, in terms of all human rights, in terms of relations between the 'First', 'Second' and 'Third World'. We cannot stand idly by when thousands of human beings are dying of hunger. Nor can we remain indifferent when the rights of the human spirit are trampled upon, when violence is done to the human conscience in matters of truth, religion, and cultural creativity.

We cannot stand idly by, enjoying our own riches and freedom, if, in any place, the Lazarus of the twentieth century stands at our doors. In the light of the parable of Christ, riches and freedom mean a special responsibility. Riches and freedom create a special obligation. And so, in the name of the solidarity that binds us all together in a common humanity, I again proclaim the dignity of every human person: the rich man and Lazarus are both human beings, both of them equally created in the image and likeness of God, both of them equally redeemed by Christ, at a great price, the price of 'the precious blood of Christ' (1 Pt 1:19).

8   Brothers and sisters in Christ, with deep conviction and affection I repeat to you the words that I addressed to the world when I took up my apostolic ministry in the service of all men and women: 'Do not be afraid. Open wide the doors for Christ. to his saving power open the boundaries of states, economic and political systems, the vast fields of culture, civilization and development. Do not be afraid. Christ knows what is in man. He alone knows it' (22 October 1978).

As I said to you at the beginning, Christ is our Justice and our Peace, and all our works of justice and peace draw from this source the irreplaceable energy and light for the great task before us. As we resolutely commit ourselves to the service of all the needs of individuals and of peoples – for Christ urges us to do so – we shall nevertheless remind ourselves that the Church's mission is not limited to this witness to social fruitfulness of the Gospel. Along this road that leads the Church to man, she does not offer, in the matter of justice and peace, only the earthly fruits of the Gospel; she brings to man – to every human person – their very source – Jesus Christ himself, our Justice and our Peace.

Wednesday, 3 October

Pope John Paul II began his second
day in New York, 3 October, with
morning prayer in St Patrick's
Cathedral. There he gave the
following address on the value of
the divine office:

Dear brothers and sisters,

Saint Paul asks: 'who will separate us from the love of Christ?'
    As long as we remain what we are this morning – a community of prayer united in Christ, an ecclesial community of praise and worship of the Father – we shall understand and experience the answer: that no one – nothing at all – will ever separate us from the love of Christ. For us today, the Church's Morning Prayer is a joyful, communal celebration of God's love in Christ.
    The value of the Liturgy of the Hours is enormous. Through it, all the faithful, but especially the clergy and religious, fulfil a role of prime importance: Christ's prayer goes on in the world. The Holy Spirit himself intercedes for God's people (cf. Rom 8:27). The Christian community, with praise and thanksgiving, glorifies the wisdom, the power, the providence and the salvation of our God.
    In this prayer of praise we lift up our hearts to the Father of our Lord Jesus Christ, bringing with us the anguish and hopes, the joys and sorrows of all our brothers and sisters in the world.
    And our prayer becomes likewise a school of sensitivity, making us aware of how much our destinies are linked together in the human family. Our prayer becomes a school of love – a special kind of Christian consecrated love, by which we love the world, but with the heart of Christ.
    Through this prayer of Christ to which we give voice, our day is sanctified, our activities transformed, our actions made holy. We pray the same psalms that Jesus prayed, and come into personal contact with him – the person to whom all Scripture points, the goal to which all history is directed.
    In our celebration of the word of God, the mystery of Christ opens up before us and envelops us. And through union with our Head, Jesus Christ, we become ever more increasingly one with all the members of his Body. As never before, it becomes possible for us to reach out and embrace the world, but to embrace it with Christ: with authentic generosity, with pure and effective love, in service, in healing and in reconciliation.
    The efficacy of our prayer renders special honour to the Father because it is made always through Christ, and for the glory of his name: 'We ask this through our

Lord Jesus Christ, your Son, who lives and reigns with you and the Holy Spirit, one God, for ever and ever.'

As a community of prayer and praise, with the Liturgy of the Hours among the highest priorities of our day – each day – we can be sure that nothing will separate us from the love of God that is in Christ Jesus our Lord.

NEW YORK, TO HIGH SCHOOL STUDENTS IN MADISON SQUARE GARDEN

After the brief morning prayer in St Patrick's Cathedral, the papal cavalcade set off for Madison Square Garden. Despite the rain there were large crowds along Fifth Avenue. Twenty thousand young people were waiting for John Paul in Madison Square Garden. He first watched a 'multi-media' presentation about the hopes and aspirations of American youth. Then he was presented with a tee-shirt, a pair of jeans, a guitar and a medal on a chain—'as symbols of the youth culture of America'. Before starting his address, the Pope diverted the young people with a noise that sounded like 'wooo' and rose half an octave. 'This is a charismatic moment' he said. Then, at the invitation of Cardinal Terence Cooke, he began his address as follows:

Dear young people,

I am happy to be with you in Madison Square Garden. Today this is a garden of life, where young people are alive: alive with hope and love, alive with the life of Christ. And it is in the name of Christ that I greet each one of you today.

I have been told that most of you come from Catholic high schools. For this reason I would like to say something about Catholic education, to tell you why the Church considers it so important and expends so much energy in order to provide you and millions of other young people with a Catholic education. The answer can be summarized in one word, in one person, Jesus Christ. The Church wants to communicate Christ to you.

92

1   This is what education is all about, this is the meaning of life: to know Christ. To know Christ as a friend: as someone who cares about you and the person next to you, and all the people here and everywhere – no matter what language they speak, or what clothes they wear, or what colour their skin is.

And so the purpose of Catholic education is to communicate Christ to you, so that your attitude towards others will be that of Christ. You are approaching that stage in your life when you must take personal responsibility for your own destiny. Soon you will be making major decisions which will affect the whole course of your life. If these decisions reflect Christ's attitude, then your education will be a success.

We have to learn to meet challenges and even crises in the light of Christ's Cross and Resurrection. Part of our Catholic education is to learn to see the needs of others, to have the courage to practice what we believe in. With the support of a Catholic education we try to meet every circumstance of life with the attitude of Christ. Yes, the Church wants to communicate Christ to you so that you will come to full maturity in him who is the perfect human being, and at the same time, the Son of God.

2   Dear young people: you and I and all of us together make up the Church, and we are convinced that only in Christ do we find real love, and the fullness of life.

And so I invite you today to look to Christ.

When you wonder about the mystery of yourself, look to Christ who gives you the meaning of life.

When you wonder what it means to be a mature person, look to Christ who is the fullness of humanity.

And when you wonder about your role in the future of the world and of the United States, look to Christ. Only in Christ will you fulfil your potential as an American citizen and as a citizen of the world community.

3   With the aid of your Catholic education, you have received the greatest of gifts: the knowledge of Christ. Of this gift Saint Paul wrote: 'I believe nothing can happen that will outweigh the supreme advantage of knowing Christ Jesus my Lord. For him I have accepted the loss of everything and I look on everything as so much rubbish if only I can have Christ and be given a place in him' (Phil 3:8–9).

Be always grateful to God for this gift of knowing Christ. Be grateful also to your parents and to the community of the Church for making possible, through many sacrifices, your Catholic education. People have placed a lot of hope in you, and they now look forward to your collaboration in giving witness to Christ, and in transmitting the Gospel to others. The Church needs you. The world needs you, because it needs Christ, and you belong to Christ. And so I ask you to accept your responsibility in the Church, the responsibility of your Catholic education: to help – by your words, and, above all, by the example of your lives – to spread the Gospel. You do this by praying, and by being just and truthful and pure.

Dear young people: by a real Christian life, by the practice of your religion you are called to give witness to your faith. And because actions speak louder than words, you are called to proclaim, by the conduct of your daily lives that you really do believe that Jesus Christ is Lord!

NEW YORK, BATTERY PARK

The rain was falling heavily between
the skyscrapers as the Pope went to
Battery Park. Here, with the Statue of
Liberty in the background and close
to Ellis Island, where so many
immigrants caught their first glimpse
of the United States, the Pope was
to meet the people of New York who,
in their great ethnic diversity, are
like a microcosm of the whole world.
An estimated three hundred thousand
people heard the Pope's address, and
his remarks to the Jewish
community, so important in New
York, were especially noted.

Dear friends,

1　My visit to your city would not have been complete without coming to Battery
Park, without seeing Ellis Island and the Statue of Liberty in the distance. Every
nation has its historical symbols. They may be shrines or statues or documents; but
their significance lies in the truths they represent to the citizens of a nation and in
the image they convey to other nations. Such a symbol in the United States is the
Statue of Liberty. This is an impressive symbol of what the United States has stood
for from the very beginning of its history; this is a symbol of freedom. It reflects the
immigrant history of the United States, for it was freedom that millions of human
beings were looking for on these shores. And it was freedom that the young
Republic offered in compassion. On this spot, I wish to pay homage to this noble
trait of America and its people: its desire to be free, its determination to preserve
freedom, and its willingness to share this freedom with others. May the ideal of
liberty, of freedom remain a moving force for your nation and for all the nations in
the world today!

2　It greatly honours your country and its citizens that on this foundation of liberty
you have built a nation where the dignity of every human person is to be respected,
where a religious sense and a strong family structure are fostered, where duty and
honest work are held in high esteem, where generosity and hospitality are no idle
words, and where the right to religious liberty is deeply rooted in your history.
　　Yesterday, before the General Assembly of the United Nations, I made a plea for
peace and justice based on the full respect of all the fundamental rights of the human
person. I also spoke of religious freedom because it regards a person's relationship
to God, and because it is related in a special way to other human rights. It is closely
allied with the right to freedom of conscience. If conscience is not secure in society,
then the security of all other rights is threatened.
　　Liberty, in all its aspects, must be based on truth. I want to repeat here the
words of Jesus 'the truth will make you free' (Jn 8:32). It is then my wish that your
sense of freedom may always go hand in hand with a profound sense of truth and

honesty about yourselves and about the realities of your society. Past achievements can never be an acceptable substitute for present responsibilities towards the common good of the society you live in and towards your fellow-citizens. Just as the desire for freedom is a universal aspiration in the world today, so is the quest for justice. No institution or organization can credibly stand for freedom today if it does not also support the quest for justice, for both are essential demands of the human spirit.

3 It will always remain one of the glorious achievements of this nation that, when people looked towards America, they received together with freedom also a chance for their own advancement. This tradition must be honoured also today. The freedom that was gained, must be ratified each day by the firm rejection of whatever wounds, weakens or dishonours human life. And so I appeal to all who love freedom and justice to give a chance to all in need, to the poor and the powerless. Break open the hopeless cycles of poverty and ignorance that are still the lot of too many of our brothers and sisters; the hopeless cycles of prejudices that linger on despite enormous progress towards effective equality in education and employment; the cycles of despair in which are imprisoned all those that lack decent food, shelter or employment; the cycles of underdevelopment that are the consequence of international mechanisms that subordinate the human existence to the domination of partially conceived economic progress; and finally the inhuman cycles of war that springs from the violation of man's fundamental rights and produces still graver violation of them.

Freedom in justice will bring a new dawn of hope for the present generation as it has done before: for the homeless, for the unemployed, for the ageing, for the sick and the handicapped, for the migrants and the undocumented workers, for all who hunger for human dignity in this land and in the world.

4 With sentiments of admiration and with confidence in your potential for true human greatness, I wish to greet in you the rich variety of your nation, where people of different ethnic origins and creeds can live, work and prosper together in freedom and mutual respect. I greet and I thank for the cordial welcome of all those who joined me here, businessmen and labourers, scholars and managers, social workers and civil servants, old and young, I greet you with respect, esteem and love. My warm greetings go to each and every group. To my fellow Catholics, to the members of the different Christian Churches with whom I am united in the faith in Jesus Christ.

And I address a special word of greeting to the leaders of the Jewish community whose presence here honours me greatly. A few months ago, I met with an international group of Jewish representatives in Rome. On that occasion, recalling the initiatives undertaken following the Second Vatican Council under my predecessor Paul VI, I stated that 'our two communities are connected and closely related at the very level of their respective religious identities', and that on this basis 'we recognize with utmost clarity that the path along which we should proceed is one of fraternal dialogue and fruitful collaboration' (L'Osservatore Romano, 12–13 March 1979). I am glad to ascertain that this same path has been followed here, in the United States, by large sections of both communities and their respective authorities and representative bodies. Several common programmes of study, mutual knowledge, a common determination to reject all forms of anti-semitism and discrimination, and various forms of collaboration for the human advancement, inspired by our common biblical heritage, have created deep and permanent links between Jews and Catholics. As one who in my homeland has shared the suffering of your brethren, I greet you with the word taken from the Hebrew language: *Shalom*! Peace be with you!

And to everyone here I offer the expression of my respect, my esteem and my fraternal love. May God bless all of you! May God bless New York!

NEW YORK, ADDRESS IN SHEA STADIUM

The Pope's last engagement in New York was at the Shea Stadium in the Queen's area of the city. It has many immigrant groups, and the Pope was greeted not only in English but in Polish and Italian. He improvized a brief greeting in both languages and then made his farewell to the city of New York.

Dear friends,

It gives me great joy to have the opportunity to come and greet you on my way to La Guardia Airport, at the end of my visit to the Archdiocese and to the metropolis of New York.

Thank you for your warm welcome. In you I wish to greet once again all the people of New York, Long Island, New Jersey and Connecticut-Brooklyn: all your parishes, hospitals, schools and organizations, your sick and aged. And with special affection I greet the young people and the children.

From Rome I bring you a message of faith and love. 'May the peace of Christ reign in your hearts!' (Col 3:15). Make peace the desire of your heart, for if you love peace, you will love all humanity, without distinction of race, colour or creed.

My greeting is also an invitation to all of you to feel personally responsible for the wellbeing and the community spirit of your city. A visitor to New York is always impressed by the special character of this metropolis: skyscrapers, endless streets, large residential areas, housing blocks, and above all the millions of people who live here or who look here for the work that will sustain them and their family.

Large concentrations of people create special problems and special needs. The personal effort and loyal collaboration of everybody are needed to find the right solutions, so that all men, women and children can live in dignity and develop to the full their potential without having to suffer for lack of education, housing, employment, and cultural opportunities. Above all, a city needs a soul if it is to become a true home for human beings. You, the people, must give it this soul. And

how do you do this? By loving each other. Love for each other must be the hallmark of your lives. In the Gospel Jesus Christ tells us: 'You shall love your neighbour as yourself' (Mt 22:39). This commandment of the Lord must be your inspiration in forming true human relationships among yourselves, so that nobody will ever feel alone or unwanted, or much less, rejected, despised or hated. Jesus himself will give you the power of fraternal love. And every neighbourhood, every block, every street will become a true community because you will want it so, and Jesus will help you to bring it about.

Keep Jesus Christ in your hearts, and you will recognize his face in every human being. You will want to help him out in all his needs: the needs of your brothers and sisters. This is the way we prepare ourselves to meet Jesus, when he will come again, on the last day, as the Judge of the living and the dead and he will say to us: 'Come, you have my Father's blessing! Inherit the kingdom prepared for you from the creation of the world. For I was hungry and you gave me food, I was thirsty and you gave me drink. I was a stranger and you welcomed me, naked and you clothed me. I was ill and you comforted me, in prison and you came to visit me. . . . I assure you as often as you did it for one of my least brethren, you did it for ME' (Mt 25:34–35, 39).

I now wish to address a very cordial welcome to each and every member of the Spanish-speaking colony, coming from various countries, here in this stadium.

In you, I see and I wish to greet, with great affection, the whole of the numerous Hispanic community living in New York and many other places in the United States.

I wish to assure you that I am well aware of the place that you occupy in American society, and that I follow with lively interest your accomplishments, aspirations and difficulties within the social fabric of this nation, which is your homeland of adoption or the land that welcomes you. For this reason, from the very moment that I accepted the invitation to visit this country, I thought of you, who are an integral and specific part of this society, a very considerable part of the Church in this vast nation.

I wish to exhort you, as Catholics, always to maintain very clearly your Christian identity, with a constant reference to the value of your faith, values that must enlighten the legitimate quest for a worthy material position for yourselves and your families.

Since you are generally immersed in the environment of heavily populated cities and in a social climate where sometimes technology and material values take first place, make an effort to provide a spiritual contribution to your life and your neighbourhood. Keep close to God in your lives, to the God who calls you to be ever more worthy of your condition as human beings with an eternal vocation, to the God who invites you to solidarity and to collaboration in building up an ever more human, just and fraternal world.

I pray for you, for your families and friends, above all for your children, for the sick and suffering, and to all of you I give my Blessing. May God be with you always!

Goodbye, and God bless you.

PHILADELPHIA, VISIT TO
THE CATHEDRAL OF SAINTS PETER AND PAUL

The flight from New York to
Philadelphia took 35 minutes. The
Pope was greeted by Cardinal John
Krol, the State Governor and the
Mayor of Philadelphia. He then went
immediately to the Cathedral of
Saints Peter and Paul. In his address
he spoke of Saint John Neumann,
who was once Bishop of
Philadelphia.

Dear brothers and sisters in Christ,

I give thanks to the Lord for permitting me to come back to this city of
Philadelphia, to this state of Pennsylvania. I have very happy memories of being
here before as your guest, and I remember especially the Eucharistic Congress and
the Bicentennial celebration in 1976 that I attended as Archbishop of Cracow.
Today, by the grace of God, I come here as Successor of Peter to bring you a
message of love and to strengthen you in your faith. In your kind welcome I feel
that you want to honour in me the Christ whom I represent and who lives in all of
us – all of us who through the Holy Spirit form one community, one communion in
faith and love. I feel moreover that I am truly among friends, and I feel very much
at home in your midst.

In a very particular way I wish to thank you, Cardinal Krol, Archbishop of
Philadelphia, for the invitation you extended to me, to come here and celebrate the
Eucharist together with you and your people. A heartfelt greeting also goes to the
clergy, religious and laity, of this local church. I have come as your Brother in
Christ, bringing with me the same message that the Lord Jesus himself brought to
the villages and cities in the Holy Land: let us praise the Lord our God and Father,
and let us love one another!

It gives me great pleasure to meet you here in the Cathedral of Philadelphia, for
it has a deep meaning for me. Above all, it means *you*: the living Church of Christ,
here and now, alive in faith, united in the love of Jesus Christ.

This Cathedral recalls the memory of Saint John Neumann, once Bishop of this
See, and now and for ever a saint of the universal Church. In this edifice, his
message and his example of holiness must continually be transmitted to every new
generation of young people. And if we listen carefully today we can hear Saint John
Neumann speaking to all of us in the words of the Letter to the Hebrews:
'Remember your leaders who spoke the word of God to you; consider how their
lives ended, and imitate their faith. Jesus Christ is the same yesterday, today and
forever' (Heb 13:8).

Finally, this Cathedral links you to the great Apostles of Rome, Peter and Paul.
They, in turn, continue to give you their testimony to Christ, to proclaim to you
Christ's divinity, to acknowledge him before the world. Here today in Philadelphia,
the confession of Peter becomes for all of us a personal act of faith, and this act of
faith we make together, as we say to Jesus: 'You are the Christ, the Son of the

living God' (Mt 16:16). And with Saint Paul, each one of us is called to say in the depths of our hearts and before the world: 'I still live my human life, but it is a life of faith in the Son of God, who loved me and gave himself for me' (Gal 2:20).

This Cathedral is also linked in religion to the heritage of this historic city. Every service to morality and spirituality is a service to the civilization of man; it is a contribution to human happiness and to true wellbeing.

And so, from this Cathedral I offer my greetings to the whole city of Philadelphia, the civil authorities and all the people. As the city of brotherly love, as the first capital of the United States of America, you are a symbol of freedom and fraternal relations. My greeting is also a prayer. May the common dedication and the united efforts of all your citizens – Catholics, Protestants and Jews alike – succeed in making your inner city and suburbs places where people are not strangers to each other, where every man, woman and child feel respected; where nobody feels abandoned, rejected or alone.

Asking for your prayerful support for my visit of friendship and pastoral concern, I extend my blessing to all of you, to those present here today, to your dear ones at home, to the aged and the sick, and in a very special way to all the young people and the children.

God bless Philadelphia!

PHILADELPHIA, HOMILY FOR EUCHARISTIC CELEBRATION AT LOGAN CIRCLE

The Pope then went to Logan Circle, a vast park, where hundreds of thousands awaited him. He concelebrated Mass with Cardinal Krol and the Bishops of Pennsylvania, Trenton and Camden, New Jersey. American commentators spoke of the visit to Philadelphia as 'a visit of the heart' since the Pope already knew Cardinal Krol well and had twice been to Philadelphia in 1969 and 1976. The Pope again used the symbols of the American experience —the Constitution and the Liberty Bell—to develop the Christian message.

Dear brothers and sisters of the Church in Philadelphia,

1 It is a great joy for me to celebrate the Eucharist with you today. All of us are gathered together as one community, one people in the grace and peace of God our

Father and of the Lord Jesus Christ; we are gathered in the fellowship of the Holy Spirit. We have come together to proclaim the Gospel in all its power, for the Eucharistic Sacrifice is the summit and enactment of our proclamation:

Christ has died, Christ is risen, Christ will come again! From this altar of Sacrifice, there arises a hymn of praise and thanksgiving to God through Jesus Christ. We who belong to Christ are all part of this hymn, this Sacrifice of praise. The sacrifice of Calvary is renewed on this altar, and it becomes our offering too – an offering for the benefit of the living and the dead, an offering for the universal Church.

Assembled in the charity of Christ, we are all one in his Sacrifice: the Cardinal Archbishop who is called to lead this Church in the path of truth and love; his Auxiliary Bishops and the diocesan and religious clergy, who share with the Bishops in the preaching of the word; men and women religious, who through the consecration of their lives show the world what it means to be faithful to the message of the Beatitudes; fathers and mothers, with their great mission of building up the Church in love; every category of the laity with their particular task in the Church's mission of evangelization and salvation. This Sacrifice offered today in Philadelphia is the expression of our praying community. In union with Jesus Christ we make intercession for the universal Church, for the wellbeing of all our fellow men and women, and today, in particular, for the preservation of all the human and Christian values that are the heritage of this land, this country and this very city.

2   Philadelphia is the city of the Declaration of Independence, that remarkable document, containing a solemn attestation of the equality of all human beings, endowed by their Creator with certain inalienable rights: life, liberty and the pursuit of happiness, expressing a 'firm reliance on the protection of divine Providence'. These are the sound moral principles formulated by your Founding Fathers and enshrined forever in your history. In the human and civil values that are contained in the spirit of this Declaration there are easily recognized strong connections with basic religious and Christian values. A sense of religion itself is part of this heritage. The Liberty Bell which I visited on another occasion, proudly bears the words of the Bible: 'Proclaim liberty throughout the land' (Lev 25:10). This tradition poses for all future generations of America a noble challenge: 'One Nation under God, indivisible, with liberty and justice for all.'

3   As citizens, you must strive to preserve these human values, to understand them better and to define their consequences for the whole community, and as a worthy contribution to the world. As Christians, you must strengthen these human values and complement them by confronting them with the Gospel message, so that you may discover their deeper meaning, and thus assume more fully your duties and obligations towards your fellow human beings, with whom you are bound in a common destiny. In a way, for us, who know Jesus Christ, human and Christian values are but two aspects of the same reality: the reality of man, redeemed by Christ and called to the fullness of eternal life.

In my first Encyclical Letter, I stated this important truth: 'Christ, the Redeemer of the world, is the one who penetrated in a unique unrepeatable way into the mystery of man and entered his "heart". Rightly therefore does the Second Vatican Council teach: "The truth is that only in the mystery of the Incarnate Word does the mystery of man take on light. For Adam, the first man, was a type of him who was to come (Rom 5:14), Christ the Lord. Christ the new Adam, in the very revelation of the mystery of the Father and his love, fully reveals man to himself and brings to light his most high calling" ' (*Redemptor Hominis*, 8). It is then in Jesus Christ that every man, woman and child is called to find the answer to the questions regarding the values that will inspire his or her personal and social relations.

4 How then can a Christian, inspired and guided by the mystery of the Incarnation and Redemption of Christ, strengthen his or her own values and those that are embodied in the heritage of this nation? The answer to that question, in order to be complete, would have to be long. Let me, however, just touch upon a few important points. These values are strengthened: when power and authority are exercised in full respect for all the fundamental rights of the human person, whose dignity is the dignity of one created in the image and likeness of God (Gen 1:26); when freedom is accepted, not as an absolute end in itself, but as a gift that enables self-giving and service; when the family is protected and strengthened, when its unity is preserved, and when its role as the basic cell of society is recognized and honoured. Human-Christian values are fostered when every effort is made so that no child anywhere in the world faces death because of lack of food, or faces a diminished intellectual and physical potential for want of sufficient nourishment, or has to bear all through life the scars of deprivation. Human-Christian values triumph when any system is reformed that authorizes the exploitation of any human being; when upright service and honesty in public servants is promoted; when the dispensing of justice is fair and the same for all; when responsible use is made of the material and energy resources of the world – resources that are meant for the benefit of all; when the environment is preserved intact for the future generations. Human-Christian values triumph by subjecting political and economic considerations to human dignity, by making them serve the cause of man – every person created by God, every brother and sister redeemed by Christ.

5 I have mentioned the Declaration of Independence and the Liberty Bell, two monuments that exemplify the spirit of freedom on which this country was founded. Your attachment to liberty, to freedom, is part of your heritage. When the Liberty Bell rang for the first time in 1776, it was to announce the freedom of your nation, the beginning of the pursuit of a common destiny independent of any outside coercion. This principle of freedom is paramount in the political and social order, in relationships between the government and the people, and between individual and individual. However, man's life is also lived in another order of reality: in the order of his relationship to what is objectively true and morally good. Freedom thus acquires a deeper meaning when it is referred to the human person. It concerns in the first place the relation of man to himself. Every human person, endowed with reason, is free when he is the master of his own actions, when he is capable of choosing that good which is in conformity with reason, and therefore with his own human dignity.
   Freedom can never tolerate an offence against the rights of others, and one of the fundamental rights of man is the right to worship God. In the Declaration on Religious Freedom, the Second Vatican Council stated that the 'demand for freedom in human society chiefly regards the quest for the values proper to the human spirit. It regards in the first place, the free exercise of religion in society. . . . Religious freedom, which men demand as necessary to fulfil their duty to worship God, has to do with immunity from coercion in civil society. Therefore it leaves untouched traditional Catholic teaching on the moral duty of men and societies towards the true religion and towards the one Church of Christ' (*Dignitatis Humanae*, 1).

6   Christ himself linked freedom with the knowledge of truth. 'You will know the truth and the truth will make you free' (Jn 8:32). In my first Encyclical I wrote in this regard: 'These words contain both a fundamental requirement and a warning: the requirement of an honest relationship with regard to truth as a condition for authentic freedom, and the warning to avoid every kind of illusory freedom, every superficial unilateral freedom, every freedom that fails to enter into the whole truth about man and the world' (*Redemptor Hominis*, 12).

Freedom can therefore never be construed without relation to the truth as revealed by Jesus Christ, and proposed by his Church, nor can it be seen as a pretext for moral anarchy, for every moral order must remain linked to truth. Saint Peter, in his first letter, says: 'Live as free men, but do not use your freedom for malice' (1 Pt 2:16). No freedom can exist when it goes against man in what he is, or against man in his relationship to others and to God.

This is especially relevant when one considers the domain of human sexuality. Here, as in any other field, there can be no true freedom without respect for the truth regarding the nature of human sexuality and marriage. In today's society, we see so many disturbing tendencies and so much laxity regarding the Christian view on sexuality that have all one thing in common: recourse to the concept of freedom to justify any behaviour that is no longer consonant with the true moral order and the teaching of the Church. Moral norms do not militate against the freedom of the person or the couple; on the contrary they exist precisely for that freedom, since they are given to ensure the right use of freedom. Whoever refuses to accept these norms and to act accordingly, whoever seeks to liberate himself or herself from these norms, is not truly free. Free indeed is the person who models his or her behaviour in a responsible way according to the exigencies of the objective good. What I have said here regards the whole of conjugal morality, but it applies as well to the priests with regard to the obligations of celibacy. The cohesion of freedom and ethics has also its consequences for the pursuit of the common good in society and for the national independence which the Liberty Bell announced two centuries ago.

7   Divine law is the sole standard of human liberty and is given to us in the Gospel of Christ, the Gospel of Redemption. But fidelity to this Gospel of Redemption will never be possible without the action of the Holy Spirit. It is the Holy Spirit who guards the life-giving message entrusted to the Church. It is the Holy Spirit who ensures the faithful transmission of the Gospel into the lives of all of us. It is by the action of the Holy Spirit that the Church is built up day after day into a kingdom: a kingdom of truth and life, a kingdom of holiness and grace, a universal kingdom of justice, love and peace.

Today, therefore, we come before the Father to offer him the petitions and desires of our hearts, to offer him praise and thanksgiving. We do this from the city of Philadelphia for the universal Church and for the world. We do this as 'members of the household of God' (Eph 2:19) in union with the Sacrifice of Christ Jesus, our cornerstone, for the glory of the Most Holy Trinity. Amen.

PHILADELPHIA, AT THE SEMINARY

The final engagement on the evening
of 3 October was a meeting with
priests, religious and seminarians of
the Archdiocese of Philadelphia. It
took place at St Charles Seminary.
The Pope's main message was
directed to the seminarians.

Beloved brothers and sons in Christ,

One of the things I wanted most to do during my visit to the United States has now
arrived. I wanted to visit a seminary and meet the seminarians; and through you I
would like to communicate to all seminarians how much you mean to me, and how
much you mean for the future of the Church – for the future of the mission given to
us by Christ.

You hold a special place in my thoughts and prayers. In your lives there is great
promise for the future of evangelization. And you give us hope that the authentic
renewal of the Church which was begun by the Second Vatican Council will be
brought to fruition. But in order for this to happen, you must receive a solid and
well-rounded preparation in the seminary. This personal conviction about the
importance of seminaries prompted me to write these words in my Holy Thursday
Letter to the Bishops of the Church:

> The full reconstitution of the life of the seminaries throughout the Church
> will be the best proof of the achievement of the renewal to which the Council
> directed the Church.

1   If seminaries are to fulfil their mission in the Church two activities in the overall
programme of the seminary are crucially important: the teaching of God's word,
and discipline.

The intellectual formation of the priest, which is so vital for the times in which
we live, embraces a number of the human sciences as well as the various sacred
sciences. These all have an important place in your preparation for the priesthood.
But the first priority for seminaries today is the teaching of God's word in all its
purity and integrity, with all its demands and in all its power. This was clearly
affirmed by my beloved predecessor Paul VI, when he stated that sacred scripture is
'a perpetual source of spiritual life, the chief instrument for handing down
Christian doctrine, and the centre of all theological study' (Apostolic Constitution
Missale Romanum, 3 April 1969). Therefore if you, the seminarians of this
generation, are to be adequately prepared to take on the heritage and challenge of
the Second Vatican Council, you will need to be well trained in the word of God.

Secondly, the seminary must provide a sound discipline to prepare for a life of
consecrated service in the image of Christ. Its purpose was well-defined by the
Second Vatican Council:

> The discipline required by seminary life should not be regarded merely as a
> strong support of community life and of charity. For it is a necessary part of
> the whole training programme designed to provide self-mastery, to foster solid

maturity of personality, and to develop other traits of character which are extremely serviceable for the ordered and productive activity of the Church (*Optatam Totius*, 11).

When discipline is properly exercised, it can create an atmosphere of recollection which enables the seminarian to develop interiorly those attitudes which are so desirable in a priest, such as joyful obedience, generosity and self-sacrifice. In the different forms of community life that are appropriate for the seminary, you will learn the art of dialogue: the capacity to listen to others and to discover the richness of their personality, and the ability to give of yourself. Seminary discipline will reinforce, rather than diminish your freedom, for it will help develop in you those traits and attitudes of mind and heart which God has given you, and which enrich your humanity and help you to serve more effectively his people. Discipline will also assist you in ratifying day after day in your hearts the obedience you owe to Christ and his Church.

2 I want to remind you of the importance of fidelity. Before you can be ordained, you are called by Christ to make a free and irrevocable commitment to be faithful to him and to his Church. Human dignity requires that you maintain this commitment, that you keep your promise to Christ no matter what difficulties you may encounter, and no matter what temptations you may be exposed to. The seriousness of this irrevocable commitment places a special obligation upon the rector and faculty of the seminary – and in a particular way on the spiritual director – to help you to evaluate your own suitability for Ordination. It is then the responsibility of the Bishop to judge whether you should be called to the priesthood.

It is important that one's commitment be made with full awareness and personal freedom. And so during these years in the seminary, take time to reflect on the serious obligations and the difficulties which are part of the priest's life. Consider whether Christ is calling you to the celibate life. You can make a responsible decision for celibacy only after you have reached the firm conviction that Christ is indeed offering you this gift, which is intended for the good of the Church and for the service of others (cf. Letter to Priests, 9).

To understand what it means to be faithful we must look to Christ, the 'faithful witness' (Rev 1:5), the Son who 'learned to obey through what he suffered' (Heb 5:8); to Jesus who said: 'My aim is to do not my own will, but the will of him who sent me' (Jn 5:30). We look to Jesus, not only to see and contemplate his fidelity to the Father despite all opposition (cf. Heb. 23:3), but also to learn from him the means he employed in order to be faithful: especially prayer and abandonment to God's will (cf. Lk 22:39 ff).

Remember that in the final analysis perseverenace in fidelity is a proof, not of human strength and courage, but of the efficacy of Christ's grace. And so if we are going to persevere we shall have to be men of prayer who, through the Eucharist, the liturgy of the hours and our personal encounters with Christ, find the courage and grace to be faithful. Let us be confident then, remembering the words of Saint Paul: 'There is nothing that I cannot master with the help of the one who gives me strength' (Phil 4:13).

3 My brothers and sons in Christ, keep in mind the priorities of the priesthood to which you aspire: namely prayer and the ministry of the word (Acts 6:4).

It is the prayer that shows the essential style of the priest; without prayer this style becomes deformed. Prayer helps us always to find the light that has led us since the beginning of our priestly vocation, and which never ceases to lead us. . . . Prayer enables us to be converted continually, to remain in a state of continuous reaching out to God, which is essential if we wish to lead others to him. Prayer helps us to believe, to hope and to love . . . (Letter to Priests, 10).

It is my hope that during your years in the seminary you will develop an ever greater hunger for the word of God (cf. Amos 8:11). Meditate on this word daily and study it continually, so that your whole life may become a proclamation of Christ, the Word made flesh (cf. Jn 1:14). In this word of God are the beginning and end of all ministry, the purpose of all pastoral activity, the rejuvenating source for faithful perseverance and the one thing which can give meaning and unity to the varied activities of a priest.

4 'Let the message of Christ, in all its richness, find a home with you' (Col 3:16). In the knowledge of Christ you have the key to the Gospel. In the knowledge of Christ you have an understanding of the needs of the world. Since he became one with us in all things but sin, your union with Jesus of Nazareth could never, and will never be an obstacle to understanding and responding to the needs of the world. And finally, in the knowledge of Christ, you will not only discover and come to understand the limitations of human wisdom and of human solutions to the needs of humanity, but you will also experience the power of Jesus, and the value of human reason and human endeavour when they are taken up in the strength of Jesus, when they are redeemed in Christ.

May our Blessed Mother Mary protect you today and always.

5 May I also take this opportunity to greet the lay people who are present today at Saint Charles Seminary. Your presence here is a sign of your esteem for the ministerial priesthood, as well as being a reminder of that close cooperation between laity and priests which is needed if the mission of Christ is to be fulfilled in our time. I am happy that you are present and I am grateful for all that you do for the Church in Philadelphia. In particular I ask you to pray for these young men, and for all seminarians that they may persevere in their calling. Please pray for all priests and for the success of their ministry among God's people. And please pray the Lord of the harvest to send more labourers into his vineyard, the Church.

Thursday, 4 October

PHILADELPHIA, IN THE CHURCH OF SAINT PETER

Thursday, 4 October, was one of the busiest days in a week of intensive activity. It began with a short prayer in St Peter's, Philadelphia, where are to be found the mortal remains of St John Neumann. In a brief speech, Pope John Paul explained why he had wanted to pray at the tomb.

Dear brothers and sisters in Christ,

I have come to Saint Peter's Church to pray at the tomb of Saint John Neumann, a zealous missionary, a dedicated pastor, a faithful son of Saint Alphonsus in the Congregation of the Most Holy Redeemer, and the fourth Bishop of Philadelphia.

As I stand in this Church, I am reminded of the one thing which motivated Saint John Neumann throughout his life: his love for Christ. His own prayers show us this love; for from the time he was a child he used to say: 'Jesus, for you I want to live; for you I want to die; I want to be all yours in life; I want to be all yours in death' (Nicola Ferrante, *S Giovanni Neumann, CSSR Pioniere del Vangelo*, p. 25). And at the First Mass he celebrated as a priest, he prayed in these words: 'Lord, give me holiness.'

My brothers and sisters in Christ: this is the lesson we learn from the life of Saint John Neumann, and the message which I leave with you today: what really matters in life is that we are loved by Christ, and that we love him in return. In comparison to the love of Jesus, everything else is secondary. And without the love of Jesus, everything else is useless.

May Mary, our Mother of Perpetual Help intercede for us; may Saint John Neumann pray for us; and with the help of their prayers may we persevere in faith, be joyful in hope and be strengthened in our love for Jesus Christ, our Redeemer and our Lord.

PHILADELPHIA, GREETING TO SPANISH-SPEAKING PEOPLE AT SAINT PETER'S CHURCH

In the time of St John Neumann, the parishioners of St Peter's were mostly of German origin. Now they are predominantly Spanish, so after his address in English, Pope John Paul spoke to the 'Hispanics', as they are known in the United States, in their own language.

Dear Spanish-speaking brothers and sisters,

I greet you with joy and I thank you for your enthusiastic presence here, in the church of Saint Peter, which houses the remains of Saint John Neumann, the first American man to be canonized a saint.

You, members of the Spanish-speaking community, have gathered in great numbers in this place, you who arrived in this country as immigrants, or who were born here of immigrant ancestors, but who preserve the Christian faith as the greatest treasure of your tradition.

Saint John Neumann too was an immigrant, and he experienced many of the difficulties that you yourselves have encountered: the difficulties of language, of a different culture, of social adaptation.

Everyone knows about your efforts and perseverance in preserving your own religious heritage, which is also at the same time placed at the service of the whole national community, so that it may be a witness of unity within a pluralism of religion, culture and social living.

In their fidelity to the saving message of Jesus Christ, your ecclesial communities will find the proper path for experiencing membership in the universal Church and for taking care of this world.

May devotion to Mary our Mother, and your communion with the Vicar of Christ, continue to be, as in the past, the power that fosters and increases your Christian faith.

To all of you here present, to those who have not been able to come, in particular to the sick and the aged, who are spiritually united with this meeting, with all my heart I impart my special Apostolic Blessing.

PHILADELPHIA, IN THE UKRAINIAN CHURCH
OF THE IMMACULATE CONCEPTION

From St Peter's the Pope went the
short distance to the Ukrainian
Cathedral of the Immaculate
Conception. There he was welcomed
in English by the Administrator and
Archbishop-elect Lubachevtsky of
the Ukrainian Archeparchy of
Philadelphia. After a brief introduction
in Ukrainian, Pope John Paul II gave
the following address in English. It
was of great importance since it was
his first major statement on the
Ukrainian Catholic Church which has
suffered greatly, both from persecution
in Soviet Russia and from internal
disputes.

Dear brothers and sisters,

'Now in Christ Jesus . . . you are citizens like all the saints, and part of God's
household. You are part of a building that has the apostles and prophets for its
foundations, and Christ Jesus himself for its main cornerstone' (Eph 2:13, 19–20).
With these words the Apostle Paul reminded the Ephesians of the tremendous
blessing they had received in becoming members of the Church. And those words
are still true today. You are part of the household of God. You, members of the
Ukrainian tradition, are part of a building that has the apostles and prophets for its
foundations, and Christ Jesus himself for its main cornerstone. This has all occurred
according to the providential plan of God.

Several years ago, my beloved predecessor, Paul VI, gave a stone from the tomb
of Saint Peter to be included in the construction of this beautiful Cathedral dedicated
to Mary Immaculate. Pope Paul intended this gift to be a visible symbol of the love
and esteem of the Apostolic See of Rome for the Ukrainian Church. At the same
time, this stone was meant to serve as a sign of the fidelity of the Ukrainian Church
to the See of Peter. In this profound symbolic gesture, Paul VI was re-affirming the
teaching of the Apostle Paul in the letter to the Ephesians.

Today, as successor to Paul VI in the Chair of Saint Peter, I come to visit you in
this magnificent new Cathedral. I am happy for this opportunity. I welcome the
occasion to assure you, as universal pastor of the Church, that all who have inherited
the Ukrainian tradition have an important and distinguished part to fulfil in the
Catholic Church.

As history testifies, the Church developed a number of rites and traditions as in
the course of time she spread from Jerusalem to the nations and took flesh in the
language, culture and human traditions of the individual peoples who accepted the
Gospel with open hearts. These various rites and traditions, far from being a sign of
deviation, infidelity or disunity, were in fact unfailing proof of the presence of the
Holy Spirit who continually renews and enriches the Church, the kingdom of

Christ already present in mystery (cf. *Lumen Gentium*, 3).

The various traditions within the Church give expression to the multitude of ways the Gospel can take root and flower in the lives of God's people. They are living evidence of the richness of the Church. Each one, while united to all the others in the 'same faith, the same sacraments and the same government' (*Orientalium Ecclesiarum*, 2), is nevertheless manifested in its own liturgy, ecclesiastical discipline and spiritual patrimony. Each tradition combined particular artistic expressions and unique spiritual insights with an unparalleled lived experience of being faithful to Christ. It was in view of these considerations that the Second Vatican Council declared: 'History, tradition, and numerous ecclesiastical institutions clearly manifest how much the universal Church is indebted to the Eastern Churches. Thus this sacred Synod not only honours this ecclesiastical and spiritual heritage with merited esteem and rightful praise, but also unhesitatingly looks upon it as the heritage of Christ's universal Church (*Orientalium Ecclesiarum*, 5).

For many years, I have highly esteemed the Ukrainian people. I have known of the many sufferings and injustices you have endured. These have been and continue to be matters of great concern to me. I am also mindful of the struggles of the Ukrainian Catholic Church, throughout its history, to remain faithful to the Gospel and to be in union with the successor of Saint Peter. I cannot forget the countless Ukrainian martyrs, in ancient and more recent times, most of whose names are unknown, who gave up their lives rather than abandon their faith. I mention these in order to show my profound esteem for the Ukrainian Church and its proved fidelity in suffering.

I also wish to mention those things which you have preserved as your special spiritual patrimony: the Slavonic liturgical language, the ecclesiastical music and the numerous forms of piety which have developed over the centuries and continue to nourish your lives. Your appreciation of these treasures of the Ukrainian tradition is demonstrated by the way that you have maintained your attachment with the Ukrainian Church and have continued to live the faith according to its unique tradition.

My brothers and sisters in Christ, I want to recall in your presence the words Jesus prayed on the vigil of his death upon the cross: 'Father . . . that they may be one' (Jn 17:11). We must never forget this prayer; in fact we must continually search for still better ways to safeguard and strengthen the bonds of union which unite us in the one Catholic Church.

Remember the words of Saint Paul: 'you form part of a building that has the apostles and prophets for its foundations, and Christ Jesus himself for its main cornerstone' (Eph 2:20). The unity of this spiritual building, which is the Church, is preserved by fidelity to the cornerstone, who is Christ, and to the teaching of the apostles preserved and explained in the tradition of the Church. A real unity of doctrine binds us as one.

Catholic unity also entails a recognition of the successor of Saint Peter and his ministry of strengthening and preserving intact the communion of the universal Church, while safeguarding the existence of legitimate individual traditions within it. The Ukrainian Church, as well as the other Eastern Churches, has a right and duty, in accordance with the teaching of the Council (cf. *Orientalium Ecclesiarum*, 5), to preserve its own ecclesiastical and spiritual patrimony. It is precisely because these individual traditions are also intended for the enrichment of the universal Church that the Apostolic See of Rome takes great care to protect and foster each one. In turn, the ecclesial communities that follow these traditions are called to adhere with love and respect to certain particular forms of discipline which my predecessors and I, in fulfilling our pastoral responsibility to the universal Church, have judged necessary for the wellbeing of the whole Body of Christ.

To a great extent, our Catholic unity depends on mutual charity. Let us remember that the unity of the Church originated on the Cross of Christ, which broke down the barriers of sin and division and reconciled us with God and with one another. Jesus foretold this unifying act when he said: '. . . and I, if I be lifted up from the earth, will draw all men to myself' (Jn 12:32). If we continue to imitate the love of Jesus, our Saviour, on the Cross, and if we persevere in love for one another, then we shall preserve the bonds of unity in the Church and witness the fulfilment of Jesus' prayer: 'Father . . . that they may be one' (Jn 17:11).

As for the future, I entrust you to the protection of Mary Immaculate, the Mother of God, the Mother of the Church. I know that you honour her with great devotion. This magnificent Cathedral dedicated to the Immaculate Conception bears eloquent witness to your filial love. And for centuries, our Blessed Mother has been the strength of your people throughout their sufferings, and her loving intercession has been a cause of their joy.

Continue to entrust yourselves to her protection.

Continue to be faithful to her son, our Lord Jesus Christ, the Redeemer of the world.

And may the grace of our Lord Jesus Christ be with you all.

PHILADELPHIA, HOMILY TO PRIESTS

The Pope's final engagement in Philadelphia was a Mass in the great hall of the Civic Center. It was concelebrated with priests representing all the dioceses of the United States and twenty religious orders. Many others priests, religious and seminarians were present. This determined the theme of the papal homily.

Dear brother Priests,

1   As we celebrate this Mass, which brings together the presidents or chairmen of the Priests' Senates, or Councils, of all the dioceses of the United States, the theme that suggests itself to our reflection is a vital one: the priesthood itself and its central importance to the task of the Church. In the Encyclical Letter *Redemptor Hominis*, I described this task in these words: 'The Church's fundamental function in every age and particularly in ours is to direct man's gaze, to point the awareness and experience of the whole of humanity towards the mystery of God, to help men to be

familiar with the profundity of the Redemption taking place in Christ Jesus' (*Redemptor Hominis*, 10).

Priests' Senates are a new structure in the Church, called for by the Second Vatican Council and recent Church legislation. This new structure gives a concrete expression to the unity of Bishop and priests in the service of shepherding the flock of Christ, and it assists the Bishop in his distinctive role of governing the diocese, by guaranteeing for him the counsel of representative advisors from among the presbyterium. Our concelebration of today's Eucharist is intended to be a mark of affirmation for the good that has been achieved by your Priests' Senates during these past years, as well as an encouragement to pursue with enthusiasm and determination this important aim, which is 'to bring the life and activity of the People of God into greater conformity with the Gospel' (cf. *Ecclesiae Sanctae*, 16:1). Most of all, however, I want this Mass to be the special occasion on which I can speak through you to all my brother priests throughout this nation about our priesthood. With great love I repeat the words that I wrote to you on Holy Thursday: 'For you I am a Bishop, with you I am a priest.'

Our priestly vocation is given by the Lord Jesus himself. It is a call which is personal and individual: we are called by name as was Jeremiah. It is a call to service: we are sent out to preach the Good News, to 'give God's flock a shepherd's care'. It is a call to communion of purpose and of action: to be one priesthood with Jesus and with one another, just as Jesus and his Father are one – a unity so beautifully symbolized in this concelebrated Mass.

Priesthood is not merely a task which has been assigned; it is a vocation, a call to be heard again and again. To hear this call and to respond generously to what this call entails is a task for each priest, but it is also a responsibility for the Senates of Priests. This responsibility means deepening our understanding of the priesthood as Christ instituted it, as he wanted it to be and to remain, and as the Church faithfully explains it and transmits it. Fidelity to the call to the priesthood means building up this priesthood with God's people by a life of service according to apostolic priorities: concentration 'on prayer and the ministry of the word' (Acts 6:4).

In the Gospel of Saint Mark the priestly call of the Twelve Apostles is like a bud whose flowering displays a whole theology of priesthood. In the midst of Jesus' ministry, we read that 'he went up the mountain and summoned the men he himself had decided on, who came and joined him. He named twelve as his companions whom he would send to preach the good news . . .' The passage then lists the names of the Twelve (Mk 3:13–14). Here we see three significant aspects of the call given by Jesus: he called his first priests individually and by name; he called them for the service of his word, to preach the Gospel; and he made them his own companions, drawing them into that unity of life and action which he shares with his Father in the very life of the Trinity.

2 Let us explore these three dimensions of our priesthood by reflecting on today's Scripture readings. For it is in the tradition of the prophetic call that the Gospel places the priestly vocation of the Twelve Apostles by Jesus. When the priest reflects on Jeremiah's call to be a prophet, he is both reassured and disturbed. 'Have no fear . . . because I am with you to deliver you', says the Lord to the one whom he calls . . . 'for look, I place my words in your mouth'. Who would not take heart at hearing such divine assurance? Yet when we consider why such reassurance is needed, do we not see in ourselves that same reluctance we find in Jeremiah's reply? Like him, at times, our concept of this ministry is too earthbound; we lack

confidence in him who calls us. We can also become too attached to our own vision of ministry, thinking that it depends too much on our own talents and abilities, and at times forgetting that it is God who calls us, as he called Jeremiah from the womb. Nor is it our work or our ability that is primary: we are called to speak the words of God and not our own; to minister the sacraments he has given to his Church; and to call people to a love which he has first made possible.

Hence the surrender to God's call can be made with utmost confidence and without reservation. Our surrender to God's will must be total – the 'yes' given once for all which has as its pattern the 'yes' spoken by Jesus himself. As Saint Paul tells us, 'As God keeps his word, I declare that my word to you is not "yes" one minute and "no" the next. Jesus Christ . . . was not alternately "yes" and "no"; he was never anything but "yes"' (1 Cor 1:18–19).

This call of God is grace: it is a gift, a treasure 'possessed in earthen vessels to make it clear that its surpassing power comes from God and not from us' (2 Cor 4:7). But this gift is not primarily for the priest himself; it is rather a gift of God for the whole Church and for her mission to the world. Priesthood is an abiding sacramental sign which shows that the love of the Good Shepherd for his flock will never be absent. In my letter to you priests last Holy Thursday, I developed this aspect of the priesthood as God's gift: our priesthood, I said, 'constitutes a special *ministerium*, that is to say "service", in relation to the community of believers. It does not however take its origin from that community, as though it were the community that "called" or "delegated". The sacramental priesthood is truly a gift for this community and comes from Christ himself, from the fullness of his priesthood' (Letter, No. 5). In this gift-giving to his people, it is the divine giver who takes the initiative; it is he who calls the ones 'he himself had decided on'.

Hence when we reflect on the intimacy between the Lord and his prophet, his priest – an intimacy arising as a result of the call which he has initiated – we can better understand certain characteristics of the priesthood and realize their appropriateness for the Church's mission today as well as in times past:

a) Priesthood is forever – *tu es sacerdos in aeternum* – we do not return the gift once given. It cannot be that God who gave the impulse to say 'yes' now wishes to hear 'no'.

b) Nor should it surprise the world that the call of God through the Church continues to offer us a celibate ministry of love and service after the example of our Lord Jesus Christ. God's call has indeed stirred us to the depths of our being. And after centuries of experience, the Church knows how deeply fitting it is that priests should give this concrete response in their lives to express the totality of the 'yes' they have spoken to the Lord who calls them by name to his service.

c) The fact that there is a personal individual call to the priesthood given by the Lord to 'the men he himself had decided on' is in accord with the prophetic tradition. It should help us too to understand that the Church's traditional decision to call men to the priesthood, and not to call women, is not a statement about human rights, nor an exclusion of women from holiness and mission in the Church. Rather this decision expresses the conviction of the Church about this particular dimension of the gift of priesthood by which God has chosen to shepherd his flock.

3   Dear brothers: 'God's flock is in your midst; give it a shepherd's care.' How close to the essence of our understanding of priesthood is the role of shepherd; throughout the history of salvation it is a recurring image of God's care for his people. And only in the role of Jesus, the Good Shepherd, can our pastoral

ministry as priests be understood. Recall how, in the call of the Twelve, Jesus summoned them to be his companions precisely in order to 'send them out to preach the good news'. Priesthood is mission and service; it is being 'sent out' from Jesus to 'give his flock a shepherd's care'. This characteristic of the priest – to apply an excellent phrase about Jesus as the 'man-for-others' – shows us the true sense of what it means to 'give a shepherd's care'. It means pointing the awareness of humanity to the mystery of God, to the profundity of Redemption taking place in Christ Jesus. Priestly ministry is missionary in its very core: it means being sent out for others, like Christ sent from his Father, for the sake of the Gospel, sent to evangelize. In the words of Paul VI, 'evangelizing means bringing the Good News into all the strata of humanity . . . and making it new' (*Evangelii Nuntiandi*, 18). At the foundation and centre of its dynamism, evangelization contains a clear proclamation that salvation is in Jesus Christ the Son of God. It is his name, his teaching, his life, his promises, his kingdom and his mystery that we proclaim to the world. And the effectiveness of our proclamation, and hence the very success of our priesthood, depends on our fidelity to the Magisterium, through which the Church guards 'the rich deposit of faith with the help of the Holy Spirit who dwells within us' (2 Tim 1:14).

As a pattern for every ministry and apostolate in the Church, priestly ministry is never to be conceived in terms of an acquisition; in so far as it is a gift, it is a gift to be proclaimed and shared with others. Do we not see this clearly in Jesus' teaching when the mother of James and John asked that her sons sit on his right hand and his left in his kingdom? 'You know how those who exercise authority among the Gentiles lord it over them; their great ones make their importance felt. It cannot be like that with you. Anyone who aspires to greatness must serve the rest, and whoever wants to rank first among you must serve the needs of all. Such is the case with the Son of Man who has come, not to be served by others, but to serve, to give his own life as a ransom for the many' (Mt 20:25–28).

Just as Jesus was most perfectly a 'man-for-others' in giving himself up totally on the cross, so the priest is most of all servant and 'man-for-others' when he acts *in persona Christi* in the Eucharist, leading the Church in that celebration in which this Sacrifice of the Cross is renewed. For in the Church's daily Eucharistic worship the 'Good News' that the Apostles were sent out to proclaim is preached in its fullness; the work of our Redemption is re-enacted.

How perfectly the Fathers at the Second Vatican Council captured this fundamental truth in their Decree on Priestly Life and Ministry: 'The other sacraments, as every ministry of the Church and every work of the apostolate, are linked with the holy Eucharist and are directed towards it. . . . Hence the Eucharist shows itself to be the source and the summit of all evangelization' (*Presbyterorum Ordinis*, 5). In the celebration of the Eucharist, we priests are at the very heart of our ministry of service, of 'giving God's flock a shepherd's care'. All our pastoral endeavours are incomplete until our people are led to the full and active participation in the Eucharistic Sacrifice.

4   Let us recall how Jesus named twelve as his companions. The call to priestly service includes an invitation to special intimacy with Christ. The lived experience of priests in every generation has led them to discover in their own lives and ministry the absolute centrality of their personal union with Jesus, of being his companions. No one can effectively bring the good news of Jesus to others unless he himself has first been his constant companion through personal prayer, unless he has learned from Jesus the mystery to be proclaimed.

This union with Jesus, modelled on his oneness with his Father, has a further intrinsic dimension, as his own prayer at the Last Supper reveals: 'that they may be one, Father, even as we are one' (Jn 17:11). His priesthood is one, and this unity must be actual and effective among his chosen companions. Hence unity among priests, lived out in fraternity and friendship, becomes a demand and an integral part of the life of a priest.

Unity among priests is not a unity or fraternity that is directed towards itself. It is for the sake of the Gospel, to symbolize, in the living out of the priesthood, the essential direction to which the Gospel calls all people: to the union of love with him and one another. And this union alone can guarantee peace and justice and dignity to every human being. Surely this is the underlying sense of the prayer of Jesus when he continues: 'I pray also for those who believe in me through their word, that all may be one as you, Father, are in me, and I in you' (Jn 17:20–21). Indeed, how will the world come to believe that the Father has sent Jesus unless people can see in visible ways that those who believe in Jesus have heard his commandment to 'love one another'? And how will believers receive a witness that such love is a concrete possibility unless they find it in the example of the unity of their priestly ministers, of those whom Jesus himself forms into one priesthood as his own companions?

My brother priests: have we not here touched upon the heart of the matter – our zeal for the priesthood itself? It is inseparable from our zeal for the service of the people. This concelebrated Mass, which so beautifully symbolizes the unity of our priesthood, gives to the whole world the witness of the unity for which Jesus prayed to his Father on our behalf. But it must not become a merely transient manifestation, which would render fruitless the prayer of Jesus. Every Eucharist renews this prayer for our unity: 'Lord, remember your Church throughout the world; make us grow in love, together with John Paul our Pope, . . . our Bishop, and all the clergy.'

Your Priests' Senates, as new structures in the Church, provide a wonderful opportunity to give visible witness to the one priesthood you share with your Bishops and with one another, and to demonstrate what must be at the heart of the renewal of every structure in the Church: the unity for which Jesus himself prayed.

5   At the beginning of this homily, I charged you with the task of taking responsibility for your priesthood, a task for each one of you personally, a charge to be shared with all the priests, and especially to be a concern for your Priests' Councils. The faith of the whole Church needs to have clearly in focus the proper understanding of the priesthood and of its place in the mission of the Church. So the Church depends on you to deepen ever more this understanding, and to put it into practice in your lives and ministry: in other words, to share the gift of your priesthood with the Church by renewing the response you have already made to Christ's invitation – 'come, follow me' – by giving yourselves as totally as he did.

At times we hear the words, 'Pray for priests'. And today I address these words as an appeal, as a plea, to all the faithful of the Church in the United States. Pray for priests, so that each and every one of them will repeatedly say *yes* to the call he has received, remain constant in preaching the Gospel message, and be faithful forever as the companion of our Lord Jesus Christ.

Dear Brother Priests: as we renew the Paschal Mystery and stand as disciples at the foot of the Cross with Mary the Mother of Jesus, let us entrust ourselves to her. In her love we shall find strength for our weakness and joy for our hearts.

DES MOINES, SAINT PATRICK'S CHURCH

The next stage of Pope John Paul's
pilgrimage took him to Des Moines,
Iowa, in the Midwest, the 'heartland
of America'. The first stop was at
St Patrick's, a white-painted wooden-
frame church which began as the
'Irish settlement' 127 years ago. The
Pope addressed the 205 parishioners
including its newest member, 11-day-
old John Paul Banks. He spoke as a
parish priest talking familiarly to his
congregation. The sun shone, there
was health and vigour in the air.
There was a new — and astonished —
parish priest, 28-year-old Father
John Richter.

Dear brothers and sisters,

It gives me great pleasure to be here today with you, in the heartland of America, in
this lovely Saint Patrick's Church at the Irish Settlement. My pastoral journey
through the United States would have seemed incomplete without a visit, although
short, to a rural community like this. Let me share with you some thoughts that this
particular setting brings to mind, and that are prompted by my meeting with the
families who make up this rural parish.

To proclaim Jesus Christ and his Gospel is the fundamental task which the
Church has received from her Founder, and which she has taken up ever since the
dawn of the first Pentecost. The early Christians were faithful to this mission which
the Lord Jesus gave them through his Apostles: 'They devoted themselves to the
apostles' teaching and fellowship, to the breaking of the bread and the prayers'
(Acts 2:42). This is what every community of believers must do: proclaim Christ
and his Gospel in fellowship and apostolic faith, in prayer and in the celebration of
the Eucharist.

How many Catholic parishes have been started like yours in the early
beginnings of the settlement of this region: a small, unpretentious church at the
centre of a group of family farms, a place and a symbol of prayer and fellowship, the
heart of a real Christian community where people know each other personally,
share each other's problems, and give witness together to the love of Jesus Christ.

On your farms you are close to God's nature; in your work on the land you
follow the rhythm of the seasons; and in your hearts you feel close to each other as
children of a common Father and as brothers and sisters in Christ. How privileged
you are, that in such a setting you can worship God together, celebrate your
spiritual unity and help to carry each other's burdens. The 1974 Synod of Bishops in
Rome and Paul VI in his Apostolic Exhortation *Evangelii Nuntiandi* have devoted
considerable attention to the small communities where a more human dimension is
achieved than is possible in a big city or in a sprawling metropolis. Let your small
community be a true place of Christian living and of evangelization, not isolating

yourselves from the diocese or from the universal Church, knowing that a community with a human face must also reflect the face of Christ.

Feel grateful to God for the blessings he gives you, not least for the blessing of belonging to this rural parish community. May our heavenly Father bless you, each and every one of you. May the simplicity of your life style and the closeness of your community be the fertile ground for a growing commitment to Jesus Christ, Son of God and Saviour of the world.

I for my part thank the Lord for the opportunity he gave me to come and visit you, and as Vicar of Christ to represent him in your midst. Thank you also for your warm welcome and for offering me your hospitality as I prepare for my encounter with the larger group of people at the Living Farms.

My gratitude goes in a special way to the Bishop of Des Moines for his most cordial invitation. He pointed out many reasons why a visit to Des Moines would be so meaningful: a city that is one of the major agricultural centres of this country; the headquarters also of the dynamic and deserving Catholic Rural Life Conference, whose history is so closely linked to the name of a pastor and a friend of the rural people, Monsignor Luigi Ligutti; a region distinguished by community involvement and family-centred activity; a diocese that is involved, together with all the Catholic Bishops of the heartland, in a major effort to build community.

My greetings and best wishes go also to the whole State of Iowa, to the civil authorities and to all the people, who have so generously extended to me a hospitality marked by kindness.

May God bless you through the intercession of Mary, the Mother of Jesus and the Mother of his Church.

DES MOINES, HOMILY AT LIVING HISTORY FARMS

From St Patrick's it was a short helicopter ride to Living History Farms which, as its name indicates, summarizes the different stages of the development of farming in the United States. That it is not merely nostalgic is proved by the fact that it has a section devoted to 'the farm of the future'. Here 350,000 people had gathered — by far the largest crowd in the history of Iowa. The National Catholic Rural Life Conference, presided over by the Bishop of Des Moines, Maurice Dingman, has been trying to apply Christian principles to contemporary agricultural problems: the vanishing family homestead, ever larger units and agribusiness, problems of conservation. Some of these themes were touched upon in the Pope's homily after the sermon.

Dear brothers and sisters in Christ,

Here in the heartland of America, in the middle of the bountiful fields at harvest time, I come to celebrate the Eucharist. As I stand in your presence in this period of autumn harvest, those words which are repeated whenever people gather for the Eucharist seem to be so appropriate:

> Blessed are you, Lord God of all creation,
> through your goodness we have this bread to
> offer which earth has given and human hands
> have made.

As one who has always been close to nature, let me speak to you today about the land, the earth, and that 'which earth has given and human hands have made'.

1   The land is God's gift entrusted to people from the very beginning. It is God's gift, given by a loving Creator as a means of sustaining the life which he had created. But the land is not only God's gift; it is also man's responsibility. Man, himself created from the dust of the earth (cf. Gen 3:7), was made its master (cf. Gen 1:26). In order to bring forth fruit, the land would depend upon the genius and skilfulness, the sweat and the toil of the people to whom God would entrust it. Thus the food which would sustain life on earth is willed by God to be both that 'which earth has given and human hands have made'.

To all of you who are farmers and all who are associated with agricultural production I want to say this: the Church highly esteems your work. Christ himself showed his esteem for agricultural life when he described God his Father as 'the vinedresser' (Jn 15:1). You cooperate with the Creator, the 'vinedresser', in sustaining and nurturing life. You fulfil the command of God given at the very beginning: 'Fill the earth and subdue it' (Gen 1:28). Here in the heartland of America, the valleys and hills have been blanketed with grain, the herds and the flocks have multiplied many times over. By hard work you have become masters of the earth and you have subdued it. By reason of the abundant fruitfulness which modern agricultural advances have made possible, you support the lives of millions who themselves do not work on the land, but who live because of what you produce. Mindful of this, I make my own the words of my beloved predecessor Paul VI:

> It is the dignity of those who work on the land and of all those engaged in different levels of research and action in the field of agricultural development which must be unceasingly proclaimed and promoted (Address to the World Food Conference, 9 November 1974, no. 4).

What then are the attitudes that should pervade man's relationship to the land? As always we must look for the answer beginning with Jesus, for, as Saint Paul says: 'In your minds you must be the same as Christ Jesus' (Phil 2:5). In the life of Jesus, we see a real closeness to the land. In his teaching, he referred to the 'birds of the air' (Mt 6:26), the 'lilies of the field' (Mt 7:17). He talked about the farmer who went out to sow the seed (Mt 13:4 ff); and he referred to his heavenly father as the 'vinedresser' (Jn 15:1), and to himself as the 'good shepherd' (Jn 10:14). This closeness to nature, this spontaneous awareness of creation as a gift from God, as well as the blessing of a close-knit family – characteristics of farm life in every age including our own – these were part of the life of Jesus. Therefore I invite you to let your attitudes always be the same as those of Christ Jesus.

2   Three attitudes in particular are appropriate for rural life. In the first place: gratitude. Recall the first words of Jesus in the Gospel we have just heard, words of gratitude to his heavenly father: 'Father, Lord of heaven and earth, to you I offer

praise.' Let this be your attitude as well. Every day the farmer is reminded of how much he depends upon God. From the heavens come the rain, the wind and the sunshine. They occur without the farmer's command or control. The farmer prepares the soil, plants the seed, and cultivates the crop. But God makes it grow; he alone is the source of life. Even the natural disasters, such as hailstorms and drought, tornados or floods, remind the farmer of his dependence upon God. Surely it was this awareness that prompted the early pilgrims to America to establish the feast which you call 'Thanksgiving'. After every harvest, whatever it may have been that year, with humility and thankfulness the farmer makes his own the prayer of Jesus: 'Father, Lord of heaven and earth, to you I offer praise.'

Secondly, the land must be conserved with care since it is intended to be fruitful for generation upon generation. You who live in the heartland of America have been entrusted with some of the earth's best land: the soil so rich in minerals, the climate so favourable for producing bountiful crops, with fresh water and unpolluted air available all around you. You are stewards of some of the most important resources God has given to the world. Therefore conserve the land well, so that your children's children and generations after them will inherit an even richer land than was entrusted to you. But also remember what the heart of your vocation is. While it is true here that farming today provides an economic livelihood for the farmer, still it will always be more than an enterprise of profit-making. In farming, you cooperate with the Creator in the very sustenance of life on earth.

In the third place, I want to speak about generosity, a generosity which arises from the fact that 'God destined the earth and all it contains for all men and all peoples so that all created things would be shared fairly by all mankind under the guidance of justice tempered by charity' (*Gaudium et Spes*, 69). You who are farmers today are stewards of a gift from God which was intended for the good of all humanity. You have the potential to provide food for the millions who have nothing to eat and thus help to rid the world of famine. To you I direct the same question asked by Paul VI five years ago:

> . . . if the potential of nature is immense, if that of the mastery of the human genius over the universe seems almost unlimited, what is it that is too often missing . . . except that generosity, that anxiety which is stimulated by the sight of the sufferings and the miseries of the poor, that deep conviction that the whole family suffers when one of its members is in distress? (Address to the World Food Conference, 9 November 1974, no. 9).

Recall the time when Jesus saw the hungry crowd gathered on the hillside. What was his response? He did not content himself with expressing his compassion. He gave his disciples the command: 'Give them something to eat yourselves' (Mt 14:16). Did he not intend those same words for us today, for us who live at the closing of the twentieth century, for us who have the means available to feed the hungry of the world? Let us respond generously to his command by sharing the fruit of our labour, by contributing to others the knowledge we have gained, by being the promotors of rural development everywhere and by defending the right to work of the rural population, since every person has a right to useful employment.

3 Farmers everywhere provide bread for all humanity, but it is Christ alone who is the bread of life. He alone satisfies the deepest hunger of humanity. As Saint Augustine said: 'Our hearts are restless until they rest in you' (*Confessions* I, 1).

While we are mindful of the physical hunger of millions of our brothers and sisters on all continents, at this Eucharist we are reminded that the deepest hunger lies in the human soul. To all who acknowledge this hunger within them Jesus says: 'Come to me, all you who are weary and find life burdensome, and I will refresh you.' My brothers and sisters in Christ: let us listen to these words with all our heart. They are directed to everyone of us. To all who till the soil, to all who benefit from the fruit of their labours, to every man and woman on earth, Jesus says: 'Come to me . . . and I will refresh you.' Even if all the physical hunger of the world were satisfied, even if everyone who is hungry were fed by his or her own labour or by the generosity of others, the deepest hunger of man would still exist.

We are reminded in the letter of Saint Paul to the Galatians: 'All that matters is that one is created anew.' Only Christ can create one anew; and this new creation finds its beginning only in his Cross and Resurrection. In Christ alone all creation is restored to its proper order. Therefore, I say: Come, all of you, to Christ. He is the bread of life. Come to Christ and you will never be hungry again.

Bring with you to Christ the products of your hands, the fruit of the land, that 'which earth has given and human hands have made'. At this altar these gifts will be transformed into the Eucharist of the Lord.

Bring with you your efforts to make fruitful the land, your labour and your weariness. At this altar, because of the life, death and Resurrection of Christ, all human activity is sanctified, lifted up and fulfilled.

Bring with you the poor, the sick, the exiled and the hungry; bring all who are weary and find life burdensome. At this altar they will be refreshed, for his yoke is easy and his burden light.

Above all, bring your families and dedicate them anew to Christ, so that they may continue to be the working, living and loving community where nature is revered, where burdens are shared and where the Lord is praised in gratitude.

CHICAGO, VISIT TO HOLY NAME CATHEDRAL

But the Pope's pilgrimage on 4 October was still not complete. He flew from Des Moines to O'Hare Airport, Chicago, in *Shepherd I* – an hour behind schedule – and went immediately to the Holy Name Cathedral where, after a brief address of welcome from Cardinal John Patrick Cody, he replied:

Dear brothers and sisters in Christ,

From Philadelphia to Des Moines, from Des Moines to Chicago! In one day I have seen a great part of your spacious land, and I have thanked God for the faith and the achievements of its people. This evening brings me to Chicago, to Holy Name Cathedral. I am grateful to the Lord for the joy of this encounter.

My special gratitude goes to you, Cardinal Cody, my Brother for many years in the College of Bishops, the Pastor of this great See of Chicago. I thank you for your kind invitation and for all you have done to prepare for my coming. A greeting of esteem and love goes also to all the priests, both diocesan and religious, who share so particularly and intimately in the responsibility of bringing the message of salvation to all the people. I am likewise looking forward to meeting people from all categories in the Church: deacons and seminarians, religious brothers and women religious, husbands and wives, mothers and fathers, the single, the widowed, the young and the children: so that we can celebrate together our ecclesial unity in Christ.

It is with a special joy that I greet all of you who are present here in Holy Name Cathedral, to which, by God's grace, I return once more. Here there is symbolized and actuated the unity of this Archdiocese, this local church – rich in history and in fidelity, rich in generosity to the Gospel, rich in the faith of millions of men, women and children who over the decades have found holiness and justice in our Lord Jesus Christ.

And today I wish to celebrate with you the great mystery expressed in the title of your Cathedral: the Holy Name of Jesus, Son of God and Son of Mary.

I have come to you to speak of salvation in Jesus Christ. I have come to proclaim it anew: to proclaim this message to you and with you and for you – and for all the people. As Successor of the Apostle Peter speaking in the Holy Spirit, I too proclaim: 'There is salvation in no one else, for there is no other name under heaven given by which we must be saved' (Acts 4:12).

It is in the name of Jesus that I come to you. Our service to the needy of the world is exercised in the name of Jesus. Repentance and the forgiveness of sins are preached in his name (cf. Lk 24:27). And through faith, all of us have 'life in his name' (Jn 20:31).

In this name – in the holy name of Jesus – there is help for the living, consolation for the dying, and joy and hope for the whole world.

Brothers and sisters in the Church of Chicago: let us do everything 'in the name of the Lord Jesus' (Col 3:12).

May the words which I address to you on my arrival here – coming from him who is called to be the servant of the servants of God – be for all of Chicago, the authorities and the people, an expression of my fraternal solidarity. How greatly I would like to meet each one of you personally, to visit you in your homes, to walk your streets so that I may better understand the richness of your personalities and the depth of your aspirations. May my words to you be an encouragement for all those who strive to bring to your community a sense of brotherhood, dignity, and unity. For in coming here I want to show my respect – beyond the limit of the Catholic faith, even beyond all religion – for man, for the humanity that is in every human being. The Christ, whom I unworthily represent, taught me to do this. I must obey his command of fraternal love. And I do it with great joy.

May God uplift humanity in this great City of Chicago!

CHICAGO, TO RELIGIOUS BROTHERS

The liturgy at Living History Farms
had already reminded us that
4 October was the Feast of St Francis
of Assisi ('Make me a channel of
your peace' was one of the hymns).
For his last engagement on that day,
a meeting with several thousand
religious men and women in the
Church of St Peter (110 West
Madison), the Pope addressed himself directly to the question of
religious brothers in the Church.

Brothers in Christ,

'I thank my God whenever I think of you; and every time I pray for you, I pray
with joy, remembering how you have helped to spread the Good News from the
day you first heard it right up to the present' (Phil 1:3–5). These words of Saint
Paul express my feelings this evening. It is good to be with you. And I am grateful
to God for your presence in the Church and for your collaboration in proclaiming
the Good News.

Brothers, Christ is the purpose and the measure of our lives. In the knowledge
of Christ, your vocation took its origin; and in his love, your life is sustained. For
he has called you to follow him more closely in a life consecrated through the gift
of the evangelical counsels. You follow him in sacrifice and willing generosity. You
follow him in joy 'singing gratefully to God from your hearts in psalms, hymns,
and inspired songs' (Col 3:16). And you follow him in fidelity, even considering it
an honour to suffer humiliation for the sake of his name (cf. Acts 5:42).

Your religious consecration is essentially an act of love. It is an imitation of
Christ who gave himself to his Father for the salvation of the world. In Christ, the
love of his Father and his love for mankind are united. And so it is with you. Your
religious consecration has not only deepened your Baptismal gift of union with the
Trinity, but it has also called you to greater service of the people of God. You are
united more closely to the person of Christ, and you share more fully in his mission
for the salvation of the world.

It is about your share in the mission of Christ that I wish to speak this evening.

1   Let me begin by reminding you of the personal qualities needed to share
effectively with Christ in his mission. In the first place, you must be interiorly free,
spiritually free. The freedom of which I speak is a paradox to many; it is even
misunderstood by some who are members of the Church. Nevertheless it is the
fundamental human freedom, and it was won for us by Christ on the Cross. As
Saint Paul said, 'We were still helpless when at his appointed moment Christ died
for sinful men' (Rom 5:6).

This spiritual freedom which you received in Baptism you have sought to
increase and strengthen through your willing acceptance of the call to follow Jesus
more closely in poverty, chastity and obedience. No matter what others may

contend or the world may believe, your promises to observe the evangelical counsels have not shackled your freedom: you are not less free because you are obedient; and you are not less loving because of your celibacy. On the contrary. The faithful practice of the evangelical counsels accentuates your human dignity, liberates the human heart and causes your spirit to burn with undivided love for Christ and for his brothers and sisters in the world (cf. *Perfectae Caritatis*, 1, 12).

But this freedom of an undivided heart (cf. 1 Cor 7:32–35) must be maintained by continual vigilance and fervent prayer. If you unite yourself continually to Christ in prayer, you shall always be free and ever more eager to share in his mission.

2   Secondly, you must centre your life around the Eucharist. While you share in many ways in the passion, death and Resurrection of Christ, it is especially in the Eucharist where this is celebrated and made effective. At the Eucharist, your spirit is renewed, your mind and heart are refreshed and you will find the strength to live day by day for him who is the Redeemer of the world.

3   Thirdly, be dedicated to God's word. Remember the words of Jesus: 'My mother and my brothers are those who hear the word of God and put it into practice' (Lk 8:21). If you sincerely listen to God's word, and humbly but persistently try to put it into practice, like the seed sown in fertile soil, his word will bear fruit in your life.

4   The fourth and final element which makes effective your sharing in Christ's mission is fraternal life. Your life in religious community is the first concrete expression of love of neighbour. It is there that the first demands of self-sacrifice and generous service are exercised in order to build up the fraternal community. This love which unites you as brothers in community becomes in turn the force which supports you in your mission for the Church.

5   Brothers in Christ, today the universal Church honours Saint Francis of Assisi. As I think of this great saint, I am reminded of his delight in God's creation, his childlike simplicity, his poetic marriage to 'Lady Poverty', his missionary zeal and his desire to share fully in the Cross of Christ. What a splendid heritage he has handed on to those among you who are Franciscans, and to all of us.

Similarly, God has raised up many other men and women outstanding in holiness. These too he destined to found religious families which, each in a distinctive way, would play an important role in the mission of the Church. The key to the effectiveness of every one of these religious institutes has been their faithfulness to the original charism God had begun in their founder or foundress for the enrichment of the Church. For this reason, I repeat the words of Paul VI: 'Be faithful to the spirit of your founders, to their evangelical intentions and to the example of their holiness. . . . It is precisely here that the dynamism proper to each religious family finds its origin' (*Evangelica Testificatio*, 11–12). And this remains a secure basis for judging what specific ecclesial activities each institute, and every individual member, should undertake in order to fulfil the mission of Christ.

6   Never forget the specific and ultimate aim of all apostolic service: to lead the men and women of our day to communion with the Most Holy Trinity. In the present age, mankind is increasingly tempted to seek security in possessions, knowledge and power. By the witness of your life consecrated to Christ in poverty,

chastity and obedience, you challenge this false security. You are a living reminder that Christ alone is 'the way, the truth and the life' (Jn 14:6).

7 Religious brothers today are involved in a wide range of activities: teaching in Catholic schools, spreading God's word in missionary activity, responding to a variety of human needs by both your witness and your actions, and serving by prayer and sacrifice. As you go forward in your particular service, keep in mind the advice of Saint Paul: 'Whatever you do, work at it with your whole being. Do it for the Lord rather than for men' (Col 3:23). For the measure of your effectiveness will be the degree of your love for Jesus Christ.

8 Finally, every form of apostolic service, of either an individual or a community, must be in accord with the Gospels as it is put forward by the Magisterium. For all Christian service is aimed at spreading the Gospel; and all Christian service incorporates Gospel values. Therefore be men of God's word: men whose hearts burn within them when they hear the word proclaimed (cf. Lk 24:32); who shape every action according to its demands; and who desire to see the Good News proclaimed to the ends of the earth.

Brothers, your presence in the Church and your collaboration in promoting the Gospel are an encouragement and joy to me in my role as Pastor of the whole Church. May God give each of you long life. May he call many others to follow Christ in the religious life. And may the Virgin Mary, Mother of the Church and model of consecrated life, obtain for you the joy and consolation of Christ, her son.

Friday, 5 October

CHICAGO, ADDRESS AT THE PROVIDENCE OF GOD CHURCH

The Pope's first full day in Chicago began somewhat later than foreseen. The visit to the Providence of God Church on West 18th Street was designed to pay tribute to the Campaign for Human Development, which works among the under-privileged, on its tenth anniversary. The conclusion of the Pope's discourse was in Spanish.

Dear brothers and sisters, dear friends in Christ,

Thank you for your welcome!

I am happy to greet and bless those groups which the Campaign for Human Development has assisted and whose representatives are here today.

This Campaign has been a witness to the Church's living presence in the world among the most needy, and to her commitment to continuing the mission of Christ, who was sent 'to bring glad tidings to the poor, to proclaim liberty to the captives, . . . and release to the prisoners' (Lk 4:18–19).

I commend the Bishops of the United States for their wisdom and compassion in establishing the Campaign for Human Development ten years ago; and I thank the whole Catholic community for the generous support given to this initiative during all these years.

Nearly fifteen hundred groups and organizations, I have been told, have received Campaign funding. The efforts aimed at establishing self-help projects deserve praise and encouragement, for in this way an effective contribution is made to removing the causes and not merely the evil effects of injustice. The projects assisted by the Campaign have helped to create a more human and just social order, and they enable many people to achieve an increased measure of rightful self-reliance. They remain in the life of the Church a witness to the love and concern of our Lord Jesus Christ.

May God give you strength, courage and wisdom to continue this work for justice. God bless you all.

Dear Spanish-speaking brothers and sisters,

I am very happy to be here among you in the course of my brief but eventful journey in this great and beautiful country.

My visit is intended to be primarily pastoral. It is meant to be a call to live together as brothers and sisters, a call for the peaceful development of good relations between individuals and peoples, a call to look to Christ for our source and our energy, so that we may fulfil God's vocation in our lives as human beings and as Christians.

I place much trust in your prayers, especially in the prayers of the children, of the aged, of the sick and of all whose physical or moral suffering brings them closer to Christ, our Saviour and Redeemer.

I greet you all with affection and give you my most cordial Blessing.

CHICAGO, MASS FOR THE POLISH COMMUNITY

Chicago has been called 'the second largest Polish city after Warsaw'. It was natural that John Paul II should wish to meet the Polish community in Chicago. He went therefore to the Five Holy Martyrs Church (South Richmond) where he gave the following address in Polish:

Dear brothers and sisters,

In a while we shall be offering to God bread and wine. I shall accept those gifts from your hands to offer them to the heavenly Father. We do so during every Holy Mass. But although we do it each time in the same way, the offering nevertheless each time has another content, it sounds a different voice on our lips and reveals different secrets of our hearts. Today it speaks in a very special way.

By accepting your offertory gifts and placing them on this altar, I would like to express through them all the contributions that the sons and daughters of our first homeland, Poland, have made to the history and to the life of their second homeland across the ocean: all their toil, efforts, struggles and sufferings; all the fruits of their minds, hearts and hands; all the achievements of the individuals, families and communities. But also all the failures, pains and disappointments; all the nostalgia for their homes, when forced by great poverty they went across the ocean; all the price of love they had to part with in order to look here anew for multiplied family, social and all human threads.

I wish to include in this Eucharistic Sacrifice all the pastoral care of the Church, all the work done by the clergy and the Seminary which has prepared priests through many years; the work of men and especially women religious, who had followed their fellow-countrymen from Poland. And also the activities of various organizations that proved the strength of spirit, the initiative and abilities, and above all the readiness to serve a good cause – a common one, though divided by the ocean between the new and the old homeland.

I have mentioned already here so many things, and I am aware that I have not yet listed them all. And that is why I ask you all, and each one of you: complete the missing items. I would like to place on this altar an offering of everything that you – the American Polonia – have represented from the very beginning, from the time of Kościuszko and Pułaski throughout the generations, and of everything you represent today.

I wish to offer to God this Holy Sacrifice as a Bishop of Rome and as a Pope who is as well a son of the same nation that you came from.

In this way I wish to fulfil a special obligation: the obligation of my heart and the obligation of history. May our Lady of Jasna Góra be with us in her maternal way during this Holy Sacrifice, as well as the patron saints of our country, whose devotion you have brought over to this land.

May this extraordinary offering of bread and wine, this unique Eucharistic Sacrifice in the story of the American Polonia reunite you in great love and great work. May it enable Jesus Christ to proceed in building your faith and your hope.

CHICAGO, QUIGLEY SOUTH SEMINARY; GREETING TO THE SICK

From the Five Holy Martyrs Church Pope John Paul went to Quigley Preparatory Seminary South where he was to meet and confer with the United States Episcopal Conference. But before that, he first addressed the crowd gathered outside the building, who included a number of invalids. He gave a brief message from the balcony:

Dear brothers and sisters,

I have desired to address a heartfelt greeting to all the sick, bedridden and handicapped in the name of the Lord Jesus, who was himself 'a man of suffering, accustomed to infirmity' (Is 53:3).

I would like to greet you, one by one, to bless you all individually, and to speak to you – to each one of you individually – about Jesus Christ, the one who took upon himself all human suffering so that he could bring salvation to the whole world. God loves you as his privileged children. For two reasons you are in a very special way my brothers and sisters: because of the love of Christ that binds us together, and particularly because you share so profoundly in the Mystery of the Cross and the Redemption of Jesus.

Thank you for the suffering you bear in your bodies and your hearts. Thank you for your example of acceptance, of patience and of union with the suffering Christ.

126

Thank you for filling up 'what is lacking in the suffering of Christ for the sake of his body, the Church' (Col 1:24).

May the peace and the joy of the Lord Jesus be always with you.

CHICAGO, TO THE STUDENTS OF THE MINOR SEMINARY

Before leaving Quigley Preparatory Seminary South, the Pope interrupted his programme in order to speak to the seminarians who study there. He gave a short address as follows:

Dear seminarians,

I extend a special greeting to all of you who are present here today. I want you to know that you have a special place in my thoughts and prayers.

Dear sons in Christ: be strong in your faith – faith in Christ, and in his Church, faith in all that the Father has revealed and accomplished through his Son and in the Holy Spirit.

During your years in the minor seminary, you have the privilege of studying and deepening your understanding of the faith. Since baptism you have lived the faith, aided by your parents, your brothers and sisters, and the whole Christian community. And yet today I call upon you to live by faith even more profoundly. For it is faith in God which makes the essential difference in your lives and in the life of every priest.

Be faithful to your daily prayers; they will keep your faith alive and vibrant.

Study the faith diligently so that your knowledge and love of Christ will continually increase.

And nourish your faith each day at Mass, for in the Eucharist we have the source and greatest expression of our faith.

God bless you.

CHICAGO, MEETING WITH THE BISHOPS
OF THE UNITED STATES OF AMERICA

The meeting with the United States
Episcopal Conference – some 350
Bishops – was arguably the most
important of the entire visit. It was
also the only one that was 'private'
in the sense that it was not televised.
But the text was released with the
usual embargo. It was a discourse of
international importance for in it John
Paul II developed an aspect of
collegiality that is sometimes
overlooked: the Pope does not act
as though all initiatives had to come
from above, but confirms and ratifies
what the local bishops are teaching.

Dear brothers in our Lord Jesus Christ,

1   May I tell you very simply how grateful I am to you for your invitation to come
to the United States. It is an immense joy for me to make this pastoral visit, and in
particular, to be here with you today.
      On this occasion I thank you, not only for your invitation, not only for
everything you have done to prepare for my visit, but also for your partnership in
the Gospel from the time of my election as Pope. I thank you for your service to
God's holy people, for your fidelity to Christ our Lord, and for your unity with my
predecessors and with me in the Church and in the College of Bishops.
      I wish at this time to render public homage to a long tradition of fidelity to the
Apostolic See on the part of the American Hierarchy. During the course of two
centuries, this tradition has edified your people, authenticated your apostolate, and
enriched the universal Church.
      Moreover, in your presence today, I wish to acknowledge with deep
appreciation the fidelity of your faithful and the renowned vitality that they have
shown in Christian life. This vitality has been manifested not only in the sacramental
practice of communities but also in abundant fruits of the Holy Spirit. With great
zeal your people have endeavoured to build up the Kingdom of God by means of
the Catholic school and through all catechetical efforts. An evident concern for
others has been a real part of American Catholicism, and today I thank the
American Catholics for their generosity. Their support has benefited the dioceses of
the United States, and a widespread network of charitable works and self-help
projects, including those sponsored by Catholic Relief Services and the Campaign
for Human Development. Moreover, the help given to the missions by the Church
in the United States remains a lasting contribution to the cause of Christ's Gospel.
Because your faithful have been very generous to the Apostolic See, my
predecessors have been assisted in meeting the burdens of their office; and thus, in
the exercise of their worldwide mission of charity, they have been able to extend
help to those in need, thereby showing the concern of the universal Church for all
humanity. For me then this is an hour of solemn gratitude.

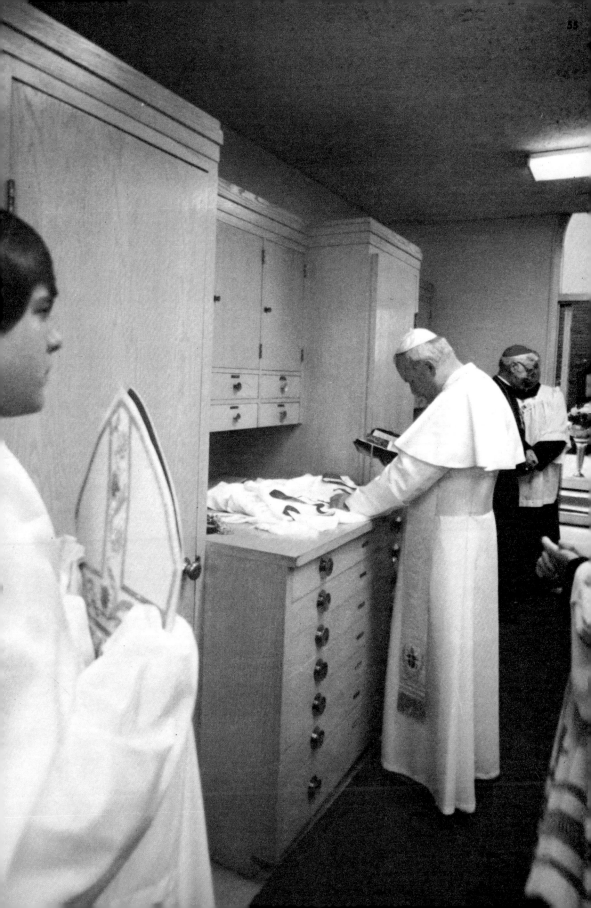

56

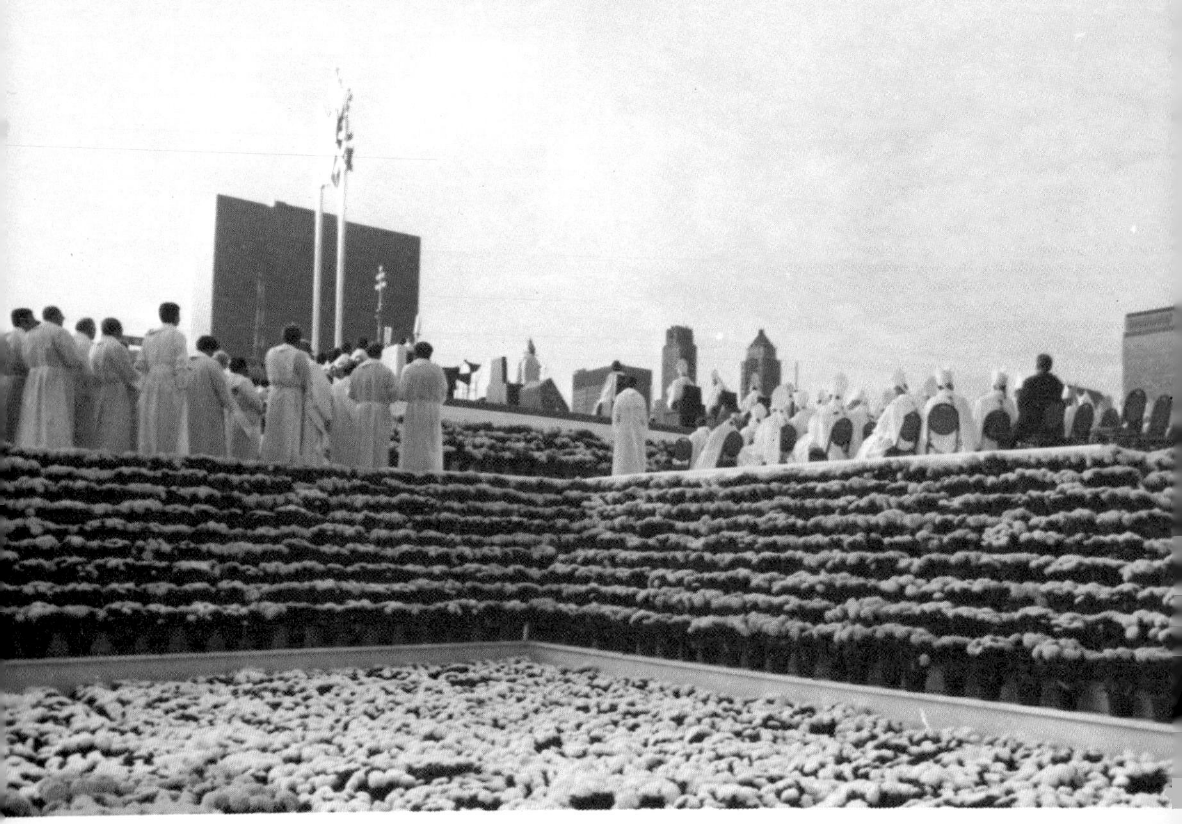

57

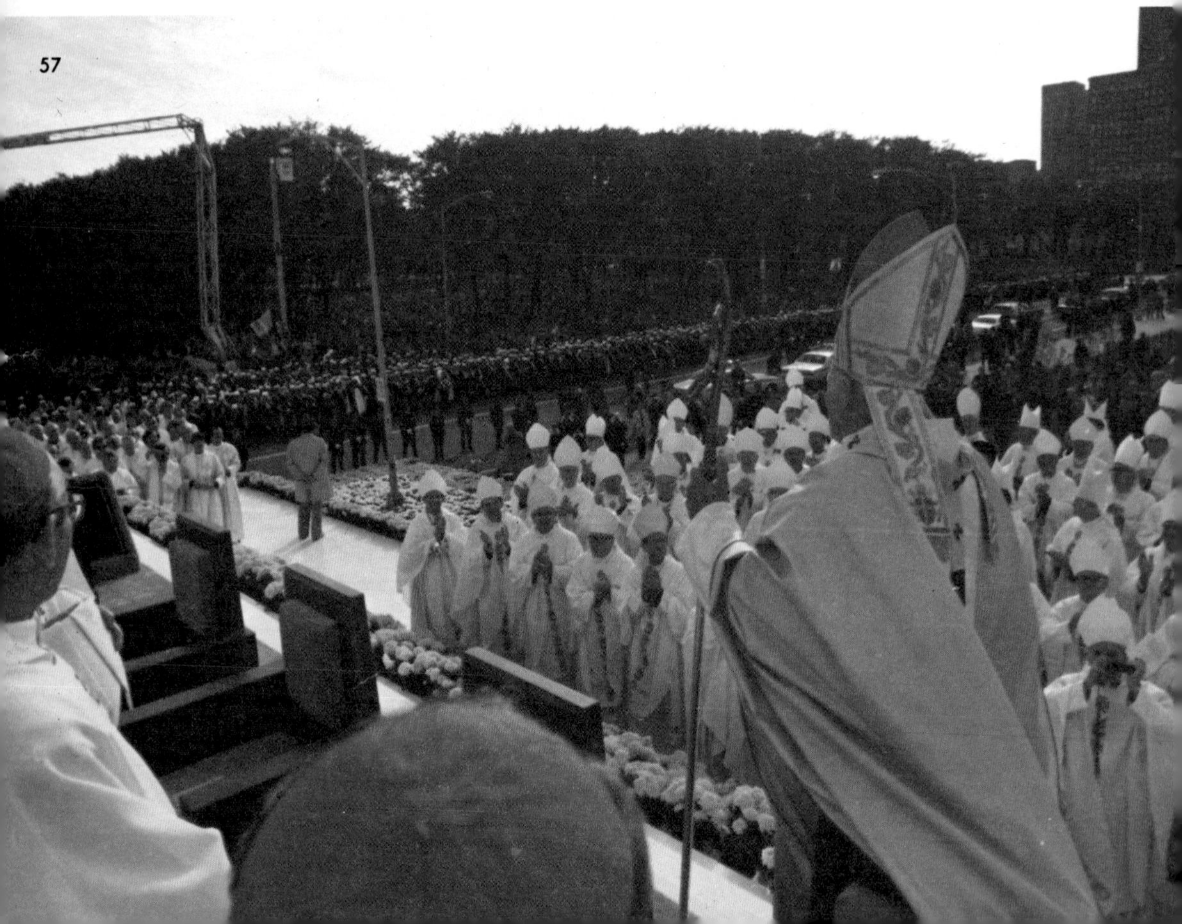

62

2   But even more, this is an hour of ecclesial communion and fraternal love. I come to you as a brother Bishop: one who, like yourselves, has known the hopes and challenges of a local Church; one who has worked within the structures of a diocese, who has collaborated within the framework of an Episcopal Conference; one who has known the exhilarating experience of collegiality in an Ecumenical Council as exercised by Bishops together with him who both presided over this collegial assembly and was recognized by it as *totius Ecclesiae Pastor* – invested with 'full, supreme and universal power over the Church' (cf. *Lumen Gentium*, 22). I come to you as one who has been personally edified and enriched by participation in the Synod of Bishops; one who was supported and assisted by the fraternal interest and self-giving of American Bishops who travelled to Poland in order to express solidarity with the Church in my country. I come as one who found deep spiritual consolation for my pastoral activity in the encouragement of the Roman Pontiffs with whom, and under whom, I served God's people, and in particular in the encouragement of Paul VI, whom I looked upon not only as Head of the College of Bishops, but also as my own spiritual father. And today, under the sign of collegiality and because of a mysterious design of God's providence, I, your brother in Jesus, now come to you as Successor of Peter in the See of Rome, and therefore as Pastor of the whole Church.

Because of my personal pastoral responsibility, and because of our common pastoral responsibility for the people of God in the United States, I desire to strengthen you in your ministry of faith as local Pastors, and to support you in your individual and joint pastoral activities by encouraging you to stand fast in the holiness and truth of our Lord Jesus Christ. And in you I desire to honour Jesus Christ, the Shepherd and Bishop of our souls (cf. 1 Pt 2:25).

Because we have been called to be shepherds of the flock, we realize that we must present ourselves as humble servants of the Gospel. Our leadership will be effective only to the extent that our own discipleship is genuine – to the extent that the Beatitudes have become the inspiration of our lives, to the extent that our people really find in us the kindness, simplicity of life and universal charity that they expect.

We who, by divine mandate, must proclaim the duties of the Christian law, and who must call our people to constant conversion and renewal, know that Saint Paul's invitation applies above all to ourselves: 'You must put on the new man created in God's image, whose justice and holiness are born of truth' (Eph 4:24).

3   The holiness of personal conversion is indeed the condition for our fruitful ministry as Bishops of the Church. It is our union with Jesus Christ that determines the credibility of our witness to the Gospel and the supernatural effectiveness of our activity. We can convincingly proclaim 'the unsearchable riches of Christ' (Eph 3:8) only if we maintain fidelity to the love and friendship of Jesus, only if we continue to live in the faith of the Son of God.

God has given a great gift to the American Hierarchy in recent years: the canonization of John Neumann. An American Bishop is officially held up by the Catholic Church to be an examplary servant of the Gospel and shepherd of God's people, above all because of his great love of Christ. On the occasion of the canonization, Paul VI asked: 'What is the meaning of this extraordinary event, the meaning of this canonization?' And he answered, saying: 'It is the celebration of holiness.' And this holiness of Saint John Neumann was expressed in brotherly love, in pastoral charity, and in zealous service by one who was the Bishop of a Diocese and an authentic disciple of Christ.

During the canonization, Paul VI went on to say: 'Our ceremony today is indeed the celebration of holiness. At the same time, it is a prophetic anticipation – for the Church, for the United States, for the world – of a renewal of love: love for God, love for neighbour.' As Bishops, we are called to exercise in the Church this prophetic role of love and, therefore, of holiness.

Guided by the Holy Spirit, we must all be deeply convinced that holiness is the first priority in our lives and in our ministry. In this context, as Bishops we see the immense value of prayer: the liturgical prayer of the Church, our prayer together, our prayer alone. In recent times many of you have found that the practice of making spiritual retreats together with your brother Bishops is indeed a help to that holiness born of truth. May God sustain you in this initiative: so that each of you, and all of you together, may fulfil your role as a sign of holiness offered to God's people on their pilgrimage to the Father. May you yourselves, like Saint John Neumann, also be a prophetic anticipation of holiness. The people need to have Bishops whom they can look upon as leaders in the quest for holiness – Bishops who are trying to anticipate prophetically in their own lives the attainment of the goal to which they are leading the faithful.

4 Saint Paul points out the relationship of justice and holiness to truth (cf. Eph 4:24). Jesus himself, in his priestly prayer, asks his Father to consecrate his disciples by means of truth; and he adds: 'Your word is truth' – *Sermo tuus veritas est* (Jn 17:17). And he goes on to say that he consecrates himself for the sake of the disciples, so that they themselves may be consecrated in truth. Jesus consecrated himself so that the disciples might be consecrated, set apart, by the communication of what he was: the Truth. Jesus tells his Father: 'I gave them your word' – 'Your word is truth' (Jn 17:14, 17).

The holy word of God, which is truth, is communicated by Jesus to his disciples. This word is entrusted as a sacred deposit to his Church, but only after he had implanted in his Church, through the power of the Holy Spirit, a special charism to guard and transmit intact the word of God.

With great wisdom, John XXIII convoked the Second Vatican Council. Reading the signs of the times, he knew that what was needed was a Council of a pastoral nature, a Council that would reflect the great pastoral love and care of Jesus Christ the Good Shepherd for his people. But he knew that a pastoral Council – to be genuinely effective – would need a strong doctrinal basis. And precisely for this reason, precisely because the word of God is the only basis for every pastoral initiative, John XXIII on the opening day of the Council – 11 October 1962 – made the following statement: 'The greatest concern of the Ecumenical Council is this: that the sacred desposit of Christian doctrine should be more effectively guarded and taught.'

This explains Pope John's inspiration; this is what the new Pentecost was to be: this is why the Bishops of the Church – in the greatest manifestation of collegiality in the history of the world – were called together: 'so that the sacred desposit of Christian doctrine should be more effectively guarded and taught.'

In our time, Jesus was consecrating anew his disciples by truth; and he was doing it by means of an Ecumenical Council; he was transmitting by the power of the Holy Spirit his Father's word to new generations. And, what John XXIII considered to be the aim of the Council, I consider as the aim of this postconciliar period.

For this reason, in my first meeting last November with American Bishops on their *ad limina* visit I stated: 'This then is my own deepest hope today for the pastors of the Church in America, as well as for all the pastors of the universal Church: that the sacred deposit of Christian doctrine should be more effectively guarded and taught.' In the word of God is the salvation of the world. By means of the proclamation of the word of God, the Lord continues in his Church and through his Church to consecrate his disciples, communicating to them the truth that he himself is.

For this reason the Vatican Council emphasized the Bishop's role of announcing the full truth of the Gospel and proclaiming 'the whole mystery of Christ' (*Christus Dominus*, 12). This teaching was constantly repeated by Paul VI for the edification of the universal Church. It was explicitly proclaimed by John Paul I on the very day he died and I too have frequently reaffirmed it in my own pontificate. And I am sure that my successors and your successors will hold this teaching until Christ comes again in glory.

5   Among the papers that were left to me by Paul VI there is a letter written to him by a Bishop, on the occasion of the latter's appointment to the Episcopacy. It is a beautiful letter; and in the form of a resolution it includes a clear affirmation of the Bishop's role of guarding and teaching the deposit of Christian doctrine, of proclaiming the whole mystery of Christ. Because of the splendid insights that this letter offers, I would like to share part of it with you.

As he pledged himself to be loyal in obedience to Paul VI and to his successors, the Bishop wrote: 'I am resolved:

To be faithful and constant in proclaiming the Gospel of Christ. To maintain the content of faith, entire and uncorrupted, as handed down by the Apostles and professed by the Church at all times and places.'

And then with equal insight, this Bishop went on to tell Paul VI that, with the help of Almighty God, he was determined:

'To build up the Church as the Body of Christ, and to remain united to it by your link, with the Order of Bishops, under the authority of the Successor of Saint Peter the Apostle.
To show kindness and compassion in the name of the Lord to the poor and to strangers and to all who are in need.
To seek out the sheep who stray and to gather them into the fold of the Lord.
To pray without ceasing for the people of God, to carry out the highest duties of the priesthood in such a way as to afford no grounds for reproof.'

This then is the edifying witness of a Bishop, an American Bishop, to the episcopal ministry of holiness and truth. These words are a credit to him and a credit to all of you.

A challenge for our age – and for every age in the Church – is to bring the message of the Gospel to the very core of our people's lives – so that they may live the full truth of their humanity, their Redemption and their adoption in Jesus Christ – that they may be enriched with 'the justice and holiness of truth'.

6   In the exercise of your ministry of truth, as Bishops of the United States you have, through statements and pastoral letters, collectively offered the word of God to your people, showing its relevance to daily life, pointing to the power it has to uplift and heal, and at the same time upholding its inherent demands. Three years ago you did this in a very special way through your Pastoral Letter, so beautifully entitled 'To Live in Christ Jesus'. This Letter, in which you offered your people the

service of truth, contains a number of points to which I wish to allude today. With compassion, understanding and love, you transmitted a message that is linked to Revelation and to the mystery of faith. And so with great pastoral charity you spoke of God's love, of humanity and of sin – and of the meaning of Redemption and of life in Christ. You spoke of the word of Christ as it affects individuals, the family, the community and nations. You spoke of justice and peace, of charity, of truth and friendship. And you spoke of some special questions affecting the moral life of Christians: the moral life in both its individual and social aspects.

You spoke explicitly of the Church's duty to be faithful to the mission entrusted to her. And precisely for this reason you spoke of certain issues that needed a clear reaffirmation, because Catholic teaching in their regard had been challenged, denied, or in practice violated. You repeatedly proclaimed human rights and human dignity and the incomparable worth of people of every racial and ethnic origin, declaring that 'racial antagonism and discrimination are among the most persistent and destructive evils of our nation'. You forcefully rejected the oppression of the weak, the manipulation of the vulnerable, the waste of goods and resources, the ceaseless preparations for war, unjust social structures and policies, and all crimes by and against individuals and against creation.

With the candour of the Gospels, the compassion of pastors and the charity of Christ, you faced the question of the indissolubility of marriage, rightly stating: 'The covenant between a man and a woman joined in Christian marriage is as indissoluble and irrevocable as God's love for his people and Christ's love for his Church.'

In exalting the beauty of marriage you rightly spoke against both the ideology of contraception and contraceptive acts, as did the Encyclical *Humanae Vitae*. And I myself today, with the same conviction of Paul VI, ratify the teaching of this Encyclical, which was put forth by my predecessor 'by virtue of the mandate entrusted to us by Christ' (*AAS*, 60, 1968, p. 485).

In portraying the sexual union between husband and wife as a special expression of their covenanted love, you rightly stated: 'Sexual intercourse is a moral and human good only within marriage, outside marriage it is wrong.'

As 'men with the message of truth and the power of God' (2 Cor 6:7), as authentic teachers of God's law and as compassionate pastors you also rightly stated: 'Homosexual activity . . . as distinguished from homosexual orientation, is morally wrong.' In the clarity of this truth, you exemplified the real charity of Christ; you did not betray those people who, because of homosexuality, are confronted with difficult moral problems, as would have happened if, in the name of understanding and compassion, or for any other reason, you had held out false hope to any brother or sister. Rather, by your witness to the truth of humanity in God's plan, you effectively manifested fraternal love, upholding the true dignity, the true human dignity, of those who look to Christ's Church for the guidance which comes from the light of God's word.

You also gave witness to the truth, thereby serving all humanity, when, echoing the teaching of the Council – 'From the moment of conception life must be guarded with the greatest care' (*Gaudium et Spes*, 51), – you reaffirmed the right to life and the inviolability of every human life, including the life of unborn children. You clearly said: 'To destroy these innocent unborn children is an unspeakable crime. . . . Their right to life must be recognized and fully protected by the law.'

And just as you defended the unborn in the truth of their being, so also you clearly spoke up for the aged, asserting: 'Euthanasia or mercy killing . . . is a grave moral evil. . . . Such killing is incompatible with respect for human dignity and reverence for life.'

And in your pastoral interest for your people in all their needs – including housing, education, health care, employment, and the administration of justice – you gave further witness to the fact that all aspects of human life are sacred. You were, in effect, proclaiming that the Church will never abandon man, nor his temporal needs, as she leads humanity to salvation and eternal life. And because the Church's greatest act of fidelity to humanity and her 'fundamental function in every age and particularly in ours is to direct man's gaze, to point the awareness and experience of the whole of humanity toward the mystery of God' (*Redemptor Hominis*, 10) – because of this you rightly alluded to the dimension of eternal life. It is indeed in this proclamation of eternal life that we hold up a great motive of hope for our people. Against the onslaughts of materialism, against rampant secularism and against moral permissiveness.

7   A sense of pastoral responsibility has also been genuinely expressed by individual Bishops in their ministry as local pastors. To the great credit of their authors I would cite but two recent examples of Pastoral Letters issued in the United States. Both are examples of responsible pastoral initiatives. One of them deals with the issue of racism and vigorously denounces it. The other refers to homosexuality and deals with the issue, as should be done, with clarity and great pastoral charity, thus rendering a real service to truth and to those who are seeking this liberating truth.

Brothers in Christ: as we proclaim the truth in love, it is not possible for us to avoid all criticism; nor is it possible to please everyone. But it is possible to work for the real benefit of everyone. And so we are humbly convinced that God is with us in our ministry of truth, and that he 'did not give us a spirit of timidity but a spirit of power and love and self-control' (2 Tim 1:7).

One of the greatest rights of the faithful is to receive the word of God in its purity and integrity as guaranteed by the Magisterium of the universal Church: the authentic Magisterium of the Bishops of the Catholic Church teaching in union with the Pope. Dear Brothers: we can be assured that the Holy Spirit is assisting us in our teaching if we remain absolutely faithful to the universal Magisterium.

In this regard I wish to add an extremely important point which I recently emphasized in speaking to a group of Bishops making their *ad limina* visit: 'In the community of the faithful – which must always maintain Catholic unity with the Bishops and the Apostolic See – there are great insights of faith. The Holy Spirit is active in enlightening the minds of the faithful with his truth, and in inflaming their hearts with his love. But these insights of faith and this *sensus fidelium* are not independent of the magisterium of the Church, which is an instrument of the same Holy Spirit and is assisted by him. It is only when the faithful have been nourished by the word of God, faithfully transmitted in its purity and integrity, that their own charisms are fully operative and fruitful. Once the word of God is faithfully proclaimed to the community and is accepted, it brings forth fruits of justice and holiness of life in abundance. But the dynamism of the community in understanding and living the word of God depends on its receiving intact the *depositum fidei*; and for this precise purpose a special apostolic and pastoral charism has been given to the Church. It is one and the same Spirit of truth who directs the hearts of the faithful and who guarantees the magisterium of the pastors of the flock' (Address to Indian Bishops, 31 May 1979).

8   One of the greatest truths of which we are the humble custodians is the doctrine of the Church's unity – that unity which is tarnished on the human face of the

Church by every form of sin, but which subsists indestructibly in the Catholic Church (cf. *Lumen Gentium*, 8; *Unitatis Redintegratio*, 2, 3). A consciousness of sin calls us incessantly to conversion. The will of Christ impels us to work earnestly and perseveringly for unity with all our Christian brethren, being mindful that the unity we seek is one of perfect faith, a unity in truth and love. We must pray and study together, knowing however that intercommunion between divided Christians is not the answer to Christ's appeal for perfect unity. And with God's help we will continue to work humbly and resolutely to remove the real divisions that still exist, and thus to restore that full unity in faith which is the condition for sharing in the Eucharist (cf. Address of 4 May 1979). The commitment of the Ecumenical Council belongs to each of us; as does the Testament of Paul VI, who writing on Ecumenism stated: 'Let the work of drawing near to our separated brethren go on, with much understanding, with much patience, with great love; but without deviating from the true Catholic doctrine.'

9   As Bishops who are servants of truth, we are also called to be servants of unity, in the communion of the Church.

In the communion of holiness we ourselves are called, as I mentioned above, to conversion, so that we may preach with convincing power the message of Jesus: 'Reform your lives and believe in the Gospel.' We have a special role to play in safeguarding the Sacrament of Reconciliation, so that, in fidelity to a divine precept, we and our people may experience in our innermost being that 'grace has far surpassed sin' (Rom 5:20). I, too, ratify the prophetic call of Paul VI, who urged the Bishops to help their priests to 'deeply understand how closely they collaborate through the Sacrament of Penance with the Saviour in the work of conversion' (Address of 20 April 1978). In this regard I confirm again the Norms of *Sacramentum Paenitentiae* which so wisely emphasize the ecclesial dimension of the Sacrament of Penance and indicate the precise limits of General Absolution, just as Paul VI did in his *ad limina* address to the American Bishops.

Conversion by its very nature is the condition for that union with God which reaches its greatest expression in the Eucharist. Our union with Christ in the Eucharist presupposes, in turn, that our hearts are set on conversion, that they are pure. This is indeed an important part of our preaching to the people. In my Encyclical I endeavoured to express it in these words: 'The Christ who calls to the Eucharistic banquet is always the same Christ who exhorts us to penance and repeats his "Repent". Without this constant and ever-renewed endeavour for conversion, partaking of the Eucharist would lack its full redeeming effectiveness . . .' (*Redemptor Hominis*, 20). In the face of a widespread phenomenon of our time, namely that many of our people who are among the great numbers who receive Communion make little use of Confession, we must emphasize Christ's basic call to conversion. We must also stress that the personal encounter with the forgiving Jesus in the Sacrament of Reconciliation is a divine means which keeps alive in our hearts and in our communities a consciousness of sin in its perennial and tragic reality, and which actually brings forth, by the action of Jesus and the power of his Spirit, fruits of conversion in justice and holiness of life. By this Sacrament we are renewed in fervour, strengthened in our resolves and buoyed up by divine encouragement.

10   As chosen leaders in a community of praise and prayer, it is our special joy to offer the Eucharist and to give our people a sense of their vocation as an Easter people, with the 'alleluia' as their song. And let us always recall that the validity of

all liturgical development and the effectiveness of every liturgical sign presupposes the great principle that the Catholic liturgy is theocentric, and that it is above all 'the worship of divine majesty' (cf. *Sacrosanctum Concilium*, 33), in union with Jesus Christ. Our people have a supernatural sense whereby they look for reverence in all liturgy, especially in what touches the mystery of the Eucharist. With deep faith our people understand that the Eucharist – in the Mass and outside the Mass – is the Body and Blood of Jesus Christ, and therefore deserves the worship that is given to the living God and to him alone.

As ministers of a community of service, it is our privilege to proclaim the truth of Christ's union with his members in his Body, the Church. Hence we commend all service rendered in his name and to his brethren (cf. Mt 25:45).

In a community of witness and evangelization may our testimony be clear and without reproach. In this regard the Catholic press and the other means of social communication are called to fulfil a special role of great dignity at the service of truth and charity. The Church's aim in employing and sponsoring these media is linked to her mission of evangelization and of service to humanity; through the media the Church hopes to promote ever more effectively the uplifting message of the Gospel.

11 And each individual Church over which you preside and which you serve is a community founded on the word of God and acting in the truth of this word. It is in fidelity to the communion of the universal Church that our local unity is authenticated and made stable. In the communion of the universal Church local Churches find their own identity and enrichment ever more clearly. But all of this requires that the individual Churches should maintain complete openness towards the universal Church.

And this is the mystery that we celebrate today in proclaiming the holiness and truth and unity of the episcopal ministry.

Brothers: this ministry of ours makes us accountable to Christ and to his Church. Jesus Christ, the chief Shepherd (1 Pt 5:4), loves us and sustains us. It is he who transmits his Father's word and consecrates us in truth, so that each of us may say in turn of our people: 'For them I consecrate myself for their sake now, that they may be consecrated in truth' (Jn 17:19).

Let us pray for and devote special energy to promoting and maintaining vocations to the sacred priesthood, so that the pastoral care of the priestly ministry may be ensured for future generations. I ask you to call upon parents and families, upon priests, religious and laity to unite in fulfilling this vital responsibility of the entire community. And to the young people themselves let us hold up the full challenge of following Christ and of embracing his invitation with full generosity.

As we ourselves pursue every day the justice and holiness born of truth, let us look to Mary, Mother of Jesus, Queen of Apostles, and Cause of our Joy. May Saint Frances Xavier Cabrini, Saint Elizabeth Ann Seton and Saint John Neumann pray for you, and for all the people whom you are called to serve in holiness and truth and in the unity of Christ and his Church.

Dear Brothers: 'Grace be with all who love our Lord Jesus Christ with unfailing love' (Eph 6:24).

CHICAGO, HOMILY AT GRANT PARK

In the afternoon of 5 October Pope John Paul presided over a joyous liturgy in Grant Park, Chicago, by the shore of Lake Michigan. It was quickly dubbed, with biblical overtones, 'the Mass by the lakeside'. The crowd, numbering over a million, was orderly and good-humoured and the discreet but ever-present police were surprised at the peaceful way in which they departed. They attributed it to the contagious goodness of the Pope who delivered a homily after the Gospel. In it, he took pains to balance the stress on 'ethnicity' which earlier discourses might have suggested and compared the American 'melting-pot' experience with the task of the Church in 'making unity out of diversity'

My brothers and sisters in Jesus Christ,

1   The readings of today's celebration place us immediately before the deep mystery of our calling as Christians.

Before Jesus was taken up to heaven, he gathered his disciples around him, and he explained to them once more the meaning of his mission of salvation: 'Thus it is written', – he said – 'that the Messiah must suffer and rise from the dead on the third day. In his name, penance for the remission of sins is to be preached to all nations' (Lk 24:46–47). At the moment that he took leave of his Apostles he commanded them, and through them the whole Church, each one of us: to go out and bring the message of redemption to all nations. Saint Paul expresses this forcefully in his second letter to the Corinthians: 'He has entrusted the message of reconciliation to us. This makes us ambassadors of Christ. God as it were appealing through us' (2 Cor 5:19–20).

Once again, the Lord places us fully in the mystery of humanity, a humanity that is in need of salvation. And God has willed that the salvation of humanity should take place through the humanity of Christ, who for our sake died and was raised up (cf. 2 Cor 5:15), and who also entrusted his redeeming mission to us. Yes, we are truly 'ambassadors for Christ', and workers for evangelization.

In the Apostolic Exhortation *Evangelii Nuntiandi*, which he wrote at the request of the Third General Assembly of the Synod of Bishops, my predecessor in the See of Saint Peter, Paul VI, invited the whole People of God to meditate on their basic duty of evangelization. He invited each one of us to examine in what way we might be true witnesses to the message of redemption, in what we might communicate to others the Good News that we have received from Jesus through his Church.

2   There are certain conditions that are necessary if we are to share in the evangelizing mission of the Church. This afternoon, I wish to stress one of these conditions in particular. I am speaking about the unity of the Church, our unity in Jesus Christ. Let me repeat what Paul VI said about this unity: 'The Lord's spiritual testament tells us that unity among his followers is not only the proof that we are his, but also the proof that he is sent by the Father. It is the test of credibility of Christians and of Christ himself . . . Yes, the destiny of evangelization is certainly bound up with the witness of unity given by the Church' (*Evangelii Nuntiandi*, 77).

I am prompted to choose this particular aspect of evangelization by looking at the thousands of people whom I see gathered around me today. When I lift up my eyes, I see in you the People of God, united to sing the praises of the Lord and to celebrate his Eucharist. I see also the whole people of America, one nation formed of many people: *E pluribus unum.*

3   In the first two centuries of your history as a nation, you have travelled a long road, always in search of a better future, in search of stable employment, in search of a homestead. You have travelled 'From sea to shining sea' to find your identity, to discover each other along the way, and to find your own place in this immense country.

Your ancestors came from many different countries across the oceans to meet here with the people of different communities that were already established here. In every generation, the process has been repeated: new groups arrive, each one with a different history, to settle here and become part of something new. The same process still goes on when families move from the south to the north, from the east to the west. Each time they come with their own past to a new town or a new city, to become part of a new community. The pattern repeats itself over and over: *E pluribus unum* – the many form a new unity.

4   Yes, something new was created every time. You brought with you a different culture and you contributed your own distinctive richness to the whole; you had different skills and you put them to work, complementing each other, to create industry, agriculture and business; each group carried with it different human values and shared them with the others for the enrichment of your nation. *E pluribus unum*: you became a new entity, a new people, the true nature of which cannot be adequately explained as a mere putting together of various communities.

And so, looking at you, I see people who have thrown their destinies together and now write a common history. Different as you are, you have come to accept each other, at times imperfectly and even to the point of subjecting each other to various forms of discrimination; at times only after a long period of misunderstanding and rejection; even now still growing in understanding and appreciation of each other's differences. In expressing gratitude for the many blessings you have received, you also become aware of the duty you have towards the less favoured in your own midst and in the rest of the world – a duty of sharing, of loving, of serving. As a people, you recognize God as the source of your many blessings, and you are open to his love and his law.

This is America in her ideal and her resolution: 'One nation, under God, indivisible, with liberty and justice for all.' This is the way America was conceived; this is what she was called to be. And for all this, we offer thanks to the Lord.

5   But there is another reality that I see when I look at you. It is even deeper, and more demanding than the common history and union which you built from the richness of your different cultural and ethnic heritages – those heritages that you now rightly want to know and to preserve. History does not exhaust itself in material progress, in technological conquest, or in cultural achievement only. Coming together around the altar of sacrifice to break the Bread of the Holy Eucharist with the Successor of Peter, you testify to this even deeper reality: to your unity as members of the People of God.

'We, though many, are one body in Christ' (Rom 12:5). The Church too is composed of many members and enriched by the diversity of those who make up the one community of faith and baptism, the one Body of Christ. What brings us together and makes us one is our faith – the one apostolic faith. We are all one, because we have accepted Jesus Christ as the Son of God, the Redeemer of the human race, the sole Mediator between God and man. By the sacrament of Baptism we have been truly incorporated into the crucified and glorified Christ, and through the action of the Holy Spirit we have become living members of his one body. Christ gave us the wonderful sacrament of the Eucharist, by which the unity of the Church is both expressed and continually brought about and perfected.

6 'One Lord, one faith, one baptism' (Eph 4:5), thus we are all bound together, as the People of God, the Body of Christ, in a unity that transcends the diversity of our origin, culture, education and personality – in a unity that does not exclude a rich diversity in ministries and services. With Saint Paul we proclaim: 'Just as each of us has one body with many members, and not all the members have the same function, so too we, though many, are one body in Christ, and individually members one of another' (Rom 12:4–5).

If then the Church, the one body of Christ, is to be a forcefully discernible sign of the Gospel message, all her members must show faith, in the words of Paul VI, that 'harmony and consistency of doctrine, life and worship which marked the first days of her existence' (*Apostolic Exhortation on Reconciliation within the Church*, 2), when Christians 'devoted themselves to the apostles' teachings and fellowship, to the breaking of bread and the prayers' (Acts 2:42).

Our unity in faith must be complete, lest we fail to give witness to the Gospel, lest we cease to be evangelizing. No local ecclesial community therefore can cut itself off from the treasure of the faith as proclaimed by the Church's teaching office, for it is to this teaching office of the Church, to this Magisterium that the deposit of faith has been especially entrusted by Christ. With Paul VI I attest to the great truth: 'While being translated into all expressions, the content of the faith must be neither impaired nor mutilated. While being clothed with the outward forms proper to each people . . . it must remain the content of the Catholic faith just exactly as the ecclesial Magisterium has received it and transmits it' (*Evangelii Nuntiandi*, 65).

7 Finally, and above all, the mission of evangelization that is mine and yours, must be carried out through a constant unselfish witnessing to the unity of love. Love is the force that opens hearts to the word of Jesus and to his Redemption: love is the only basis for human relationships that respect in one another the dignity of the children of God created in his image and saved by the death and Resurrection of Jesus; love is the only driving force that impels us to share with our brothers and sisters all that we are and have.

Love is the power that gives rise to dialogue, in which we listen to each other and learn from each other. Love gives rise, above all, to the dialogue of prayer in which we listen to God's word, which is alive in the Holy Bible and alive in the life of the Church. Let love then build the bridges across our differences and at times our contrasting positions. Let love for each other and love for truth be the answer to polarization, when factions are formed because of differing views in matters that relate to faith or to the priorities for action. No one in the ecclesial community should ever feel alienated or unloved, even when tensions arise in the course of the common efforts to bring the fruits of the Gospel to society around us. Our unity as Christians, as Catholics, must always be a unity of love in Jesus Christ our Lord.

In a few moments, we shall celebrate our unity by renewing the Sacrifice of Christ. Each one will bring a different gift to be presented in union with the offering of Jesus: dedication to the betterment of society; efforts to console those who suffer; the desire to give witness for justice; the resolve to work for peace and brotherhood; the joy of a united family; or suffering in body or mind. Different gifts, yes, but all united in the one great gift of Christ's love for his Father and for us – everything united in the unity of Christ and his Sacrifice.

And in the strength and power, in the joy and peace of this sacred unity, we pledge ourselves anew – as one people – to fulfil the command of our Lord Jesus Christ: Go and teach all people my Gospel. By word and example give witness to my name. And, behold, I am with you always, until the end of the world.

CHICAGO, CHICAGO SYMPHONY ORCHESTRA CONCERT

Chicago's farewell to Pope John
Paul was entrusted to the Chicago
Symphony Orchestra which played
Anton Bruckner's Fifth Symphony in
the unfamiliar setting of Holy Name
Cathedral. The Pope, who missed
half the concert, thanked the
orchestra as follows:

I am indeed honoured by the splendid performance of the Chicago Symphony Orchestra.

I thank you for the opportunity to express my profound admiration for the artistic beauty which you have shared with me tonight. Please accept my deep gratitude.

And I am honoured to be able, on this occasion, to join my voice to that of my predecessor Paul VI, who through the eloquent testimony of a long pontificate, showed himself to be the friend of artists. With all the intensity of his noble soul, he convincingly attested to the Church's esteem for the role of art. With consummate skill himself, he led the Catholic Church to a new level of dialogue with the artists of the world. It was his fond hope that all art and beauty would lift the gaze of man toward God, pointing the way to uncreated beauty.

For the honour of the memory of Paul VI, in my own name, and on behalf of the Church, I reiterate my respect and admiration for your uplifting contribution to humanity, for your artistic creation that exalts what is human and reaches what is religious and divine.

In the cultural and spiritual encounter of this evening, I extend my respectful greetings to all the artists of this land, extolling the role they are called to play, with prodigious capacity, for the advancement of true culture in the United States and in the whole world.

Saturday, 6 October

WASHINGTON, ARRIVAL AT ANDREWS MILITARY BASE

The flying time from O'Hare Airport, Chicago, to the Andrews Military Base, Washington, was one hour and thirty minutes. The Pope arrived at 10.38 a.m. local time and was greeted by the Vice President of the United States, Walter Mondale and Secretary of State, Cyrus Vance. He replied as follows:

Mr Vice President,
Dear friends,
Dear brothers and sisters in Christ,

I wish to express my sincere thanks for the gracious words of welcome that have been extended to me on my arrival at the nation's capital, the last stage of my first apostolic journey to the United States. I wish to say once more how grateful I am for the invitation of the Episcopal Conference and of President Carter to come and visit the United States.

I extend a cordial greeting to all those who have come to welcome me here: to you, Mr Vice President, and to the other civil authorities, in whom I greet the whole American people and in a particular way all the citizens of the state of Maryland. A fraternal greeting to you, Cardinal Baum, Pastor of the Archdiocese of Washington, and through you to all the clergy, religious and laity of the Catholic community. I am most happy to greet at the same time the President, Officers and Staff of the National Conference of Catholic Bishops that has its headquarters in this city, as well as all those who in the United States Catholic Conference provide all the indispensable services to the whole Catholic community of this country. To all my brother Bishops, a greeting and a blessing from the Bishop of Rome in the See of Saint Peter, for you and your dioceses.

I am looking forward to meeting the leaders of this young and flourishing country – in the first place, the President of the United States. I shall also be honoured to visit the headquarters of the Organization of American States to bring to this deserving body a message of peace for all the peoples they represent.

It will give me a special pleasure, during these last days on my visit and pilgrimage, to come into contact with the Catholic community of this area, and to learn about their pastoral efforts, programmes and activities.

May the blessings of Almighty God descend in abundance on all the people of this nation's capital.

WASHINGTON, CATHEDRAL OF SAINT MATTHEW

After a brief stop at the Reflecting Pool, the Pope's motorcade set off through Washington for Saint Matthew's Cathedral where were waiting the five thousand priests who work in the Archdiocese. There was no concelebration, and the Pope's homily was brief but important in that it stressed the relatedness of Mary to the Church: Our Lady is the model of faith.

Mary says to us today: 'I am the servant of the Lord. Let it be done to me as you say' (Lk 1:38).

And with those words, she expresses what was the fundamental attitude of her life: her faith! Mary believed! She trusted in God's promises and was faithful to his will. When the angel Gabriel announced that she was chosen to be the Mother of the Most High, she gave her 'Fiat' humbly and with full freedom: 'Let it be done to me as you say.'

Perhaps the best description of Mary and, at the same time the greatest tribute to her, was the greeting of her cousin Elizabeth: 'Blessed is she who trusted that God's words to her would be fulfilled' (Lk 1:45). For it was that continual trust in the providence of God which most characterized her faith.

All her earthly life was a 'pilgrimage of faith' (cf. *Lumen Gentium*, 58). For like us she walked in shadows and hoped for things unseen. She knew the contradictions of our earthly life. She was promised that her son would be given David's throne, but at his birth, there was no room even at the inn. Mary still believed. The angel said her child would be called the Son of God; but she would see him slandered, betrayed and condemned, and left to die as a thief on the cross. Even yet, Mary 'trusted that God's words to her would be fulfilled' (Lk 1:45) and that 'nothing was impossible with God' (Lk 1:37).

This woman of faith, Mary of Nazareth, the Mother of God, has been given to us as a model in our pilgrimage of faith. From Mary we learn to surrender to God's will in all things. From Mary, we learn to trust even when all hope seems gone. From Mary, we learn to love Christ, her Son and the Son of God. For Mary is not only the Mother of God, she is Mother of the Church as well. In every stage of the march through history, the Church has benefited from the prayer and protection of the Virgin Mary. Holy Scripture and the experience of the faithful see the Mother of God as the one who in a very special way is united with the Church at the most difficult moments in her history, when attacks on the Church become most threatening. Precisely in periods when Christ, and therefore his Church, provokes premeditated contradiction, Mary appears particularly close to the Church, because for her the Church is always her beloved Christ.

I therefore exhort you in Christ Jesus, to continue to look to Mary as the model of the Church, as the best example of the discipleship of Christ. Learn from her to be always faithful, to trust that God's word to you will be fulfilled, and that nothing is impossible with God. Turn to Mary frequently in your prayer 'for never was it known that anyone who fled to her protection, implored her help or sought her intercession was left unaided'.

As a great sign that has appeared in the heavens, Mary guides and sustains us on our pilgrim way, urging us on to 'the victory that overcomes the world, our faith' (1 Jn 5:5).

141

WASHINGTON, THE WHITE HOUSE; TO THE PRESIDENT, CONGRESS, CABINET, SUPREME COURT AND WHITE HOUSE STAFF

Almost on time — only three minutes
later than scheduled — the Pope
arrived at the North Portico of the
White House for his historic meeting
with President Jimmy Carter. With
the President were his wife,
Rosalynn, and his daughter, Amy.
After the President's words of
greeting, the Pope replied with the
following speech, which was
immediately followed by an address
to the Members of Congress and
other officials present:

Mr President,

I wish to express my most sincere thanks for your kind words of welcome to the White House. It is indeed a great honour for me to meet with the President of the United States during a visit of which the aims are spiritual and religious in nature. May I convey at the same time to you, and through you to all your fellow Americans, my profound respect for all the Federal and State Authorities of this nation and for its beloved people. In the course of the last few days, I have had the opportunity to see some of your cities and rural areas. My only regret is that the time is too short to bring my greetings personally to all parts of this country, but I want to assure you that my esteem and affection go out to every man, woman and child without distinction.

Divine Providence in its own designs has called me from my native Poland to be the Successor of Peter in the See of Rome and the leader of the Catholic Church. It gives me great joy to be the first Pope in history to come to the capital of this nation, and I thank Almighty God for this blessing.

In accepting your courteous invitation, Mr President, I have also hoped that our meeting today would serve the cause of world peace, international understanding and the promotion of full respect for human rights everywhere.

Mr Speaker and Honourable Members of Congress,
Distinguished Members of the Cabinet and of the Judiciary,
Ladies and Gentlemen,

Your presence here honours me greatly and I deeply appreciate the expression of respect which you thus extend to me. My gratitude goes to each one of you personally for your kind welcome, and to all I wish to say how profoundly I esteem your mission as stewards of the common good of all the people of America.

I come from a nation with a long tradition of deep Christian faith and with a national history marked by many upheavals; for more than a hundred years Poland was even erased from the political map of Europe. But it is also a country marked by a deep veneration for those values without which no society can prosper: love of freedom, cultural creativity, and the conviction that common endeavours for the good of society must be guided by a true moral sense. My own spiritual and religious mission impels me to be the messenger of peace and brotherhood, and to witness to the true greatness of every human person. This greatness derives from the love of God, who created us in his own likeness and gave us an eternal destiny. It is in this dignity of the human person that I see the meaning of history, and that I find the principle that gives sense to the role which every human being has to assume for his or her own advancement and for the wellbeing of the society to which he or she belongs. It is with those sentiments that I greet in you the whole American people, a people that bases its concept of life on spiritual and moral values, on a deep religious sense, on respect for duty and on generosity in the service of humanity – noble traits which are embodied in a particular way in the nations' capital, with its monuments dedicated to such outstanding national figures as George Washington, Abraham Lincoln and Thomas Jefferson.

I greet the American people in their elected representatives, all of you who serve in Congress to chart, through legislation, the path that will lead every citizen of this country towards the fullest development of his or her potential, and the nation as a whole towards assuming its share of the responsibility for building a world of true freedom and justice. I greet America in all who are vested with authority, which can only be seen as an opportunity for serving your fellow-citizens in the overall development of their true humanity and in the full and unimpeded enjoyment of all their fundamental rights. I salute the people of this land also in the members of the Judiciary, who are servants of humanity in the application of justice, and who thus hold in their hands the awesome power of profoundly affecting, by their decisions, the lives of every individual.

For all of you I pray to Almighty God that he may grant you the gift of wisdom in your decisions, prudence in your words and actions, and compassion in the exercise of the authority that is yours, so that in your noble office you will always render true service to the people.

God bless America!

WASHINGTON, THE WHITE HOUSE; ADDRESS AFTER MEETING WITH THE PRESIDENT OF THE UNITED STATES

After a private meeting with President Carter in the Oval Office, about which nothing was released, the Pope and the President re-emerged onto the North Lawn of the White House. There John Paul II addressed the President and the invited guests as follows:

Mr President,

I am honoured to have had, at your kind invitation, the opportunity of a meeting with you; for by your office as President of the United States of America you represent before the world the whole American nation and you hold the immense responsibility of leading this nation in the path of justice and peace. I thank you publicly for this meeting and I thank all those who have contributed to its success. I wish also to reiterate here my deep gratitude for the warm welcome and the many kindnesses which I have received from the American people on my pastoral journey through your beautiful land.

Mr President,

In responding to the kind words which you have addressed to me, I take the liberty of beginning with the passage from the Prophet Micah that you quoted at your Inauguration: 'You have been told, O man, what is good, and what the Lord requires of you: only to do right and to love goodness, and to walk humbly with your God' (Micah 6:8). In recalling these words, I wish to greet you and all the authorities in the individual States and in the nation who are committed to the good of the citizens. There is indeed no other way to put oneself at the service of the whole human person except by seeking the good of every man and woman in all their commitments and activities. Authority in the political community is based on the objective ethical principle that the basic duty of power is the solicitude of the common good of society and that it serves the inviolable rights of the human person. The individuals, families, and various groups which compose the civic community are aware that by themselves they are unable to realize their human potential to the full, and therefore they recognize in a wider community the necessary condition for the ever better attainment of the common good.

   I wish to commend those in public authority and all the people of the United States for having given, from the very beginning of the existence of the nation, a special place to some of the most important concerns of the common good. Three years ago, during the Bicentennial celebration, which I was fortunate to participate in as the Archbishop of Cracow, it was obvious to every one that concern for what is human and spiritual is one of the basic principles governing the life of this community. It is superfluous to add that respect for the freedom and the dignity of every individual, whatever his origin, race, sex or creed, has been a cherished tenet of the civil creed of America, and that it has been backed up by courageous decisions and actions.

Mr President,
Ladies and Gentlemen,

I know and appreciate this country's efforts for arms limitation, especially of nuclear weapons. Everyone is aware of the terrible risk that the stockpiling of such weapons brings upon humanity. Since it is one of the greatest nations on earth, the United States plays a particularly important part in the quest for greater security in the world and for closer international collaboration. With all my heart I hope that there will be no relaxing of its efforts both to reduce the risk of a fatal and disastrous worldwide conflagration, and to secure a prudent and progressive reduction of the destructive capacity of military arsenals. At the same time, by reason of its special position, may the United States succeed in influencing the other nations to join in a continuing commitment for disarmament. Without wholeheartedly accepting such a commitment how can any nation effectively serve humanity, whose deepest desire is true peace?

Attachment to human values and to ethical concerns, which have been a hallmark of the American people, must be situated, especially in the present context of the growing interdependence of peoples across the globe, within the framework of the view that the common good of society embraces not just the individual nation to which one belongs but the citizens of the whole world. I would encourage every action for the re-enforcement of peace in the world, a peace based on liberty and justice, on charity and truth. The present-day relationships between peoples and between nations demand the establishment of greater international cooperation also in the economic field. The more powerful a nation is, the greater becomes its international responsibility, the greater also must be its commitment to the betterment of the lot of those whose very humanity is constantly being threatened by want and need. It is my fervent hope that all the powerful nations in the world will deepen their awareness of the principle of human solidarity within the one great human family. America, which in the past decades has demonstrated goodness and generosity in providing food for the hungry of the world, will, I am sure, be able to match this generosity with an equally convincing contribution to the establishing of a world order that will create the necessary economic and trade conditions for a more just relationship between all the nations of the world, in respect for their dignity and their own personality. Since people are suffering under international inequality, there can be no question of giving up the pursuit of international solidarity, even if it involves a notable change in the attitudes and life styles of those blessed with a larger share of the world's goods.

Mr President,
Ladies and Gentlemen,

In touching upon the common good, which embodies the aspiration of all human beings to the full development of their capacities and the proper protection of their rights, I have dealt with areas where the Church that I represent and the political community that is the State share a common concern: the safeguarding of the dignity of the human person, and the search for justice and peace. In their own proper spheres, the political community and the Church are mutually independent and self-governing. Yet, by a different title, each serves the personal and social vocation of the same human beings.

For her part, the Catholic Church will continue her efforts to cooperate in promoting justice, peace and dignity through the commitment of her leaders and the members of her communities, and through her incessant proclamation that all human beings are created to the image and likeness of God, and that they are brothers and sisters, children of one heavenly Father.

May Almighty God bless and sustain America in her quest for the fullness of liberty, justice and peace.

WASHINGTON, THE ORGANIZATION OF AMERICAN STATES

From the White House, the Pope
went immediately to the OAS (the
Organization of American States),
which was established in 1947 at Rio
de Janeiro by the Inter-American
Treaty of Defence, Non-aggression
and Mutual Help. It was renewed by
the Charter of Rio de Janeiro of 1965
with the intention of guaranteeing
the security and development of the
member states in both parts of the
continent. Pope John Paul first spoke
in Spanish, the language of all the
major countries of Latin America
except Brazil.

(In Spanish)

Mr President,
Mr Secretary General,
Ladies and Gentlemen,

1   It is indeed a pleasure for me to have this opportunity to greet all the
distinguished representatives of the different Member Nations of the Organization
of American States. My sincere gratitude goes to you, Mr President, for the cordial
words of welcome you have extended to me. I thank also the Secretary General for
his thoughtful invitation to come and visit the headquarters of the oldest of the
regional international organizations. It is fitting that, after my visit to the United
Nations Organization, the Organization of American States should be the first one
among the many intergovernmental organizations and agencies to which I am
privileged to address a message of peace and friendship.
    The Holy See follows with great interest, and may I say, with special attention,
the events and developments that touch upon the wellbeing of the peoples of the
Americas. It felt therefore greatly honoured by the invitation to send its own
Permanent Observer to this institution – an invitation extended last year by a
unanimous decision of the General Assembly. The Holy See sees in regional
organizations such as yours intermediary structures that promote a greater internal
diversity and vitality in a given area within the global community of nations. The
fact that the American continent is provided with an organization concerned with
ensuring more continuity for the dialogue between governments, with promoting
peace, with advancing full development in solidarity, and with protecting man, his
dignity, and his rights is a factor contributing to the health of the whole human
family. The Gospel and Christianity have entered deeply into your history and your
cultures. I would like to call on this common tradition in order to present to you
some reflections, in full respect for your personal convictions and your own
competence, in order to bring to your endeavours an original contribution in a
spirit of service.

146

2   Peace is a most precious blessing that you seek to preserve for your peoples. You are in agreement with me that it is not by accumulating arms that this peace can be ensured in a stable way. Apart from the fact that such accumulation increases in practice the danger of having recourse to arms to settle the disputes that may arise, it takes away considerable material and human resources from the great peaceful tasks of development that are so urgent. It can also tempt some to think that the order built on arms is sufficient to ensure internal peace in the single countries.

I solemnly call on you to do everything in your power to restrain the arms race on this continent. There are no differences between your countries that cannot be peacefully overcome. What a relief it would be to your peoples, what new opportunities it would provide for their economic, social and cultural progress, and how contagious an example it would give the world, if the difficult enterprise of disarmament were here to find a realistic and resolute solution!

3   The painful experience of the history of my own country, Poland, has shown me how important national sovereignty is when it is served by a State worthy of the name and free in its decisions; how important it is for the protection not only of a people's legitimate material interests, but also of its culture and its soul. Your organization is an organization of States, founded on respect for the full national sovereignty of each, on equal participation in common tasks, and on solidarity between your peoples. The legitimate demand by the States to participate on a basis of equality in the organization's common decisions must be matched by the will to promote within each country an ever more effective participation by the citizens in the responsibility and decisions of the nation through ways that take into account particular traditions, difficulties and historical experiences.

4   However, while such difficulties and experiences can at times call for exceptional measures and a certain period of maturation in preparation for new advances in shared-responsibility, they never, never justify any attack on the inviolable dignity of the human person and on the authentic rights that protect this dignity. If certain ideologies and certain ways of interpreting legitimate concern for national security were to result in subjugating to the State man and his rights and dignity, they would to that extent cease to be human and would be unable to claim without gross deception any Christian reference. In the Church's thinking it is a fundamental principle that social organization is at the service of man, not vice versa. That holds good also for the highest levels of society, where the power of coercion is wielded and where abuses, when they occur, are particularly serious. Besides, a security in which the peoples no longer feel involved, because it no longer protects them in their very humanity, is only a sham; as it grows more and more rigid, it will show symptoms of increasing weakness and rapidly approaching ruin.

Without undue interference, your Organization can, by the spirit with which it tackles all the problems in its competence, do much throughout the continent to advance a concept of the State and its sovereignty that is truly human, and that is therefore the basis for the legitimacy of the States and of their acknowledged prerogatives for the service of man.

5   Man! Man is the decisive criterion that dictates and directs all your undertakings, the living value for whose service new initiatives are unceasingly demanded. The words that are most filled with meaning for man – words such as

justice, peace, development, solidarity, human rights – are sometimes belittled as a result of systematic suspicion or party and sectarian ideological censure. They then lose their power to mobilize and attract. They will recover it only if respect for the human person and commitment to the human person are explicitly brought back to the centre of all considerations. When we speak of the right to life, to physical and moral integrity, to nourishment, to housing, to education, to health care, to employment, to shared-responsibility in the life of the nation, we speak of the human person. It is this human person whom faith makes us recognize as created in the image of God and destined for an eternal goal. It is this human person that is often threatened and hungry, without decent housing and employment, without access to the cultural heritage of his or her people or of humanity, and without a voice to make his or her distress heard. The great cause of full development in solidarity must be given new life by those who in one degree or another enjoy these blessings, for the service of all those – and there are many of them still on your continent – who are deprived of them to a sometimes dramatic extent.

6   The challenge of development deserves your full attention. In this field too what you achieve can be an example for humanity. The problems of rural and urban areas, of industry and agriculture, and of the environment are to a large extent a common task. The energetic pursuit of these will help to spread throughout the continent a sentiment of universal fraternity that extends beyond borders and regimes. Without any disregard for the responsibilities of sovereign states, you discover that it is a logical requirement for you to deal with problems, such as unemployment, migration and trade, as common concerns whose continental dimension increasingly demands more organic solutions on a continental scale. All that you do for the human person will halt violence and the threats of subversion and destabilization. For, by accepting courageous revisions demanded by 'this single fundamental point of view, namely the welfare of man – or, let us say, of the person in the community – which must, as a fundamental factor in the common good, constitute the essential criterion for all programmes, systems and regimes' (*Redemptor Hominis*, 17), you direct the energies of your peoples towards the peaceful satisfaction of their aspirations.

7   The Holy See will always be happy to make its own disinterested contribution to this work. The local Churches in the Americas will do the same within the framework of their various responsibilities. By advancing the human person and his or her dignity and rights, they serve the earthly city, its cohesion and its lawful authorities. The full religious freedom that they ask for is in order to serve, not in order to oppose the legitimate autonomy of civil society and of its own means of action. The more all citizens are able to exercise habitually their freedoms in the life of the nation, the more readily will the Christian communities be able to dedicate themselves to the central task of evangelization, namely the preaching of the Gospel of Jesus Christ, the source of life, strength, justice and peace.

(In English)

With fervent prayers for prosperity and concord, I invoke upon this important Assembly, upon the Representatives of all the Member States and their families, upon all the beloved peoples of the Americas, the choicest favours and blessings of Almighty God.

(In French)

My visit here, in the Hall of the Americas, before this noble assembly dedicated to inter-American collaboration, expresses at the same time a wish and a prayer. My wish is that, in all the nations of this continent, no man, woman or child may ever feel abandoned by the constituted authorities, to whom they are ready to accord their full confidence to the extent that those authorities seek the good of all. My prayer is that Almighty God may grant his light to the peoples and the governments, that they may always discover new means of collaboration for building up a fraternal and just society.

(In Portuguese)

One last word before I leave you – with great regret – after this first brief visit to your esteemed Organization. When I visited Mexico, at the beginning of the year, I was amazed at the enthusiasm, spontaneity and joy of living of its people. I am convinced that you will succeed in preserving the rich human and cultural heritage of all your peoples, and thus maintain the indispensable basis for true progress, which is constituted, always and everywhere, by respect for the supreme dignity of man.

WASHINGTON, GREETING TO THE PEOPLE OUTSIDE THE OAS BUILDING

Dear friends,

Thank you for coming here to greet me. To all of you: peace and joy!

Every time I have the opportunity to meet with a group of people, it gives me great happiness, for in you I see my brothers and sisters, children of the same God, who is our Father, and who has created us with a unique beauty and richness: the great beauty of being free human beings, capable of knowing truth, of offering love and understanding to each other, and of joining hands to make the world a better place to live in.

I have met many people during the last few days, many different people: in Ireland, at the United Nations, in the cities and rural areas of America, at this great Organization of American States. I have enjoyed being with them, but above all I have rejoiced in seeing how strongly every one believes in the possibility of bringing peace and wellbeing to all men, women and children in the world. So, I would like to encourage you also in your dedication to truth and to justice, without which real peace can never exist.

One of the temptations of the modern world is a growing materialism in the outlook of people and of society itself. Many people have been deceived in this regard; they have been led to think that money, pleasure, comfort or self-indulgence can be substitutes for spiritual values.

So, I invite all of you not to lose sight of the things that really matter, the things of the spirit; and let us remember, above all, that it is God who gives meaning to our lives.

To all of you, young and old, I say: do not let the material things of life rob you of the things that really count: God's love for you, and your love for one another. God bless you!

Dear Spanish-speaking friends,

I have just visited the headquarters of the Organization of American States and I have met the Representatives of this area, bringing them a message of peace, of friendship, of encouragement and of collaboration on the part of the Church.

The Pope's interest in this regional international organization is intended to indicate his interest also in each one of your countries and in each one of yourselves, both as family groups and as individuals.

The greeting I gave the representatives of the American States now goes to you with all my heart. I also pray God to grant that you may always be able to look to this Organization with eyes of hope, as a place that will echo your lawful expectations directed to goals of greater human and Christian dignity.

I know very well that throughout my journey in the United States I have been meeting many groups of the Hispanic community spread among the great crowds and big cities. Let no one feel that he or she has been forgotten by the Pope. Let each person feel respected and loved in his or her dignity as a human being with his or her own cultural and personal values, as well as for being a Christian and a child of God.

I exhort you and your friends and all the Spanish-speaking people to have solidarity of sentiment and I encourage you to maintain your human and Christian values with valour and constancy.

Finally, I assure you of my remembrance as a friend and of my affectionate Blessing.

WASHINGTON, TO THE DIPLOMATIC CORPS

The visit to the OAS was also an occasion for John Paul II to meet the staff of the organization and the diplomats accredited to it. He addressed them in French as follows:

Your Excellencies, Ladies and Gentlemen,

It pleases me greatly that, in the midst of a programme that is at the same time demanding and enjoyable, the opportunity has been offered to me to meet tonight with the distinguished Members of the Diplomatic Corps in this city of Washington.

I thank you most cordially for the honour you bestow upon me by your presence, an honour given not only to my person but to the leader of the Catholic Church. I also see in your courteous gesture an encouragement for the activity of the Catholic Church and of the Holy See in the service of humanity.

In this cause of service to humanity the Diplomatic Corps and the Holy See stand together, each one in its own sphere, each one faithfully pursuing its own mission, but united in the great cause of understanding and solidarity among peoples and nations.

Yours is a noble task. Despite unavoidable difficulties, setbacks and failures, diplomacy retains its importance as one of the roads that must be travelled in the search for peace and progress for all mankind. 'Diplomacy', in the words of my predecessor Paul VI, 'is the art of making peace' (Address to the Diplomatic Corps, Rome, 12 January 1974). The efforts of diplomats, whether in a bilateral or in a multilateral setting, do not always succeed in establishing or in maintaining peace, but they must always be encouraged, today as in the past, so that new initiatives will be born, new paths tried with the patience and tenacity that are the eminent qualities of the deserving diplomat. As one who speaks in the name of Christ, who called himself 'the way, the truth, and the life' (Jn 14:6), I would also like to make a plea for the fostering of other qualities that are indispensable if today's diplomacy is to justify the hopes that are placed in it: the ever deeper insertion of the supreme values of the moral and spiritual order into the aims of peoples and into the methods used in pursuit of these aims.

First among the ethical imperatives that must preside over the relations among nations and peoples is *truth*. As the theme for the Thirteenth World Day of Peace (1 January 1980), I have chosen: 'Truth, the power of peace.' I am confident that the Governments and the nations which you represent will, as they have so admirably done in the past, associate themselves once again with this lofty aim: to instil truth into all relationships, be they political or economic, bilateral or multinational.

All too often, falsehood is met in personal as well as in collective life, and thus suspicion arises where truth is called for, and the ensuing reluctance to enter into dialogue makes any collaboration or understanding almost impossible. Bringing truth into all relations is to work for peace, for it will make it possible to apply to the problems of the world the solutions that are in conformity with reason and with justice – in a word, with the truth about man.

And this brings me to the second point I would like to make. If it is to be true and lasting, Peace must be truly human. The desire for peace is universal. It is embedded in the hearts of all human beings and it cannot be achieved unless the human person is placed at the centre of every effort to bring about unity and brotherhood among nations.

Your mission as diplomats is based on the mandate you receive from those who hold responsibility for the wellbeing of your nations. The power you partake of cannot be separated from the objective demands of the moral order or from the destiny of every human being. May I repeat here what I stated in my first Encyclical Letter: 'The fundamental duty of power is solicitude for the common good of society; this is what gives power its fundamental rights. Precisely in the name of these premises of the objective ethical order, the rights of power can only be understood on the basis of respect for the objective and inviolable rights of man. The common good that authority in the State serves is brought to full realization only when all the citizens are sure of their rights. The lack of this leads to the dissolution of society, opposition by citizens to authority, or a situation of oppression, intimidation, violence and terrorism, of which many examples have been provided by the totalitarianisms of this century. Thus the principle of human rights is of profound concern to the area of social justice and is the measure by which it can be tested in the life of the political bodies' (*Redemptor Hominis*, 17). These considerations assume their full relevance also in the area of your immediate concern, the quest for international peace, for justice among nations and for cooperation in solidarity by all peoples. The success of today's diplomacy will, in the final analysis, be the victory of the truth about man.

I invoke from Almighty God abundant blessings upon your mission, which requires you to foster the interests of your own nation and to place it in the context of universal peace; upon you personally – who are in such a distinguished way artisans of peace; upon your spouses and families, who support and encourage you; and finally upon all who count on your dedicated service to see their own human dignity respected and enhanced. May God's peace be always in your hearts.

Sunday, 7 October

WASHINGTON, TO THE STUDENTS OF THE CATHOLIC UNIVERSITY

Sunday, 7 October, the final day of Pope John Paul's journey to the United States, was if possible more crowded than anything that had gone before. The day began early, just after 8 o'clock, with an address to the students of the Catholic University of Washington. 'John Paul II, we like you', they chanted. To which the Pope replied, 'John Paul II, he likes you'. He then addressed them from the top of the steps at the main entrance.

Dear students of The Catholic University,

My first greeting on arriving at this campus is for you! To all of you I offer the peace and joy of our Lord Jesus Christ! I am told that you have held an all-night prayer vigil to ask God's blessing on my visit. Thank you most cordially for such a wonderful expression of communion with me, and for such a beautiful gift. I would like to talk to you at length; I would like to listen to you and know what you think about yourselves and the world. But the time I have been given is so short.

One thing you have told me already: by choosing to welcome me with the offering of your prayers, you have demonstrated that you understand what is most important in your lives – your contact with God, your searching for the meaning of life by listening to Christ as he speaks to you in the Scriptures. I am pleased to know that reflection on spiritual and religious values is part of your desire to live fully this time of your lives. Materialistic concerns and one-sided values are never sufficient to fill the heart and mind of a human person. A life reduced to the sole dimension of possessions, of consumer goods, of temporal concerns will never let you discover and enjoy the full richness of your humanity. It is only God – in Jesus, God made man – that you will fully understand what you are. He will unveil to you the true greatness of yourselves: that you are redeemed by him and taken up in his love; that you are made truly free in him who said about himself: 'If the son frees you, you will be free indeed' (Jn 8:36).

I know that you, like students all over the world, are troubled by the problems that weigh on society around you and on the whole world. Look at those problems, explore them, study them and accept them as a challenge. But do it in the light of Christ. He is 'the way, and the truth, and the life' (Jn 14:6). He put all human life in the true dimension of truth and of authentic love. True knowledge and true freedom are in Jesus. Make Jesus always part of your hunger for truth and justice, and part of your dedication to the wellbeing of your fellow human beings.

Enjoy the privileges of your youth: the right to be dynamic, creative and spontaneous; the right to be full of hope and joy; the opportunity to explore the marvellous world of science and knowledge; and above all the chance to give of yourself to others in generous and joyful service.

I leave you now with this prayer: that the Lord Jesus will reveal himself to each one of you, that he will give you the strength to go out and profess that you are Christian, that he will show you that he alone can fill your hearts. Accept his freedom and embrace his truth, and be messengers of the certainty that you have been truly liberated through the death and Resurrection of the Lord Jesus. This will be the new experience, the powerful experience, that will generate, through you, a more just society and a better world.

God bless you and may the joy of Jesus be always with you!

WASHINGTON, AT THE SHRINE OF THE IMMACULATE CONCEPTION

From the meeting with the students,
the Pope proceeded to the Shrine of
the Immaculate Conception, where
some five thousand sisters awaited
him and gave him an ecstatic
welcome. After listening to an
address of welcome by one of the
sisters, Pope John Paul invited the
sisters to look on Mary as their
model. His invocation was as follows:

My first desire, in this National Shrine of the Immaculate Conception, is to direct my thoughts, to turn my heart to the woman of salvation history. In the eternal design of God, this woman, Mary, was chosen to enter into the work of the Incarnation and Redemption. This design of God was to be actuated through her free decision given in obedience to the divine will. Through her 'yes', a 'yes' that pervades and is reflected in all history, she consented to be the Virgin Mother of our saving God, the handmaid of the Lord, and at the same time, the Mother of all the faithful who in the course of the centuries would become brothers and sisters of her Son. Through her, the Sun of justice was to rise in the world. Through her the great Healer of humanity, the reconciler of hearts and consciences, her Son, the God-Man, Jesus Christ, was to transform the human condition and by his death and resurrection uplift the entire human family. As a great sign that appeared in the heavens, in the fullness of time, the woman dominates all history as the Virgin Mother of the Son and as the Spouse of the Holy Spirit, as the Handmaid of humanity.

The woman becomes also, by association with her Son, the sign of contradiction to the world, and at the same time the sign of hope, whom all generations shall call blessed. The woman who conceived spiritually before she conceived physically, the woman who accepted the Word of God, the woman who was inserted intimately and irrevocably into the mystery of the Church, exercising a spiritual motherhood with regard to all peoples. The woman who is honoured as Queen of Apostles, without herself being inserted into the hierarchical constitution of the Church, and yet this woman made all hierarchy possible because she gave to the world the

Shepherd and Bishop of our souls. This woman, this Mary of the Gospels, who is not mentioned as being at the Last Supper, comes back again at the foot of the cross, in order to consummate her contribution to salvation history. By her courageous act she prefigures and anticipates the courage of all women throughout the ages who concur in bringing forth Christ in every generation.

At Pentecost, the Virgin Mother once again comes forward to exercise her role in union with the apostles, with and in and over the Church. Yet again, she conceived of the Holy Spirit to bring forth Jesus in the fullness of his Body, the Church, never to leave him, never to abandon him, but to continue to love and to cherish him through the ages.

This is the woman of history and destiny who inspires us today, the woman who speaks to us of femininity, human dignity and love, and who is the greatest expression of total consecration to Jesus Christ, in whose name we are gathered today.

WASHINGTON, TO RELIGIOUS WOMEN

After his invocation, the Holy Father spoke to all the sisters gathered at the Shrine of the Immaculate Conception, lauding their invaluable contribution to the life of the Church. He spoke as follows:

Dear Sisters,

May the grace, love and peace of God our Father and our Lord Jesus Christ be with you.

I welcome this opportunity to speak with you today. I am happy for this occasion because of my esteem for religious life, and my gratitude to women religious for their invaluable contribution to the mission and very life of the Church.

I am especially pleased that we are gathered here in the National Shrine of the Immaculate Conception, for the Virgin Mary is the model of the Church, the Mother of the faithful and the perfect example of consecrated life.

1   On the day of our Baptism, we received the greatest gift God can bestow on any man or woman. No other honour, no other distinction will equal its value. For we were freed from sin and incorporated into Christ Jesus and his Body, the Church. That day and every day after, we were chosen 'to live through love in his presence' (Eph 1:4).

In the years that followed our Baptism, we grew in awareness – even wonder – of the mystery of Christ. By listening to the Beatitudes, by meditating on the Cross, conversing with Christ in prayer and receiving him in the Eucharist, we progressed towards the day, that particular moment of our life, when we solemnly ratified with full awareness and freedom our Baptismal consecration. We affirmed our determination to live always in union with Christ, and to be, according to the gifts given us by the Holy Spirit, a generous and loving member of the People of God.

2   Your religious consecration builds on this common foundation which all Christians share in the Body of Christ. Desiring to perfect and intensify what God had begun in your life by Baptism, and discerning that God was indeed offering you the gift of the evangelical counsels, you willed to follow Christ more closely, to conform your life more completely to that of Jesus Christ, in and through a distinctive religious community. This is the essence of religious consecration: to profess within and for the benefit of the Church, poverty, chastity and obedience in response to God's special invitation, in order to praise and serve God in greater freedom of heart (cf. 1 Cor 7:34–35) and to have one's life more closely conformed to Christ in the manner of life chosen by him and his blessed Mother (cf. *Perfectae Caritatis*, 1; *Lumen Gentium*, 46).

3   Religious consecration not only deepens your personal commitment to Christ, but it also strengthens your relationship to his Spouse, the Church. Religious consecration is a distinctive manner of living in the Church, a particular way of fulfilling the life of faith and service begun in Baptism.

Or. her part, the Church assists you in your discernment of God's will. Having accepted and authenticated the charisms of your various Institutes, she then unites your religious profession to the celebration of Christ's Paschal Mystery.

You are called by Jesus himself to verify and manifest in your lives and in your activities your deepened relationship with his Church. This bond of union with the Church must also be shown in the spirit and apostolic endeavours of every Religious Institute. For faithfulness to Christ, especially in religious life, can never be separated from faithfulness to the Church. This ecclesial dimension of the vocation of religious consecration has many important practical consequences for institutes themselves and for each individual member. It implies, for example, a greater public witness to the Gospel, since you represent, in a special way as women religious, the spousal relationship of the Church to Christ. The ecclesial dimension also requires, on the part of individual members as well as entire institutes, a faithfulness to the original charisms which God has given to his Church, through your founders and foundresses. It means that institutes are called to continue to foster, in dynamic faithfulness, those corporate commitments which were related to the original charism, which were authenticated by the Church, and which still fulfil important needs of the People of God. A good example in this regard would be the Catholic School system which has been invaluable for the Church in the United States, an excellent means not only for communicating the Gospel of Christ to the students, but also for permeating the entire community with Christ's truth and his love. It is one of the apostolates in which women religious have made, and are still making, an incomparable contribution.

4   Dear Sisters in Christ: Jesus must always be first in your lives. His person must be at the centre of your activities – the activities of every day. No other person and no activity can take precedence over him. For the whole life has been consecrated to him. With Saint Paul you have to say: 'All I want is to know Christ and the power of his Resurrection and to share his sufferings by reproducing the pattern of his death' (Phil 3:10).

Christ remains primary in your life only when he enjoys the first place in your mind and heart. Thus you must continuously unite yourself to him in prayer. Without prayer, religious life has no meaning. It has lost contact with its source, it has emptied itself of substance, and it no longer can fulfil its goal. Without prayer there can be no joy, no hope, no peace. For prayer is what keeps us in touch with Christ. The incisive words written in *Evangelica Testificatio* cause us all to reflect: 'Do not forget the witness of history: faithfulness to prayer or its abandonment is the test of the vitality or decadence of religious life' (*Evangelica Testificatio*, 42).

5   Two dynamic forces are operative in religious life: your love for Jesus – and, in Jesus, for all who belong to him – and his love for you.

We cannot live without love. If we do not encounter love, if we do not experience it and make it our own, and if we do not participate intimately in it, our life is meaningless. Without love we remain incomprehensible to ourselves (cf. *Redemptor Hominis*, 10).

Thus every one of you needs a vibrant relationship of love to the Lord, a profound loving union with Christ, your spouse, a love like that expressed in the psalm:

God, you are my God whom I seek,
for you my flesh pines and my soul thirsts
like the earth, parched, lifeless and without
water. Thus have I gazed toward you in the
sanctuary to see your power and your glory
(PS. 63:1–2).

Yet far more important than your love for Christ is Christ's love for you. You have been called by him, made a member of his Body, consecrated in a life of the evangelical counsels and destined by him to have a share in the mission that Christ has entrusted to the Church: his own mission of salvation. For this reason, you centre your life in the Eucharist. In the Eucharist, you celebrate his death and Resurrection and receive from him the Bread of eternal life. And it is in the Eucharist especially that you are united to the one who is the object of all your love. Here, with him, you find ever greater reasons to love and serve his brothers and sisters. Here, with him – with Christ – you find greater understanding and compassion for God's people. And here you find the strength to persevere in your commitment to selfless service.

6   Your service in the Church is then an extension of Christ to whom you have dedicated your life. For it is not yourself that you put forward, but Christ Jesus as Lord. Like John the Baptist, you know that for Christ to increase, you must decrease. And so your life must be characterized by a complete availability: a readiness to serve as the needs of the Church require, a readiness to give public witness to the Christ whom you love.

The need for this public witness becomes a constant call to inner conversion, to justice and holiness of life on the part of each religious. It also becomes an invitation to each Institute to reflect on the purity of its corporate ecclesial witness. And it is for this reason that in my address last November to the International Union of Superiors General I mentioned that it is not unimportant that your consecration to God should be manifested in the permanent exterior sign of a simple and suitable religious garb. This is not only my personal conviction, but also the desire of the Church, often expressed by so many of the faithful.

As daughters of the Church – a title cherished by so many of your great saints – you are called to a generous and loving adherence to the authentic Magisterium of the Church, which is a solid guarantee of the fruitfulness of all your apostolates and an indispensable condition for the proper interpretation of the 'signs of the times'.

7 The contemplative life occupies today and for ever a place of great honour in the Church. The prayer of contemplation was found in the life of Jesus himself, and has been a part of religious life in every age. I take this opportunity therefore – as I did in Rome, in Mexico, in Poland and in Ireland – to encourage again all who are members of contemplative communities. Know that you shall always fulfil an important place in the Church, in her mission of salvation, in her service to the whole community of the People of God. Continue faithfully, confidently and prayerfully, in the rich tradition that has been handed down to you.

In closing, I remind you, with sentiments of admiration and love, that the aim of religious life is to render praise and glory to the Most Holy Trinity, and, through your consecration, to help humanity enter into fullness of life in the Father, and in the Son and in the Holy Spirit. In all your planning and in all your activities, try also to keep this aim before you. There is no greater service you can give; there is no greater fulfilment you can receive. Dear Sisters: today and forever: Praised be Jesus Christ!

This Shrine speaks to us with the voice of all America, with the voice of all the sons and daughters of America, who have come here from the various countries of the Old World. When they came, they brought with them in their hearts the same love for the Mother of God that was a characteristic of their ancestors and of themselves in their native lands. These people, speaking different languages, coming from different backgrounds of history and tradition in their own countries, came together around the heart of a Mother whom they all had in common. While their faith in Christ made all of them aware of being the one People of God, this awareness became all the more vivid through the presence of the Mother in the work of Christ and the Church.

Today, as I thank you, Mother, for this presence of yours in the midst of the men and women of this land – a presence which has lasted two hundred years – giving a new form to their social and civic lives in the United States, I commend them all to your Immaculate Heart.

With gratitude and joy I recall that you have been honoured as Patroness of the United States, under the title of your Immaculate Conception since the days of the Sixth Provincial Council of Baltimore in 1846.

I commend to you, Mother of Christ, and I entrust to you the Catholic Church: the Bishops, priests, deacons, individual religious and religious institutes, the seminarians, vocations, and the apostolate of the laity in its various aspects.

In a special way, I entrust to you the wellbeing of the Christian families of this country, the innocence of children, the future of the young, the vocation of single men and women. I ask you to communicate to all the women of the United States a deep sharing in the joy that you experienced in your closeness to Jesus Christ, your Son. I ask you to preserve all of them in freedom from sin and evil, like the freedom which was yours in a unique way from that moment of supreme liberation in your Immaculate Conception.

I entrust to you the great work of ecumenism here, in this land, in which those who confess Christ belong to different Churches and communions. I do this in order that the words of Christ's prayer may be fulfilled: 'That they may be one.' I entrust to you the consciences of men and women and the voice of public opinion, in order that they may not be opposed to the law of God but follow it as the fount of truth and good.

I add to this, Mother, the great cause of justice and peace in the modern world, in order that the force and energy of love may prevail over hatred and destructiveness, and in order that the children of light may not lack concern for the welfare of the whole human family.

Mother, I commend and entrust to you all that goes to make up earthly progress, asking that it should not be onesided, but that it should create conditions for the full spiritual advancement of individuals, families, communities and nations. I commend to you the poor, the suffering, the sick and the handicapped, the ageing and the dying. I ask you to reconcile those in sin, to heal those in pain, and to uplift those who have lost their hope and joy. Show to those who struggle in doubt the light of Christ your Son.

Bishops of the Church in the United States have chosen your Immaculate Conception as the mystery to hold the patronage over the people of God in this land. May the hope contained in this mystery overcome sin and be shared by all the sons and daughters of America, and also by the whole human family. At a time, when the struggle between good and evil, between the prince of darkness and father of lies and evangelical love is growing more acute, may the light of your Immaculate Conception show to all the way to grace and to salvation. Amen.

WASHINGTON, CATHOLIC UNIVERSITY; TO PRESIDENTS OF CATHOLIC COLLEGES AND UNIVERSITIES

The Pope then went to the Catholic University of America Field House where he was welcomed by Cardinal Baum and Dr Edmund Pelegrino, President of the University. The only significant departure from the prepared text below was when the Pope said, 'As one who for long years has been a university professor'. He added, amid laughter, 'at least I tried to be'.

Dear brothers and sisters in Christ,

1   Our meeting today gives me great pleasure, and I thank you sincerely for your cordial welcome. My own association with the university world, and more particularly with the Pontifical Theological Faculty of Cracow makes our encounter all the more gratifying for me. I cannot but feel at home with you. The sincere expressions with which the Chancellor and the President of The Catholic University of America have confirmed, in the name of all of you, the faithful adherence to Christ and the generous commitment to the service of truth and charity of your Catholic Associations and Institutions of higher learning are appreciated.

Ninety-one years ago Cardinal Gibbons and the American Bishops requested the foundation of The Catholic University of America, as a university 'destined to provide the Church with worthy ministers for the salvation of souls and the propagation of religion and to give the republic most worthy citizens'. It seems appropriate to me on this occasion to address myself not only to this great institution, so irrevocably linked to the Bishops of the United States, who have founded it and who generously support it, but also to all the Catholic universities, colleges, and academies of post-secondary learning in your land, those with formal and sometimes juridical links with the Holy See, as well as all those who are 'Catholic'.

2   Before doing so, though, allow me first to mention the Ecclesiastical Faculties, three of which are established here at The Catholic University of America. I greet these Faculties and all who dedicate their best talents in them. I offer my prayers for the prosperous development and the unfailing fidelity and success of these Faculties. In the Apostolic Constitution *Sapientia Christiana*, I have dealt directly with these institutions in order to provide guidance and to ensure that they fulfil their role in meeting the needs of the Christian community in today's rapidly changing circumstances.

I also wish to address a word of praise and admiration for the men and women, especially priests and religious, who dedicate themselves to all forms of campus ministry. Their sacrifices and efforts to bring the true message of Christ to the university world, whether secular or Catholic, cannot go unnoticed.

The Church also greatly appreciates the work and witness of those of her sons and daughters whose vocation places them in non-Catholic universities in your country. I am sure that their Christian hope and Catholic patrimony, being an enriching and irreplaceable dimension to the world of higher studies.

A special word of gratitude and appreciation also goes to the parents and students who, sometimes at the price of great personal and financial sacrifice, look towards the Catholic universities and colleges for the training that unites faith and science, culture and the Gospel values.

To all engaged in administration, teaching or study in Catholic colleges and universities I would apply the words of Daniel: 'They who are learned shall shine like the brightness of the firmament and those that instruct many in justice as stars for all eternity' (Dan 12:3). Sacrifice and generosity have accomplished heroic results in the foundation and development of these institutions. Despite immense financial strain, enrolment problems, and other obstacles, divine Providence and the commitment of the whole People of God have allowed us to see these Catholic institutions flourish and advance.

3   I would repeat here before you what I told the professors and students of the Catholic universities in Mexico when I indicated three aims that are to be pursued. A Catholic university or college must make a specific contribution to the Church and to society through high quality scientific research, in-depth study of problems, and a just sense of history, together with the concern to show the full meaning of the human person regenerated in Christ, thus favouring the complete development of the person. Furthermore, the Catholic university or college must train young men and women of outstanding knowledge who, having made a personal synthesis between faith and culture, will be both capable and willing to assume tasks in the service of the community and of society in general, and to bear witness to their faith before the world. And finally, to be what it ought to be, a Catholic college or university must set up, among its faculty and students, a real community which

bears witness to a living and operative Christianity, a community where sincere commitment to scientific research and study goes together with a deep commitment to authentic Christian living.

This is your identity. This is your vocation. Every university or college is qualified by a specific mode of being. Yours is the qualification of being Catholic, of affirming God, his revelation and the Catholic Church as the guardian and interpreter of that revelation. The term 'Catholic' will never be a mere label, either added or dropped according to the pressures of varying factors.

4   As one who for long years has been a university Professor, I will never tire of insisting on the eminent role of the university, which is to instruct but also to be a place of scientific research. In both these fields, its activity is closely related to the deepest and noblest aspiration of the human person: the desire to come to the knowledge of truth. No university can deserve the rightful esteem of the world of learning unless it applies the highest standards of scientific research, constantly updating its methods and working instruments, and unless it excels in seriousness, and therefore, in freedom of investigation. Truth and science are not gratuitous conquests, but the result of a surrender to objectivity and of the exploration of all aspects of nature and man. Whenever man himself becomes the object of investigation, no single method, or combination of methods, can fail to take into account, beyond any purely natural approach, the full nature of man. Because he is bound by the total truth on man, the Christian will, in his research and in his teaching, reject any partial vision of human reality, but he will let himself be enlightened by his faith in the creation of God and the Redemption of Christ.

The relationship to truth explains therefore the historical bond between the university and the Church. Because she herself finds her origin and her growth in the words of Christ, which are the liberating truth (cf. Jn 8:32), the Church has always tried to stand by the institutions that serve, and cannot but serve the knowledge of truth. The Church can rightfully boast of being in a sense the mother of universities. The names of Bologna, Padua, Prague and Paris shine in the earliest history of intellectual endeavour and human progress. The continuity of the historic tradition in this field has come down to our day.

5   An undiminished dedication to intellectual honesty and academic excellence are seen, in a Catholic university, in the perspective of the Church's mission of evangelization and service. This is why the Church asks these institutions, your institutions, to set out, without equivocation your Catholic nature. This is what I have desired to emphasize in my Apostolic Constitution *Sapientia Christiana*, where I stated: 'Indeed, the Church's mission of spreading the Gospel not only demands that the Good News be preached ever more widely and to ever greater numbers of men and women, but that the very power of the Gospel should permeate thought patterns, standards of judgment, and the norms of behaviour; in a word, it is necessary that the whole of human culture be steeped in the Gospel. The cultural atmosphere in which a human being lives has a great influence upon his or her way of thinking and, thus, of acting. Therefore, a division between faith and culture is more than a small impediment to evangelization, while a culture penetrated with the Christian spirit is an instrument that favours the spreading of the Good News' (*Sapientia Christiana*, I). The goals of Catholic higher education go beyond education for production, professional competence, technological and scientific competence; they aim at the ultimate destiny of the human person, at the full justice and holiness born of truth (cf. Eph 4:24).

161

6   If then your universities and colleges are institutionally committed to the Christian message, and if they are part of the Catholic community of evangelization, it follows that they have an essential relationship to the hierarchy of the Church. And here I want to say a special word of gratitude, encouragement and guidance for the theologians. The Church needs her theologians, particularly in this time and age so profoundly marked by deep changes in all areas of life and society. The Bishops of the Church, to whom the Lord has entrusted the keeping of the unity of the faith and the preaching of the message – individual Bishops for their dioceses; and Bishops collegially, with the Successor of Peter for the Universal Church – we all need your work, your dedication and the fruits of your reflection. We desire to listen to you and we are eager to receive the valued assistance of your responsible scholarship.

But true theological scholarship, and by the same token theological teaching, cannot exist and be fruitful without seeking its inspiration and its source in the word of God as contained in Sacred Scripture and in the Sacred Tradition of the Church, as interpreted by the authentic Magisterium throughout history (cf. *Dei Verbum*, 10). True academic freedom, must be seen in relation to the finality of the academic enterprise, which looks to the total truth of the human person. The theologian's contribution will be enriching for the Church only if it takes into account the proper function of the Bishops and the rights of the faithful. It devolves upon the Bishops of the Church to safeguard the Christian authenticity and unity of faith and moral teaching, in accordance with the injunction of the Apostle Paul: 'Proclaim the message and, welcome or unwelcome, insist on it. Refute falsehood, correct error, call to obedience . . .' (2 Tim 4:2). It is the right of the faithful not to be troubled by theories and hypotheses that they are not expert in judging or that are easily simplified or manipulated by public opinion for ends that are alien to the truth. On the day of his death, John Paul I stated: 'Among the rights of the faithful, one of the greatest is the right to receive God's word in all its entirety and purity . . .' (28 September 1979). It behoves the theologian to be free, but with the freedom that is openness to the truth and the light that comes from faith and from fidelity to the Church.

In concluding I express to you once more my joy in being with you today. I remain very close to your work and your concerns. May the Holy Spirit guide you. May the intercession of Mary, Seat of Wisdom, sustain you always in your irreplaceable service of humanity and the Church. God bless you.

WASHINGTON, ECUMENICAL MEETING AT TRINITY COLLEGE

Pope John Paul's next engagement was at Trinity College, a women's college run by the Sisters of Our Lady of Namur, where he met over five hundred representatives of other Christian Churches and ecclesial communities. After an address of welcome by Cardinal William Wakefield Baum, the Pope spoke as follows:

Dearly beloved in Christ,

1   I am grateful to the providence of God that permits me, on my visit to the United States of America, to have this meeting with other religious leaders, and to be able to join with you in prayer for the unity of all Christians.

It is indeed fitting that our meeting should occur just a short time before the observance of the fifteenth anniversary of the Second Vatican Council's Decree of Ecumenism, *Unitatis Redintegratio*. Since the inception of my pontificate, almost a year ago, I have endeavoured to devote myself to the service of Christian unity; for, as I stated in my first Encyclical, it is certain 'that in the present historical situation of Christianity and of the world the only possibility we see in fulfilling the Church's universal mission, with regard to ecumenical questions, is that of seeking sincerely, perseveringly, humbly and also courageously the ways of drawing closer and of union' (*Redemptor Hominis*, 6). On a previous occasion, I said that the problem of division within Christianity is 'binding in a special way on the Bishop of the ancient Church of Rome, founded on the preaching and the testimonies of the martyrdom of Saints Peter and Paul' (General Audience, 17 January 1979). And today I wish to reiterate before you the same conviction.

2   With great satisfaction and joy I welcome the opportunity to embrace you, in the charity of Christ, as beloved Christian brethren and fellow disciples of the Lord Jesus. It is a privilege to be able, in your presence and together with you, to give expression to the testimony of John, that 'Jesus Christ is the Son of God' (1 Jn 4:15), and to proclaim that 'there is one Mediator between God and men, the man Christ Jesus' (1 Tim 2:5).

In the united confession of faith in the divinity of Jesus Christ, we feel great love for each other and great hope for all humanity. We experience immense gratitude to the Father, who has sent his Son to be our Saviour, 'the expiation for our sins, and not for ours only but for the sins of the whole world' (1 Jn 2:2).

By divine grace we are united in esteem and love for Sacred Scripture, which we recognize as the inspired word of God. And it is precisely in this word of God that we learn how much he wants us to be fully one in him and in his Father. Jesus prays that his followers may be one 'so that the world may believe . . .' (Jn 17:21). That the credibility of evangelization should, by God's plan, depend on the unity of his followers is a subject of inexhaustible meditation for all of us.

3   I wish to pay homage here to the many splendid ecumenical initiatives that have been realized in this country through the action of the Holy Spirit. In the last fifteen years there has been a positive response to ecumenism by the Bishops of the United States. Through their committee for ecumenical and interreligious affairs, they have established a fraternal relationship with other Churches and ecclesial Communities – a relationship which, I pray, will continue to deepen in the coming years. Conversations are in progress with our brothers from the East, the Orthodox. Here I wish to note that this relationship has been strong in the United States and that soon a theological dialogue will begin on a worldwide basis in an attempt to resolve those difficulties which hinder full unity. There are also American dialogues with the Anglicans, the Lutherans, the Reformed Churches, the Methodists and the Disciples of Christ – all having a counterpart on the international level. A fraternal exchange exists likewise between the Southern Baptists and American theologians.

My gratitude goes to all who collaborate in the matter of joint theological investigation, the aim of which is always the full evangelical and Christian dimension of truth. It is to be hoped that, through such investigation, persons who are well prepared by a solid grounding in their own traditions will contribute to a deepening of the full historical and doctrinal understanding of the issues.

The particular climate and traditions of the United States have been conducive to joint witness in the defence of the rights of the human person, in the pursuit of goals of social justice and peace, and in questions of public morality. These areas of concern must continue to benefit from creative ecumenical action, as must the fostering of esteem for the sacredness of marriage and the support of healthy family life as a major contribution to the wellbeing of the nation. In this context, recognition must be given to the deep division which still exists over moral and ethical matters. The moral life and the life of faith are so deeply united that it is impossible to divide them.

4 Much has been accomplished but there is still much to be done. We must go forward, however, with a spirit of hope. Even the very desire for the complete unity in faith – which is lacking between us, and which must be achieved before we can lovingly celebrate the Eucharist together in truth – is itself a gift of the Holy Spirit, for which we offer humble praise to God. We are confident that through our common prayer the Lord Jesus will lead us, at a moment dependent on the sovereign action of his Holy Spirit, to the fullness of ecclesial unity.

Faithfulness to the Holy Spirit calls for interior conversion and fervent prayer. In the words of the Second Vatican Council: 'This change of heart and holiness of life, along with public and private prayer for the unity of Christians, should be regarded as the soul of the whole ecumenical movement . . .' (*Unitatis Redintegratio*, 8). It is important that every individual Christian search his or her heart to see what may obstruct the attainment of full union among Christians. And let us all pray that the genuine need for the patience to await God's hour will never occasion complacency in the status quo of division in faith. By divine grace may the need for patience never become a substitute for the definitive and generous response which God asks that there be given to his invitation to perfect unity in Christ.

And so, as we are gathered here to celebrate the love of God that is poured out in our hearts by the Holy Spirit, let us be conscious of the call to show supreme fidelity to the will of Christ. Let us together perseveringly ask the Holy Spirit to remove all divisions from our faith, to give us that perfect unity in truth and love for which Christ prayed, for which Christ died: 'to gather together in unity the scattered children of God' (Jn 11:52).

I offer my respectful greeting of grace and peace to those whom you represent, to each of your respective congregations, to all who long for the coming of 'our great God and Saviour Jesus Christ' (Tit 2:14).

WASHINGTON, TO JOURNALISTS

There was still time in the crowded
schedule for another meeting with the
journalists who had accompanied the
Pope. He met them in the garden
behind the Apostolic Delegation, and
read the following address:

My dear friends of the communications media,

Here we are together again at the end of another journey – a journey which this time
has brought me to Ireland, to the United Nations and to the United States of
America. The purpose of this journey was to permit the Pope to exercise his
function as a herald of peace, in the name of Christ, who was referred to as the
Prince of Peace. This message of peace was announced especially in those places and
before those audiences where the problem of war and peace is perceived with
particular sensitivity and where there exist the conditions of understanding, of good
will and of the means necessary to building peace and cooperation among all
nations and among all peoples.

The word 'peace' is a synthesis. It has many components. I have touched on
several of these during this journey, and you have diligently reported on these
reflections. You have commented on them: you have interpreted them: you have
performed the service of stimulating people to think about how they might
contribute to a firmer foundation for peace, for cooperation and for justice among
all persons.

Now we find ourselves at the moment of parting, in this capital city of one of
the most powerful nations in the world. The power of this country, I believe, comes
not only from material wealth but from a richness of spirit.

In fact, the name of this city and of the tall monument which dominates it recalls
the spirit of George Washington, the first President of the nation, who – with
Thomas Jefferson, for whom an imposing memorial also exists here, and with other
enlightened individuals – established this country on a foundation which was not
only human but also profoundly religious.

As a consequence, the Catholic Church has been able to flourish here. The
millions of faithful who belong to the Church testify to that fact, as they exercise the
rights and duties which flow from their faith with full freedom. The great National
Shrine of the Immaculate Conception in this city testifies to that fact. The existence
in this capital city of two Catholic universities – Georgetown and The Catholic
University of America – testifies to that fact. I have observed that the people of the
United States of America proudly and gratefully pledge allegiance to their republic
as 'One nation under God'.

This one nation is made up of many members – members of all races, of all
religions, of all conditions of life – so that it is a type of microcosm of the world
community and accurately reflects the motto *E pluribus unum*. As this country
courageously abolished the plague of slavery under the presidency of Abraham
Lincoln, may it never stop striving for the effective good of all the inhabitants of
this one nation and for that unity which reflects its national motto. For this reason,

the United States of America gives to all cause to reflect on a spirit which, if well applied, can bring beneficial results for peace in the world community.

I sincerely hope that all of you have profited from this journey, and that you have had the opportunity to reflect anew on the values which have come from Christianity to the civilization of this new continent. Most of all, however, we can draw hope for a peaceful world community from the example of persons of all races, of all nationalities, and of all religions living together in peace and in unity.

As we prepare to part, my dear friends, I am consoled by the fact that you will continue to inform and to form world public opinion with a profound consciousness of your responsibility and with the realization that so many persons depend on you.

Finally, I say goodbye to you and to America. I thank you again, and with all my heart I ask God to bless you and your families.

WASHINGTON, TO THE KNIGHTS OF COLUMBUS

Also to be greeted were the Knights
of Saint Columbus who had made
themselves useful during the Pope's
visit. He thanked them as follows:

Dear Knights of Columbus,

It gives me great pleasure to be with you on the occasion of my pastoral visit to the United States. I thank you most sincerely for the respect and love which you have manifested towards me as Successor of Peter, Bishop of Rome and Pastor of the Universal Church.

In the person of the Supreme Knight and the Members of the Supreme Board, I greet all the Knights of Columbus: the more than one million three hundred thousand Catholic laymen all over the world, who display a spirit of profound attachment to their Christian faith and of loyalty to the Apostolic See.

Many times in the past, and again today, you have given expression to your solidarity with the mission of the Pope. I see in your support a further proof – if further proof were ever necessary – of your awareness that the Knights of Columbus highly value their vocation to be part of the evangelization effort of the Church. I am happy to recall here what my revered predecessor, Paul VI, said about this task in his Apostolic Exhortation *Evangelii Nuntiandi*, as he emphasized the specific role of the laity: 'Their own field of evangelizing activity is the vast and complicated world of politics, society and economics, but also the world of culture, of the sciences and the arts, of international life, of the mass media. It also includes other realities which are open to evangelization, such as human love, the family, the education of children and adolescents, professional work and suffering' (no. 70).

These words of one who never ceased to encourage you clearly indicate the road which your association must travel. I am aware of the many efforts you make to promote the use of mass media for the spreading of the Gospel and for the wider diffusion of my own messages. May the Lord reward you, and through your efforts bring forth abundant fruits of evangelization in the Church. May your dedicated activity in turn help you to realize in yourselves those interior attitudes without which no one can truly evangelize: trust in the power of the Holy Spirit, true holiness of life, deep concern for truth, and an ever increasing love for all God's children.

May the Lord's blessing be upon you, upon your families and upon all the Knights of Columbus.

WASHINGTON, HOMILY AT CAPITOL MALL

The last major event of the final day of the Pope's visit to the United States was a Mass celebrated on the Mall at Washington, between the Capitol and the Lincoln Memorial. An estimated 175,000 people struggled to keep warm in the brisk winds. Gloomy clouds hovered overhead for much of the day, but there were only occasional sprinkles of rain. The Pope's theme — 'We celebrate life' — had an especial appropriateness in Washington where abortions out-number live births.

Dear brothers and sisters in Jesus Christ,

1   In his dialogue with his listeners, Jesus was faced one day with an attempt by some Pharisees to get him to endorse their current views regarding the nature of marriage. Jesus answered by reaffirming the teaching of Scripture: 'At the beginning of creation God made them male and female; for this reason a man shall leave his father and mother and the two shall become one. They are no longer two but one in flesh. Therefore let no man separate what God has joined' (Mk 10:6–9).

The Gospel according to Mark immediately adds the description of a scene with which we are all familiar. This scene shows Jesus becoming indignant when he noticed how his own disciples tried to prevent the people from bringing their children closer to him. And so he said: 'Let the children come to me and do not hinder them. It is to just such as these that the kingdom of God belongs. . . . Then he embraced them and blessed them, placing his hands on them' (Mk 10:14–16). In proposing these readings, today's liturgy invites all of us to reflect on the nature of marriage, on the family, and on the value of life – three themes that are so closely interconnected.

2   I shall all the more gladly lead you in reflecting on the word of God as proposed by the Church today, because all over the world the Bishops are discussing marriage and family life as they are lived in all dioceses and nations. The Bishops are doing this in preparation for the next World Synod of Bishops, which has as its theme: 'The Role of the Christian Family in the Contemporary World.' Your own Bishops have designated next year as a year of study, planning and pastoral renewal with regard to the family. For a variety of reasons there is a renewed interest throughout the world in marriage, in family life, and in the value of all human life.

This very Sunday marks the beginning of the annual Respect Life Programme, through which the Church in the United States intends to reiterate its conviction regarding the inviolability of human life in all stages. Let us then, all together, renew our esteem for the value of human life, remembering also that, through Christ, all human life has been redeemed.

3   I do not hesitate to proclaim before you and before the world that all human life – from the moment of conception and through all subsequent stages – is sacred, because human life is created in the image and likeness of God. Nothing surpasses the greatness or dignity of a human person. Human life is not just an idea or an abstraction; human life is the concrete reality of a being that lives, that acts, that grows and develops; human life is the concrete reality of a being that is capable of love, and of service to humanity.

Let me repeat what I told the people during my recent pilgrimage to my homeland: 'If a person's right to life is violated at the moment in which he is first conceived in his mother's womb, an indirect blow is struck also at the whole of the moral order, which serves to ensure the inviolable goods of man. Among those goods, life occupies the first place. The Church defends the right to life, not only in regard to the majesty of the Creator, who is the First Giver of this life, but also in respect of the essential good of the human person' (8 June 1979).

4   Human life is precious because it is the gift of a God whose love is infinite; and when God gives life, it is for ever. Life is also precious because it is the expression and the fruit of love. This is why life should spring up within the setting of marriage, and why marriage and the parents' love for one another should be marked by generosity in self-giving. The great danger for family life, in the midst of any society whose idols are pleasure, comfort and independence, lies in the fact that people close their hearts and become selfish. The fear of making permanent commitments can change the mutual love of husband and wife into two loves of self – two loves existing side by side, until they end in separation.

In the sacrament of marriage, a man and a woman – who at Baptism became members of Christ and hence have the duty of manifesting Christ's attitudes in their lives – are assured of the help they need to develop their love in a faithful and indissoluble union, and to respond with generosity to the gift of parenthood. As the Second Vatican Council declared: Through this sacrament, Christ himself becomes present in the life of the married couple and accompanies them, so that they may love each other and their children, just as Christ loved his Church by giving himself up for her (cf. *Gaudium et Spes*, 48; cf. Eph 5:25).

5   In order that Christian marriage may favour the total good and development of the married couple, it must be inspired by the Gospel, and thus be open to new life – new life to be given and accepted generously. The couple is also called to create a family atmosphere in which children can be happy, and lead full and worthy human and Christian lives.

To maintain a joyful family requires much from both the parents and the children. Each member of the family has to become, in a special way, the servant of the others and share their burdens (cf. Gal 6:2, Phil 2:2). Each one must show concern, not only for his or her own life, but also for the lives of the other members of the family: their needs, their hopes, their ideals. Decisions about the number of children and the sacrifices to be made for them must not be taken only with a view to adding to comfort and preserving a peaceful existence. Reflecting upon this matter before God, with the graces drawn from the Sacrament, and guided by the teaching of the Church, parents will remind themselves that it is certainly less serious to deny their children certain comforts or material advantages than to deprive them of the presence of brothers and sisters, who could help them to grow in humanity and to realize the beauty of life at all its ages and in all its variety.

If parents fully realized the demands and the opportunities that this great sacrament brings, they could not fail to join in Mary's hymn to the author of life – to God – who has made them his chosen fellow-workers.

6   All human beings ought to value every person for his or her uniqueness as a creature of God, called to be a brother or sister of Christ by reason of the Incarnation and the universal Redemption. For us, the sacredness of human life is based on these premises. And it is on these same premises that there is based our celebration of life – all human life. This explains our efforts to defend human life against every influence or action that threatens or weakens it, as well as our endeavours to make every life more human in all its aspects.

And so, we will stand up every time that human life is threatened. When the sacredness of life before birth is attacked, we will stand up and proclaim that no one ever has the authority to destroy unborn life. When a child is described as a burden or is looked upon only as a means to satisfy an emotional need, we will stand up and insist that every child is a unique and unrepeatable gift of God, with the right to a loving and united family. When the institution of marriage is abandoned to human selfishness or reduced to a temporary, conditional arrangement that can easily be terminated, we will stand up and affirm the indissolubility of the marriage bond. When the value of the family is threatened because of social and economic pressures, we will stand up and reaffirm that the family is 'necessary not only for the private good of every person, but also for the common good of every society, nation and state' (General Audience, 3 January 1979). When freedom is used to dominate the weak, to squander natural resources and energy, and to deny basic necessities to people, we will stand up and reaffirm the demands of justice and social love. When the sick, the aged or the dying are abandoned in loneliness, we will stand up and proclaim that they are worthy of love, care and respect.

I make my own the words which Paul VI spoke last year to the American Bishops: 'We are convinced, moreover, that all efforts made to safeguard human rights actually benefit life itself. Everything aimed at banishing discrimination – in law or in fact – which is based on race, origin, colour, culture, sex or religion (cf. *Octogesima Adveniens*, 16) is a service to life. When the rights of minorities are fostered, when the mentally or physically handicapped are assisted, when those on the margin of society are given a voice – in all these instances the dignity of life, and

169

the sacredness of human life are furthered. . . . In particular, every contribution made to better the moral climate of society, to oppose permissiveness and hedonism, and all assistance to the family, which is the source of new life, effectively uphold the values of life' (26 May 1978).

8   Much remains to be done to support those whose lives are wounded and to restore hope to those who are afraid of life. Courage is needed to resist pressures and false slogans, to proclaim the supreme dignity of all life, and to demand that society itself give it its protection. A distinguished American, Thomas Jefferson, once stated: 'The care of human life and happiness and not their destruction is the just and only legitimate object of good government' (31 March 1809). I wish therefore to praise all the members of the Catholic Church and other Christian Churches, all men and women of the Judeo-Christian heritage, as well as all people of good will who unite in common dedication for the defence of life in its fullness and for the promotion of all human rights.

Our celebration of life forms part of the celebration of the Eucharist. Our Lord and Saviour, through his death and Resurrection, has become for us 'the bread of life' and the pledge of eternal life. In him we find the courage, perseverance and inventiveness which we need in order to promote and defend life within our families and throughout the world.

Dear brothers and sisters: we are confident that Mary, the Mother of God and the Mother of Life, will give us her help so that our way of living will always reflect our admiration and gratitude for God's gift of love that is life. We know that she will help us to use every day that is given to us as an opportunity to defend the life of the unborn and to render more human the lives of all our fellow human beings, wherever they may be.

And through the intercession of Our Lady of the Rosary, whose feast we celebrate today, may we come one day to the fullness of eternal life in Christ Jesus our Lord. Amen.

WASHINGTON, DEPARTURE FOR ROME

Before leaving from the Andrews
Military Base, Pope John Paul said
farewell to America:

Mr Vice President,
My dear friends in America,
and my brothers and sisters in the faith of our Lord Jesus Christ,

As I leave this capital city of Washington, I wish to express my gratitude to the President of the United States and to all the religious and civil authorities of this country.

My thoughts turn likewise to all the American people: to all Catholics, Protestants and Jews, and to all men and women of good will; to people of every ethnic origin, and in particular to the descendants of the first inhabitants of this land, the American Indians; to all of you whom I have greeted personally; those who have been close to me through the providential media of press, radio and television; those who have opened their hearts to me in so many ways. Your hospitality has been warm and filled with love, and I am grateful for all your kindnesses.

I believe strongly in the message of hope that I have held up to you, in the justice and love and truth that I have extolled, and in the peace that I have asked the Lord to give to all of you.

And now I must leave the United States and return to Rome. But all of you will constantly be remembered in my prayers, which I look upon as the best expression of my loyalty and friendship.

Today, therefore, my final prayer is this: that God will bless America, so that she may increasingly become – and truly be – and long remain – 'One Nation, *under God*, Indivisible. With Liberty and Justice for All'.

God bless America!
God bless America!

Monday, 8 October

ROME, ARRIVAL AT FIUMICINO AIRPORT

The Pope's journey ended where it
had begun, at Fiumicino Airport. He
addressed the Cardinals and the
prelates who had come to welcome
him back as follows:

As I set foot once more on the beloved soil of Italy, after the unforgettable emotions of more than a week of liturgical celebrations, meetings and talks, I am filled with sentiments of deep gratitude and joy before the Lord, who in his provident goodness has once more enabled me to meet personally so many brothers and sisters, sons and daughters, and so many representatives and people in authority, men and women of good will.

My brief stay in Ireland enabled me to get to know that country more closely, and to admire its ancient traditions of faith, which witness to its attachment to the Apostolic See, and to appreciate its precious moral values. I am happy to have accepted the Irish Bishop's invitation to celebrate with all the faithful the centenary of the Apparition of Our Lady at Knock. In this way I was enabled to express my filial gratitude to Mary, who in every land offers clear and tangible signs of her motherly care and loving help, which we have invoked especially for peace and reconciliation in that beloved island.

I then went to the General Assembly of the United Nations, where the peoples of the world are represented and as it were come together. This meeting is a continuation of the visit fourteen years ago, as part and symbol of his persevering peace mission, by my unforgettable predecessor Paul VI. I too, willingly accepting the invitation of the Secretary General, wished to assure the United Nations that the Church is close to those who work for peace, and wishes to inspire and support their efforts, through the sole desire to serve humanity. In fact, the Church desires that peace which springs from the true idea of man, from respect for man's rights and the accomplishment of his duties, an idea that is based chiefly upon justice. The Church will never cease to urge people to think about the future destiny of society and the world, with an outlook that is ever renewed and converted.

Thirdly, in response to the desire expressed by the President of the United States and the worthy members of the American Episcopate, I spent some days in their great country. It is a country that certainly has an eminent part to play, and a grave responsibility – precisely by reason of the high level of wellbeing and technical and social progress that it has attained – in the building up of a world that is just and worthy of man. My visit was mainly an ecclesial contact with the faithful and their pastors, to refresh their spirits and increase their courage to think and to live not in man's way but in God's way.

The devoted and enthusiastic welcome given me by all the people of the United States has left me with a desire for an ever more direct and intimate contact with my dear sons and daughters in that country.

As I conclude these brief remarks, I wish to express in the first place to the President of the Council of Ministers my lively and profound thanks for the noble and cordial words with which he has welcomed me back to Italy. With deep respect I also extend my thanks to the Cardinals, the representatives of the State and the Italian Government, the members of the Diplomatic Corps, led by their worthy Dean, the members of the Roman Curia and all those who have given me this festive welcome and made the moment of my return even more pleasant by their affectionate presence.

I also feel the pleasant duty to express my satisfaction and gratitude to the directors of the airlines, to the pilots and crews of the various aircraft, and to all who have worked with generous devotion for the complete success of my journey.

Once more I offer to Christ the Lord, the Prince of Peace, aspirations and resolves for peaceful coexistence, fraternal collaboration and human and Christian solidarity of the peoples of the earth, and together with my Apostolic Blessing I invoke the divine outpouring of grace and mercy upon all of you here present, and upon the beloved sons and daughters of the city of Rome and of all humanity.

List of Illustrations

174